# Teach Yourself
## VISUAL

# Abobe® Muse

## Visual

## Rob Huddleston

WILEY

John Wiley & Sons, Inc.

**Teach Yourself VISUALLY™ Adobe® Muse™**

Published by
John Wiley & Sons, Inc.
10475 Crosspoint Boulevard
Indianapolis, IN 46256

www.wiley.com

Published simultaneously in Canada

Wiley publishes in a variety of print and electronic formats and by print-on-demand. Some material included with standard print versions of this book may not be included in e-books or in print-on-demand. If this book refers to media such as a CD or DVD that is not included in the version you purchased, you may download this material at http://booksupport.wiley.com. For more information about Wiley products, visit www.wiley.com.

*Library of Congress Control Number:* 2012936425

ISBN: 978-1-118-24051-9

Manufactured in the United States of America

10  9  8  7  6  5  4  3  2  1

## Trademark Acknowledgments

Wiley, the Wiley logo, Visual, the Visual logo, Teach Yourself VISUALLY, Read Less - Learn More and related trade dress are trademarks or registered trademarks of John Wiley & Sons, Inc. and/or its affiliates. Adobe and Muse are trademarks or registered trademarks of Adobe Systems, Inc. All other trademarks are the property of their respective owners. John Wiley & Sons, Inc. is not associated with any product or vendor mentioned in this book.

## Contact Us

For general information on our other products and services please contact our Customer Care Department within the U.S. at 877-762-2974, outside the U.S. at 317-572-3993 or fax 317-572-4002.

For technical support please visit www.wiley.com/techsupport.

**WILEY**   Sales | Contact Wiley at (877) 762-2974 or fax (317) 572-4002.

# Credits

**Sr. Acquisitions Editor**
Stephanie McComb

**Sr. Project Editor**
Sarah Hellert

**Technical Editor**
Jonathan Nutting

**Copy Editor**
Scott Tullis

**Editorial Director**
Robyn Siesky

**Business Manager**
Amy Knies

**Sr. Marketing Manager**
Sandy Smith

**Vice President and Executive Group Publisher**
Richard Swadley

**Vice President and Executive Publisher**
Barry Pruett

**Project Coordinator**
Katie Crocker

**Graphics and Production Specialists**
Ana Carrillo
Carrie A. Cesavice
Ronda David-Burroughs
Andrea Hornberger
Jennifer Mayberry
Jill A. Proll

**Quality Control Technician**
Lindsay Amones

**Proofreader**
Lisa Young Stiers

**Indexer**
Potomac Indexing, LLC

# About the Author

**Rob Huddleston** is an Adjunct Professor at the Art Institute of California, Sacramento in the Web Design and Interactive Media department, where he teaches programming and design, focusing heavily on mobile development. He has been creating web pages and applications since 1994, and worked for many years as a corporate trainer, where he taught web and graphic design to thousands of students from all walks of life.

Rob is the author of *XML: Your visual blueprint for building expert websites using XML, CSS, XHTML, and XSLT*; *HTML, XHTML, and CSS: Your visual blueprint for designing effective Web pages*; *Master VISUALLY Dreamweaver CS4 and Flash CS4 Professional*; *ActionScript: Your visual blueprint for creating interactive projects in Flash CS4 Professional*; the *Flash Catalyst CS5 Bible*; *Teach Yourself VISUALLY Web Design*; and two editions of *Android: Fully Loaded*.

When he is not writing or teaching, Rob hangs out with his wife and two children, runs the Sacramento Adobe Users Group, sees a ridiculous number of movies, and obsesses about *Firefly* and *Serenity*.

You can contact Rob via his website at www.robhuddleston.com or follow him on Twitter at http://twitter.com/robhuddles.

# Author's Acknowledgments

Writing a book is always a challenge; writing a book on a program that is still being developed is an even greater challenge. This book would not have been possible without the hard work and dedication of the wonderful people at Wiley, most importantly Stephanie McComb and Sarah Hellert. Their patience at the delays and constantly evolving table of contents made my job much easier, and I thank them. I would also be remiss in not thanking Lynn Northrup, who was instrumental in shepherding the book through its earliest phases.

I owe a huge thank you as well to my tech editor Jon Nutting. I'm pleased to have Jon as a colleague and a friend as well as a tech editor.

For several years, I resisted the idea of getting an agent. Finally, my good friend and fellow author Tom Green talked me into it, and it's one of the best things I've ever done. My agent, Margot Hutchison, takes care of the business side of things and allows me to focus on what I love doing — writing — and for that I am extremely grateful.

The Muse team at Adobe was very kind and patient at answering my seemingly never-ending stream of questions and suggestions on the forums, even going so far as to implement a few of the latter. Keep up the good work, folks. Also, thanks once again to Christine Yarrow at Adobe for providing an invaluable link between authors and the product teams.

As always, I could not do this without the love and support of my beautiful wife Kelley, with whom I've had the fortune of spending the last twenty-five years of my life, and that of my daughter Jessica and son Xander, who keep me grounded with the important things in life while understanding when I need to spend a weekend locked away at the computer.

Finally, I want to thank Olen Sanders, for close to a decade of friendship, lots of great chats, and all those midnight movie screenings.

# Author's Examples and Updates

All example files necessary to follow the examples in the book, including Muse project files for the beginning and ending states of the project in each chapter, can be downloaded for free from www.wiley.com/go/tyvmuse.

One of the advantages of Adobe's plan to make Muse available by subscription only is that it allows the company to push major upgrades to the program much more frequently than they have for past programs. You can read about the changes to the program and their impact on specific topics or sections of this book on the author's website at www.robhuddleston.com/books/tyvmuse. Additional topics and example files are also be available on that site.

# How to Use This Book

## Who This Book Is For

This book is for the reader who has never used this particular technology or software application. It is also for readers who want to expand their knowledge.

## The Conventions in This Book

### ❶ Steps

This book uses a step-by-step format to guide you easily through each task. **Numbered steps** are actions you must do; **bulleted steps** clarify a point, step, or optional feature; and **indented steps** give you the result.

### ❷ Notes

Notes give additional information — special conditions that may occur during an operation, a situation that you want to avoid, or a cross-reference to a related area of the book.

### ❸ Icons and Buttons

Icons and buttons show you exactly what you need to click to perform a step.

### ❹ Tips

Tips offer additional information, including warnings and shortcuts.

### ❺ Bold

**Bold** type shows command names or options that you must click or text or numbers you must type.

### ❻ Italics

*Italic* type introduces and defines a new term.

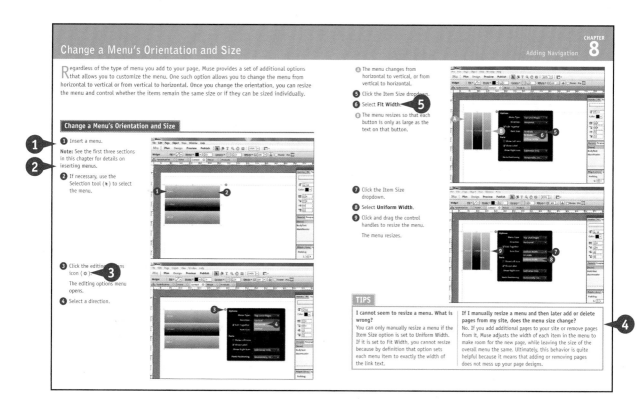

# Table of Contents

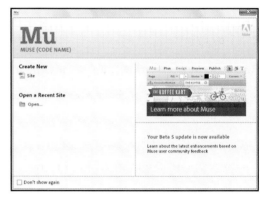

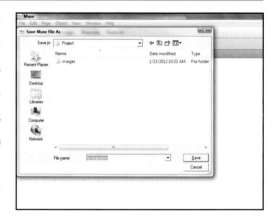

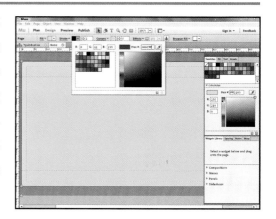

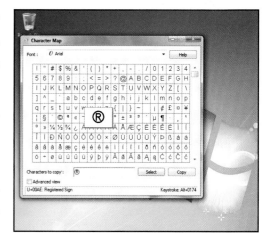

# Table of Contents

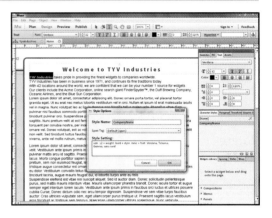

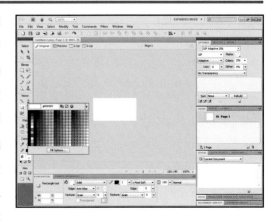

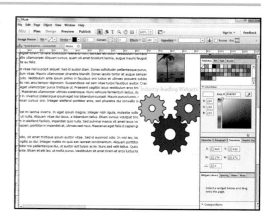

# Table of Contents

## Chapter 9    Using Master Pages

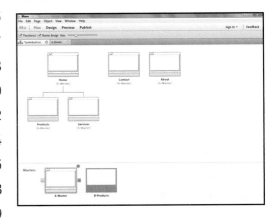

# Chapter 10 | Adding Widgets

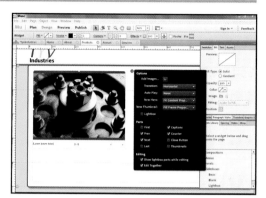

# Table of Contents

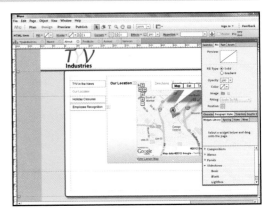

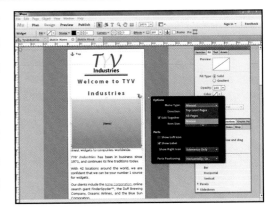

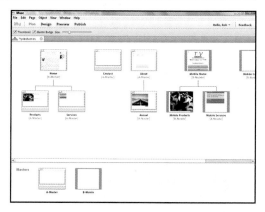

# CHAPTER 1

# Introducing Adobe Muse

From the web's earliest days, designers have wanted a tool that they could use to create websites without having to learn code. Now, with Adobe Muse, they have it. In this chapter, you will learn how to get started using Adobe Muse.

# Understanding Web Design

The web was invented by a scientist with the hopes of making it easier for other scientists to communicate. Given this background, it is really no surprise that creating web pages has always relied primarily on writing code. Thankfully, Muse changes that, letting you create sites without ever writing or even seeing the underlying code, even though the code is still there. Although designers around the world will rejoice at this, you still need to understand a few key concepts about the principles of web design before you begin building sites.

## The Web Is Not Print

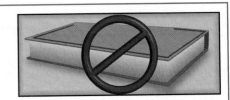

The web and print share many similar attributes. Both rely heavily on the written word. Typography plays a key — if often misunderstood and underused — role in both. Yet in the end, the web remains a very different medium from print. If you are a traditional print designer, some of your current skill set may transfer to web design, but much will not. You need to be willing to adapt.

## Accept What You Cannot Know

When you design for print, you begin the process by deciding what size paper to use, and that in turn determines much of your design. On the web, you simply cannot know how big of a screen your users have; it could be anything from a large monitor to a small smartphone. You cannot know their screen resolution. You cannot know whether they have their browser maximized. You can either waste time and energy worrying about these unknowns, or accept them as facts of life and focus on those things you can know. The choice is yours.

## Start with a Plan

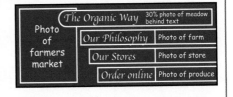

A good, effective website does not happen by accident. When you set out to create a new site, you may find the temptation to open up Muse and start designing right away hard to resist. The vast majority of the time, however, you will discover that the more time you spend planning your site, the better the end result. Just as important: A well-planned site is also almost always easier to create than one put together on the fly.

## Create a Wireframe

A *wireframe* is a simplistic representation of the layout and structure of a page that gives the designer a blueprint from which to work. Wireframes can be drawn on paper, whether as rough sketches or precise drawings. You can also create a wireframe on your computer using a tool like Adobe Fireworks; or, if you have a tablet computer, you can use Adobe Proto, available in the Android and iOS markets or as part of a Creative Cloud subscription.

## Have a Purpose

Although it may seem odd at first to state that a website should always be built with a single purpose in mind, the reality is that the web is littered with sites created simply because a person or business thought they needed a presence on the web. Avoid this trap. You do not need a presence on the web;

rather, you need a site that effectively solves some specific need either not currently fulfilled or that could be fulfilled better. Identifying this need should always be an early step in your process.

## Plan for the Future

Printed documents can easily be completely redesigned between print runs. Totally starting over with the design of a web page, although possible, almost always requires a significant commitment in time and money. Therefore, you should try to create a design that can grow with the site as needed and that can adapt to new purposes and to the ever-changing world of the web.

## Have a Maintenance Plan

Maintaining a site can at times be as big a burden as building it in the first place. The bad news is that websites can become stagnant very quickly. A stagnant website is easily noticed and can drive your users away. The good news is that a well-thought-out, well-designed site can be very easy to maintain, as long as you have a plan from the very early days of development.

## Content Is King

Think back to the last beautifully designed website you visited that did not provide you with the content you needed. Think back as well to the last time you visited a site that might have been badly designed but took you right to the content. At which one did you stay longer? Thankfully, the two are not mutually exclusive, and you can have a beautiful site that still delivers the necessary content.

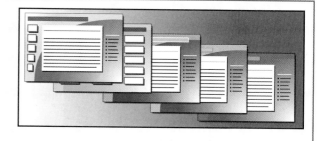

# Download Muse

M use is one of the first products to be sold exclusively online and exclusively via a service contract. This means that you cannot go to a store and purchase it in a box and you cannot request the program on a DVD. Instead, you must download it from Adobe's web server, and to continue using Muse past the end of the trial period, you need to continue paying a monthly fee to Adobe. The program is downloaded and installed on your computer, so you can use it offline later.

## Download Muse

**1** Use a web browser to go to http://muse.adobe.com.

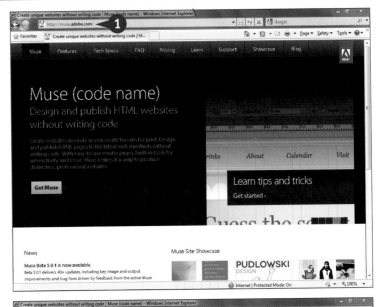

**2** Click **Get Muse**.

A dialog box appears, showing options to Open, Save, or Cancel.

③ Click **Open**.

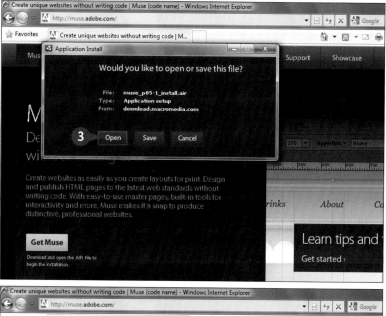

The file downloads. An installer dialog box opens.

④ Click **Install**.

Muse installs.

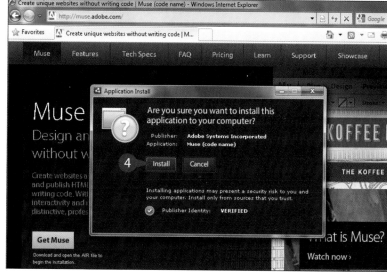

**My computer said I also needed to install Adobe AIR. What is that?**

AIR stands for Adobe Integrated Runtime, a technology Adobe developed that allows application developers to easily create programs that run on multiple operating systems. Because Muse is built in AIR, it must be installed on your system before you can install Muse. AIR is free, and over time you are likely to need it for other applications you install.

**If I have to subscribe in order to use Muse, can I still run it if my computer is not connected to the Internet?**

Yes. Muse installs on your computer just like any other program. When you launch Muse and are connected to the Internet, it checks to ensure your subscription is valid. If you are not connected, it continues to run and checks the next time you are online.

# Introducing the Welcome Screen

Muse has five primary views. The first one you see each time you launch the program is the Welcome screen. As with other Adobe products, the Welcome screen provides you with quick links to getting started with new projects, opening existing projects, getting help, and downloading updates. You can choose to disable the Welcome screen if you want, but you will most likely find that it allows you to get going in the program more quickly. You can reposition the Welcome screen if you want by dragging its title bar. You can also access the normal program menus in the main window.

**A Create New**

Allows you to create a new Muse project.

**B Open a Recent Site**

Provides quick access to your most recently opened sites.

**C Don't show again button**

Turns off the Welcome screen. It can be turned on again in the Preferences window.

**D Information box**

Messages from Adobe, most often about available program updates, appear here.

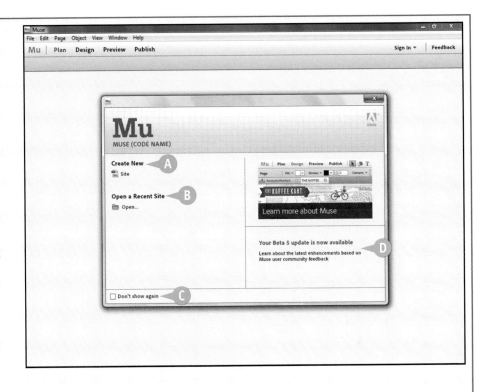

**E Muse website link**

Clicking this area takes you to the Muse home page on the web, where you can access tutorials and ask questions on the Muse forum.

**F Close button**

Clicking here closes the Welcome screen. The screen appears again the next time you launch Muse or if you close all open projects.

**G Title bar**

Dragging the title bar allows you to reposition the Welcome screen.

**H Program menus**

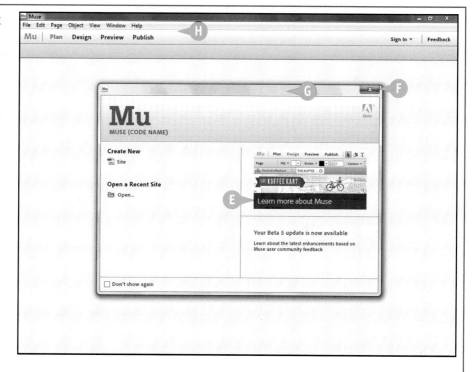

The main program menus are accessible when the Welcome screen is open. The menus on the second row — Plan, Design, Preview, Publish, Sign In, and Feedback — are not.

# CHAPTER 2

# Planning a Site

Effective web design does not happen by accident. Careful planning of your site's design, content, and navigation structure will make the process of building a site much easier while also ensuring that your site meets its goals.

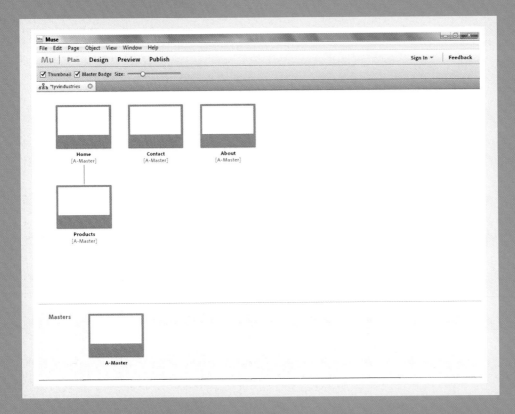

# Understanding the Importance of Planning Your Site

Although you may be tempted to sit down at your computer and simply start designing in Muse, you will find that careful planning is needed to ensure that your site's content is organized logically, that your site fits your users' needs, and that your navigation works and is intuitive. Planning a site may not be the most exciting task in the overall process, but it is perhaps the most important. In general, well-planned sites come together much more quickly and are more likely to end up being something you can be proud of.

## Brainstorm Design Concepts

Most successful finished designs are the result of taking parts from several ideas and combining them into a whole. In your brainstorming session, whether you are working alone or in a team, always remember that no idea should be rejected out-of-hand.

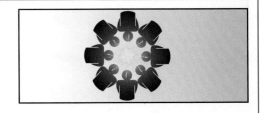

## Wireframe the Design

A wireframe is simply a representation of the site's structure and layout. It does not need to be fancy — many wireframes are simply boxes with labels — but you should try to get proportions correct to make sure the design will work. You can draw the wireframes by hand, or use a graphics program such as Adobe Fireworks or a tablet-based program such as Adobe Proto.

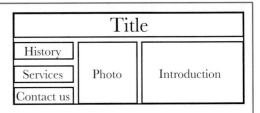

## Storyboard Pages

Storyboards provide more detailed representations of your design. You can use storyboards to see how the color scheme from your project will work and begin to get an idea of what graphics you might use. You can create a storyboard for each page in your site, although sites with animated elements may require multiple storyboards.

## Develop a Timeline for Completion

If you are working for a client or developing a website for your company, you need to discuss with your client or boss a realistic timeline that includes deadlines along the way in which you can complete the project. If you are creating a personal site, a timeline can be just as important to keep you on track.

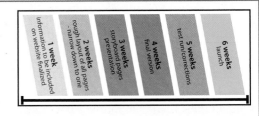

# Understanding Your Audience

The web is a user-centric environment. Almost all of your users will approach your site with a "what's in it for me" attitude. Traditional businesses can, to a point, rely on the fact that by the time a customer walks in their door, the customer has already invested something in the trip, such as time and gas. Thus, they may be more likely to endure a certain level of inconvenience. On the web, your customers have invested next to nothing in getting to your site. Understanding your audience is the key to being able to meet their needs and keep them on your site.

## Market Studies

Companies have long understood the importance of studying the market in which they plan to do business in order to target advertising and products to their important customers. Many websites, however, forego this step, to their peril. Web market studies are every bit as important as those for traditional offline businesses.

## Demographics

*Demographics* is the study of populations. You need to get an idea of the demographics of your potential audience to ensure that your site meets their needs. General questions to research include your audience's age, educational level, socio-economic background, and more.

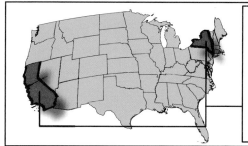

Launch from these two states, which have the largest proportion of potential customers, then grow from both coasts, meeting in the middle. Keep original bases strong, with smaller satellite stores with capabilities for growth.

## Local Businesses with Global Customers

The global scope of the web is one of its more exciting aspects. Even the smallest of businesses can now reach companies on the other side of the world, but that same global scope presents many challenges as well. How will you handle foreign orders? Will you present your site in multiple languages?

**Choose your language:**

- **English**
- **Français**
- **Deutsch**
- **Español**
- **Italiano**
- **Русский**

# Create a Site in Muse

Your first step in working in Muse is to create a site. Muse helps you plan how the pages in your site relate to one another, automatically creates navigation between pages, manages site assets such as images, and assists in uploading the entire project when you are done. When you create a site, Muse prompts you to define basic properties about the pages in the site, including their width and height, margins, and columns. It then creates the site and the site's home page for you.

## Create a Site in Muse

1 If you have not already done so, open Muse.

2 From the Start screen's Create New section, click **Site**.

A dialog box appears.

3 Set the desired width and height of your page.

4 Set the desired number of columns, column width, and gutter.

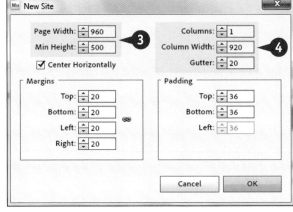

⑤ Set the desired margins.

⑥ Set the desired padding.

⑦ Click **OK**.

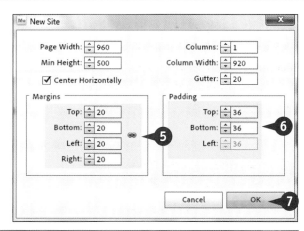

Ⓐ The Muse Plan view opens, showing a new site with a single page created.

## TIP

**What is the best size to use for my page?**

Unfortunately, you cannot know with any certainly what size you should use. In the end, your design and the content you need to fit on the page will primarily dictate your page size.

For many years, most computer monitors came with a default screen resolution of 1024 × 768, and designers created pages to attempt to fit that screen. Today, screen sizes vary greatly, from small mobile device screens that may be only 320 × 140 to giant HD screens that could be several thousand pixels wide.

# Save and Back Up Your Site

M use saves your site as a MUSE file. The file contains all the contents of your site — its pages, graphic assets, and anything else you may be working on. It is in many ways similar to the files used in such programs as Adobe InDesign. Because losing this file would require that you totally recreate your site from scratch, you should get in the habit of routinely making backups.

## Save and Back Up Your Site

### Save the Site in Muse

**1** In Muse, click **File** and then **Save Site**.

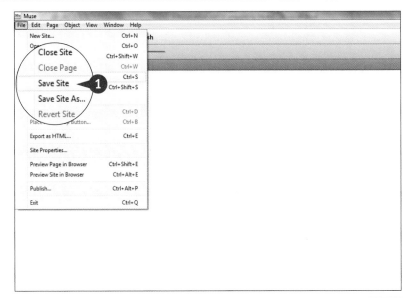

The Save Muse File As dialog box opens.

**2** Navigate to the folder into which you want to save your site.

**3** Name your site file.

**4** Click **Save**.

The site is saved.

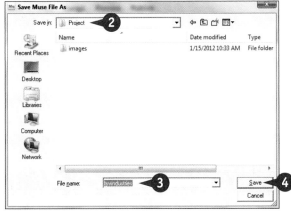

## Create a Backup

**1** Using Windows Explorer or Mac Finder, navigate to the folder into which you saved the site in the prior steps.

**2** Create a copy of the site.

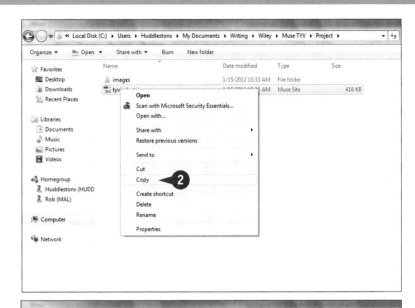
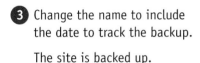

**3** Change the name to include the date to track the backup.

The site is backed up.

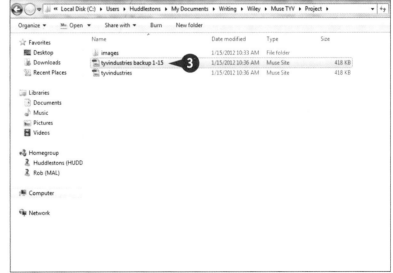

**Can I define a Muse site for a website that already exists?**

No. Muse has been created specifically to allow designers to create new sites from scratch. You can copy and paste content from existing pages into Muse pages, but it must be done page-by-page.

**How often should I re-create the backup file?**

As often as you need to feel protected. Remember that if something happens to your main MUSE file, you must start over on your site. Therefore, you should re-create your backup file frequently. You should also store copies of it on a different computer or other media in case your hard drive fails.

# Using Plan View

The Plan view in Muse provides you with a high-level overview of the pages in your site and their relationships with other pages. It also gives you access to your Master pages and easy tools to create additional pages as needed. The Plan view opens automatically when you create a new site, and can be accessed at any time using the View menu, the main toolbar, or by pressing Ctrl+M in Windows or ⌘+M on a Mac.

**A Main toolbar**

Provides access to Muse's other views.

**B View options**

Select or deselect these to change the details displayed on each page.

**C Thumbnail size slider**

Drag this to the left to decrease the size of the page thumbnails, or to the right to increase their size.

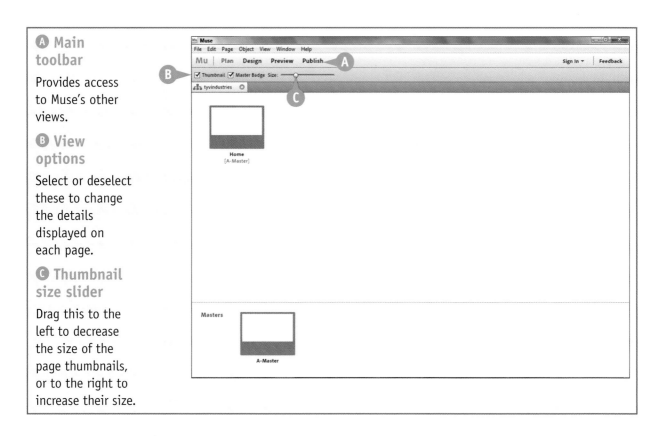

**ⓓ Site tab**

Each site or page you have open will have a tab. You can use the X on the tab to close the site without closing Muse.

**ⓔ Site page thumbnails**

Each page in your site appears as a thumbnail. Position your mouse pointer over the thumbnail to see buttons to create additional pages. Double-click a page to open it for editing.

**ⓕ Masters**

Master pages appear as thumbnails here. Double-click a Master to open it for editing.

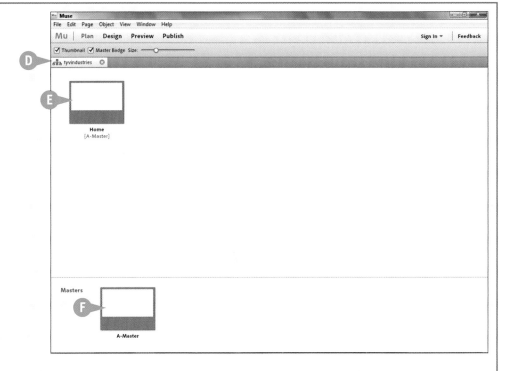

# Plan Your Navigation Structure

Carefully laid-out navigation makes your site easy and intuitive to use, which in turn ensures that users have a more successful experience in your site. You should plan your navigation early in the design process, to make sure that all important pages are navigable and to ensure that the navigation works with your design. Sites with poorly designed navigational structures quickly confuse and frustrate your users, which is likely to cause them to give up and find another site. Good navigation should be so intuitive that the user never has to consciously think about it.

## Main Navigation

Your site's main navigation is the area that contains links to the primary sections of your site, such as your home page and departmental pages. The main navigation will likely appear on every page in the site, and traditionally appears either horizontally near the top of the site or vertically along the left side.

## Section Sub-Navigation

Each section of your site will likely require its own navigation to the pages within the section. Section navigation can be presented directly below or next to the main navigation, or as an independent unit. It should be visually obvious to users that these areas represent links within the section.

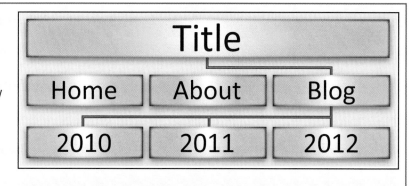

## Think Like Users

Do not organize your site's navigation based on the internal organization of your company. Rather, approach the site from an outsider's view, and organize your navigation based on the needs of your prospective users.

# Plan What Pages You Will Need

Your site will be divided into pages. In Muse, you use the Plan view to create pages. The organization of the pages resembles an organization chart or family tree. All sites will have a home page at the top of the site. From there, other pages will either be top-level, existing at the same organizational level as the home page; subpages of these top-level pages; or subpages of other subpages. You need to carefully consider what pages your site needs and how they relate to each other.

## Top-Level Pages

Your home page is the entry point for most of your users. Sites with additional top-level pages are most often those that are divided into sections, and often those sections are semi-independent of one another. In these cases, each top-level page serves as a sort of home page for its section.

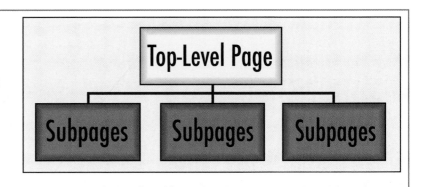

## Subpages

The bulk of your site will be made of subpages. In most cases, your users begin at either your home page or another top-level page, and then use the navigation on the page to go to its subpages. Each subpage can have one or more sibling pages; that is, pages that live at the same level as the subpage. They may also have subpages of their own.

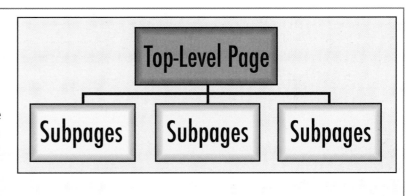

## Determine How Many Pages You Need

Once you have a good idea of what content you want for your site, you can look at how to logically divide the content. From there, determine what content would best fit on its own pages and what would best go with other content on a single page.

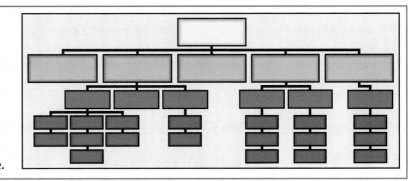

# Create a Site Map

A site map is a visual representation of the pages in your site and their relationship to one another. Although web designers have for years relied on hand-drawn site maps, Muse provides an intuitive tool in its Plan view with which to create your map. Even better is that the map is not merely a representation of your site; rather, as you add pages to the site map, those pages are created for you, ready to edit.

## Create a Site Map

### Add Top-Level Pages

1 Open an existing Muse site or create a new one.

**Note:** See the section "Create a Site in Muse" for details.

2 If necessary, click **Plan** to go to Plan view.

3 Position your mouse pointer over the Home page thumbnail.

4 Click the plus sign to the right of the Home page.

Ⓐ A new top-level page is added.

5 Type a descriptive name for the page.

6 Repeat steps **3** to **5** as needed to create additional top-level pages.

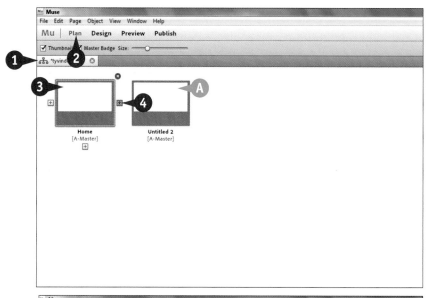

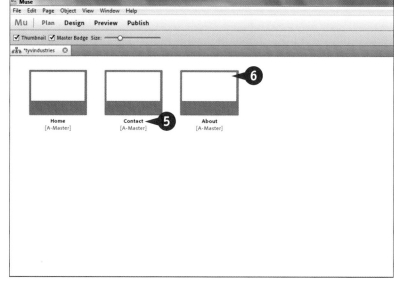

## Create Subpages

1️⃣ Position your mouse pointer over one of the top-level pages.

2️⃣ Click the plus sign on the bottom of the page.

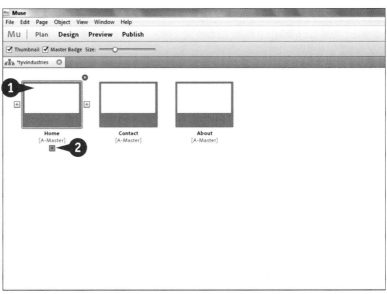

🅑 A subpage is created.

3️⃣ Type a descriptive name for the page.

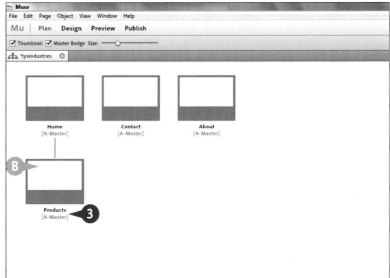

## TIPS

**Is there a limit as to how many pages I can create?**

No. Muse can be used to create sites of any size. The number of top-level and subpages that you create is dependent on the complexity of the content you want to publish and your overall vision for the site.

**Do I need to create all my pages at once?**

No. You can return to Plan view at any time and add additional pages. However, you will hopefully have invested considerable time in planning your site before you begin working in Muse, so you should have a fairly good idea of what pages you need.

# CHAPTER 3

# Designing Your Site in Adobe Muse

Once you have planned the purpose of your site and determined the content you will use, you can start the design process.

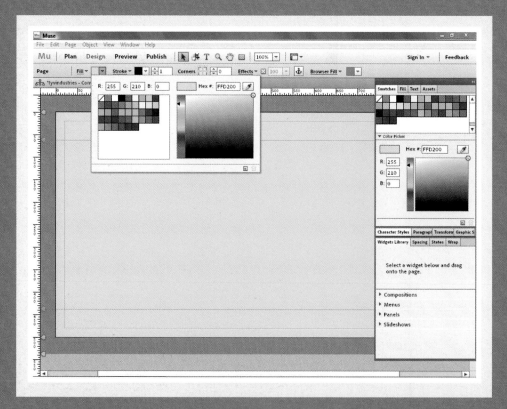

# Using Design View

Design view in Muse is your primary work surface for designing your site. You can access Design view by either double-clicking any page thumbnail in Plan view or by clicking Design from the main toolbar. Design view displays your page and the tools Muse provides for adding content and changing visual properties such as color and font formats. Design view is known as a WYSIWYG environment, so the page you see in Design view will be almost exactly what your users see when they view your page.

**Ⓐ Views menu**

Access the other views in the program.

**Ⓑ Selection tool**

Select items for editing with this tool.

**Ⓒ Crop tool**

Use this tool to crop images to the correct size.

**Ⓓ Text tool**

Add text to your design with this tool.

**Ⓔ Zoom tool**

Use this tool to zoom in on your design. Press Alt with this tool to zoom out.

**Ⓕ Hand tool**

The Hand tool allows you to move around on your canvas.

**Ⓖ Rectangle tool**

Draw rectangles in your design with this tool.

**Ⓗ Zoom levels**

Select a specific magnification level to zoom to from this list.

**Ⓘ View options**

This menu provides a set of options to change your view.

**Ⓙ Sign In**

Use this to sign into your account to upload your site.

**Ⓚ Feedback**

Click here to send feedback about Muse to the product team.

**Ⓛ Selection indicator**

This tells what item you currently have selected.

**Ⓜ Fill settings**

Select a color from the color picker or click directly on the word *Fill* for more options.

**Ⓝ Stroke settings**

Select a color from the color picker or click directly on the word *Stroke* for more options.

**Ⓞ Corner settings**

Use this set of tools to create rounded corners.

**Ⓟ Effects**

Apply special effects such as drop shadows.

**Ⓠ Transparency**

Adjust the opacity or transparency of objects.

**Ⓡ Link button**

Create a link to another page.

**Ⓢ Browser Fill**

Change the background color of your document.

**Ⓣ Page tabs**

Move between open documents by selecting them here.

**Ⓤ Rulers**

Use the rulers to precisely size and position objects.

**Ⓥ Canvas**

Your drawing area, or canvas, is represented in white or whatever background color you select.

**Ⓦ Panels**

Panels provide additional options and tools.

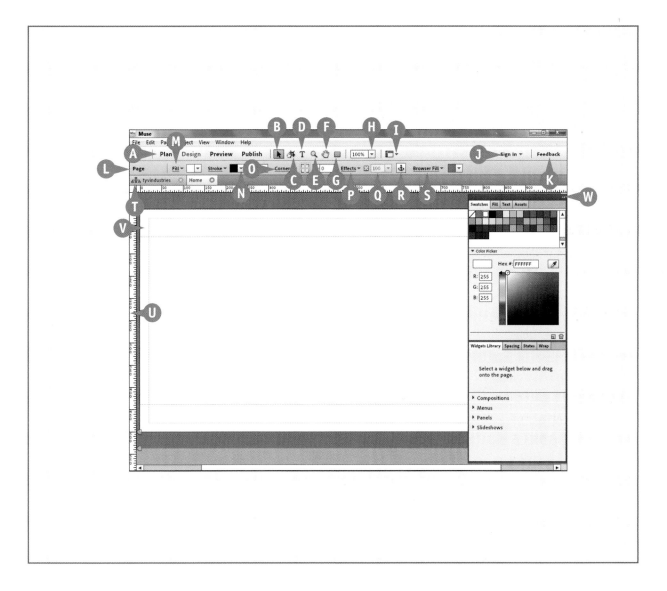

# Set a Page Fill Color

Your primary work area in building a site in Muse is the canvas. The canvas defaults to a white background, but you can set it to any color you want. Colors can be expressed in RGB or hexadecimal format. Muse presents you with a small set of predefined swatches of color, but you can use other colors as needed. Custom colors can then be added to the swatches panel to later reuse. If you set a background color on the canvas, you can also adjust its opacity so that any background on the browser will show through.

## Set a Page Fill Color

### Set a Color

**1** Click the dropdown next to Fill on the toolbar.

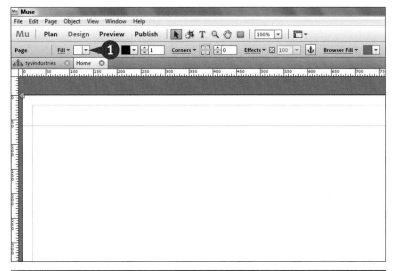

**2** Select a color from the swatches or the color picker.

**Note:** You can also manually enter RBG or hexadecimal values.

The color is applied to the canvas.

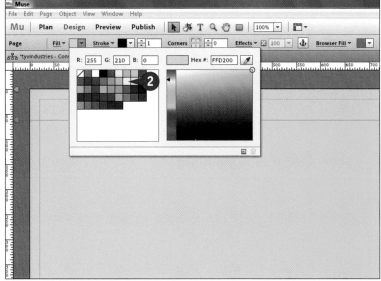

## Add a Custom Color to the Swatches

1. From the Fill dropdown, click the **New Swatch** button (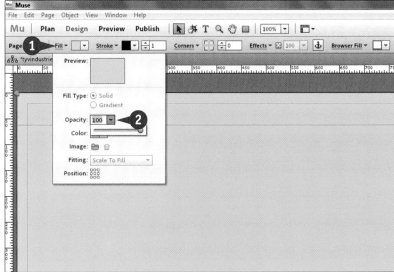) in the lower right corner.

A A new swatch is added.

## Change the Opacity of the Canvas

1. Click the word **Fill** on the toolbar.

2. Change the opacity to a new value by moving the slider or typing your own value.

**Can I use CMYK colors in Muse?**

No. CMYK is a color model used strictly for print. For on-screen designs, which Muse by definition creates, you must use the RGB color model. Muse does allow you to set colors in RGB by either specifying the exact red, green, and blue values or by entering the hexadecimal value for the color.

**Can I select a color from a logo or image to use as my background?**

Yes. When you click the Fill dropdown to access the color picker, you will see an eyedropper tool (✐). Select this, and then click an image you have imported into Muse to select the desired color.

# Add a Border

You can add a border or stroke around your canvas. Borders allow you to set off your canvas from your page background. The border can be a solid color of any width. You can set different widths on each side, and you can also control whether the border aligns with the inside edge of the canvas or the outside edge, or centers itself on the edge.

## Add a Border

1 Click the dropdown to the right of Stroke.

2 Select a color for your border.

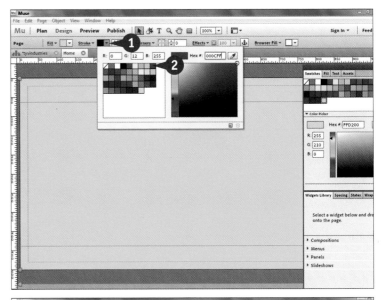

3 Click the text field to the right of the color dropdown, and enter a value for the width of the border.

**Note:** You can also use the arrows to increase or decrease the value.

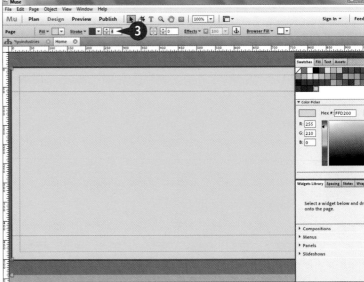

④ Click the word **Stroke**.

⑤ Select a desired alignment option.

⬚ aligns the border with the inside edge of the canvas.

⬚ aligns the border with the outside edge of the canvas.

⬚ centers the border on the edge of the canvas, as shown in this example.

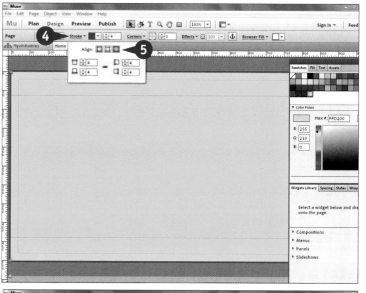

⑥ Click the **Make all stroke weight settings the same** button ( ⊕ ).

⑦ Enter new values for the stroke weight for individual sides.

Ⓐ A border is added to your canvas.

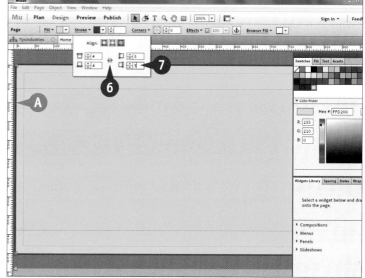

---

## TIPS

**Can I use images or gradients for the border?**
No. Borders or strokes can only be a single solid color. While there is some very limited support for gradient borders in Cascading Style Sheets, or CSS, the formatting language of the web that Muse uses, the program does not yet support them.

**Can I set different colors for each side of the border?**
No. This is also a limitation of Muse. Although CSS does allow for border colors to be different on each side, Muse does not support this. You also cannot use anything other than a solid border.

# Create Rounded Corners

For years, the web was a very boxy place. Earlier versions of CSS and HTML did not provide an easy way to create objects with rounded corners. Thankfully, that has now changed. In Muse, you can round the corners of your canvas using the toolbar. You can round the corners of your page without a border, but the page will be more visible if you have a border applied.

## Create Rounded Corners

① Apply a border, as described in the previous section.

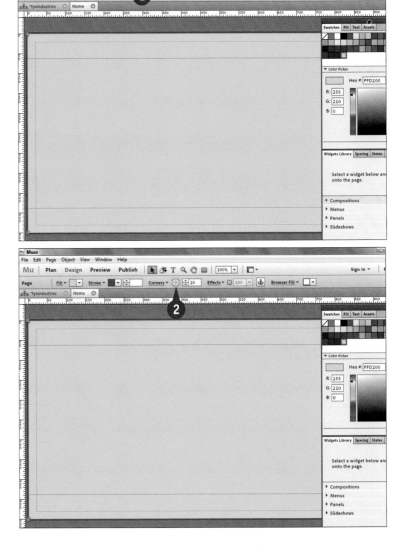

② Click one or more of the rounded corner buttons.

③ Enter a value for the radius of the corners, or use the arrows to change the value.

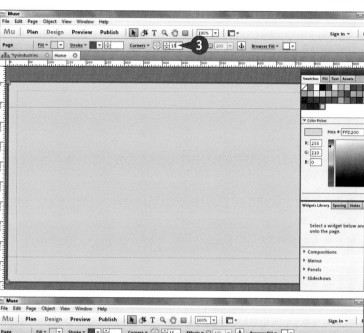

Ⓐ The border's corners are rounded.

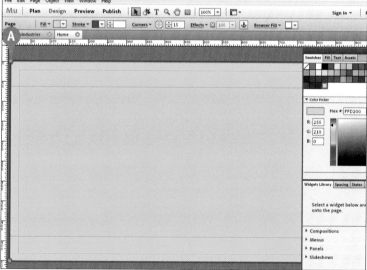

**Can I set different radii for each corner?**

No. Although CSS does allow this, Muse only has the ability to set the radius of any corners you have rounded to the same value.

# Add Effects

M use supports three effects you can apply to your page: Drop Shadow, Bevel, and Glow. All three are applied to the outside edge of your page. Drop Shadow creates the illusion of your page floating slightly above the browser window. Bevel gives it a slight 3-D look. Glow is similar to Drop Shadow but works best on a dark background. You can apply any or all of the effects at once.

## Add Effects

**Apply a Drop Shadow**

**1** Click **Effects**.

**2** Click **Shadow**.

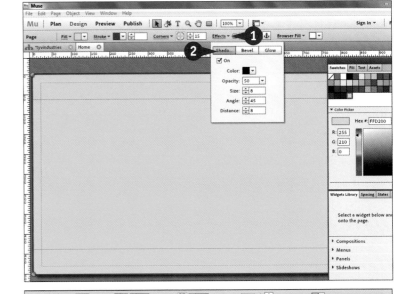

**3** Click **On** ( ☐ changes to ☑ ).

**4** Adjust any settings as desired.

**A** A shadow is applied to the page.

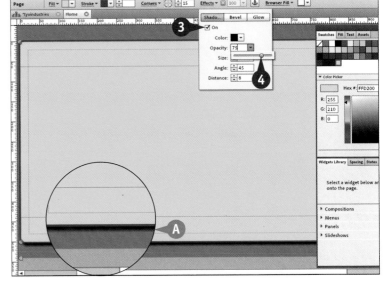

## Apply a Bevel

1 Click **Bevel**.

2 Click **On** (☐ changes to ☑).

3 Adjust any desired settings.

Ⓑ A bevel is applied.

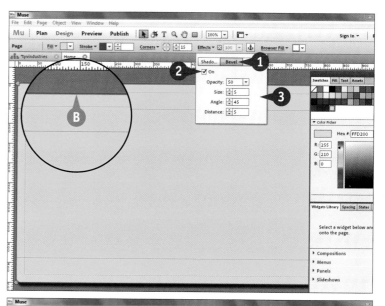

## Apply a Glow

1 Click **Glow**.

2 Click **On** (☐ changes to ☑).

3 Adjust any settings as desired.

Ⓒ A glow is applied to the page.

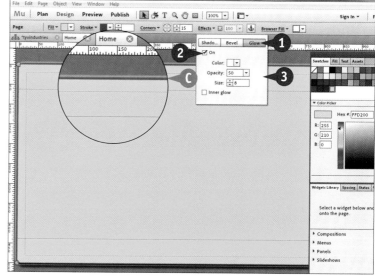

---

**TIP**

**Photoshop has dozens of possible effects. I was expecting something similar in Muse. Where are the rest of my effects?**

The current version of CSS supports only bevels, glows, and drop shadows, so these are all that Muse supports. If more effect possibilities are added as CSS continues to evolve, Adobe would likely add them to Muse. In the meantime, you could create an image with Photoshop that used other effects and then set that image as your page background.

# Add a Background Fill

The page, or canvas, fills only a portion of your user's browser window. The remainder of the browser window either will be plain white, or can be filled by a color or with an image of your choosing. You can select any image on your computer as long as it is a GIF, JPEG, or PNG file, although you should ensure that the image has been optimized for the web. See Chapter 6 for details.

## Add a Background Fill

### Add a Solid Color Fill

**1** Click the dropdown to the right of Browser Fill.

**2** Select a color.

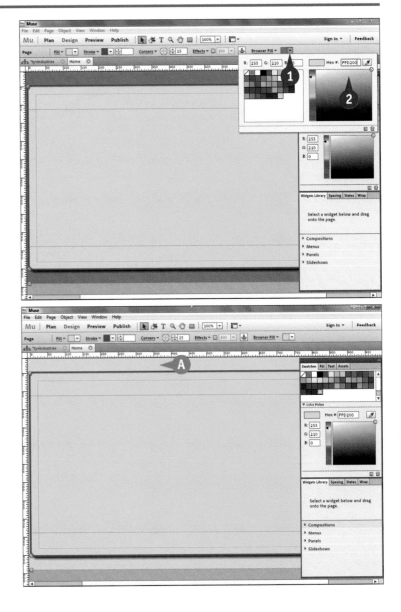

**A** The browser fill color is applied.

## Add a Background Image

**1** Click **Browser Fill**.

**2** Click the **Choose a background image** button ( 🗁 ).

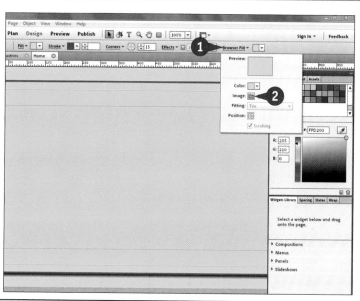

**3** Navigate to the folder in which your image is stored.

**4** Select an image.

**5** Click **Open**.

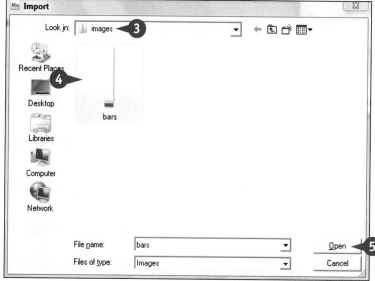

continued ▶ 37

## TIPS

**When I select a background color, it does not appear to really fill the background, but instead leaves a lot of gray area. Why is this?**

Why Muse displays the background fill color in such a small area is not known, but that is only a Muse display issue. When you eventually publish the site and view it in the browser, the color will fill the entire browser background, regardless of how big or small the browser window is.

**Can I apply a gradient color as the background?**

No. You can use an image and a solid color to create the illusion of a gradient background, but you cannot apply a gradient directly. Simply create a thin image that contains the gradient you want to use, and then set it to tile in one direction. Apply as the background color the final color in the gradient.

# Add a Background Fill (continued)

When you add a background image, it by default appears in the top left corner of the page and then tiles both horizontally and vertically from there. You can control this tiling effect, limiting the tiling to one direction or turning off tiling altogether. You can also control the initial placement of the image. If you have a background fill color selected, the color shows wherever the image does not tile.

## Add a Background Fill (continued)

Ⓐ The image appears in the background.

### Control Placement and Tiling

① Click **Browser Fill**.

② Click the **Fitting** dropdown.

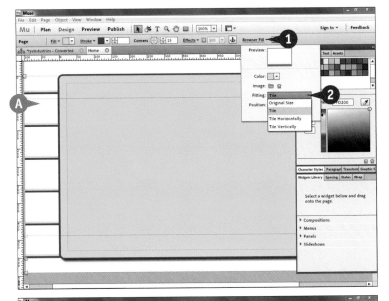

③ Select **Original Size** to turn off tiling, **Tile** to tile in both directions, **Tile Horizontally**, or **Tile Vertically**.

This example uses Tile Horizontally.

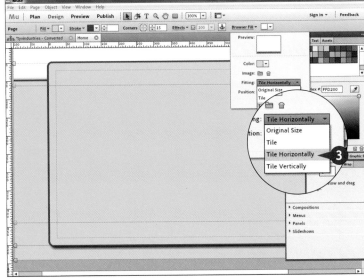

Ⓑ The image tiles appropriately.

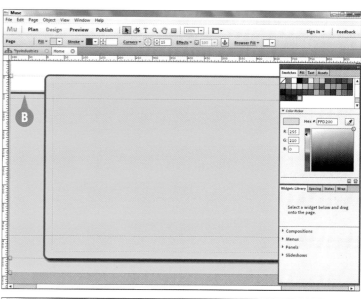

Ⓒ You can click **Browser Fill** again, and select a position option to reposition the image.

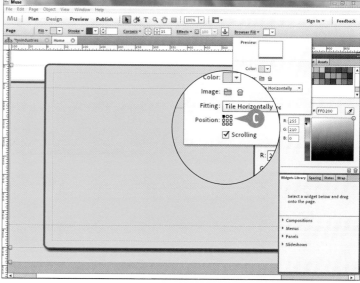

**I see only a portion of my image. How can I make my page big enough to see the whole thing?**

The page automatically expands as you add more content, so you should eventually see your entire image. If you know that you will not have a lot of content on the page, you may want to consider using a smaller background image.

**When I select Tile Vertically, I still see only one copy of my image. Why?**

This is essentially the same issue as was noted above. When you first apply your background image to a page with little or no content, the page may not be tall enough to display more than one instance of the image. As you add content, you will see the image begin to tile vertically.

# Create a Layout Comp in Adobe Proto

T he Adobe Touch Apps are a set of tablet-based applications targeted at designers. One of these apps, Adobe Proto, allows web designers to create layout comps directly on their tablet by simply drawing boxes and other elements to represent the basic layout of their page. Owners of higher-end Android tablets can purchase Proto from Google Play for $9.99. iPad owners can download them for the same price from the iTunes Store.

## Create a Layout Comp in Adobe Proto

**1** On your tablet, go to Google Play.

**2** Search for Adobe Proto.

**3** Select **Adobe Proto**.

**4** Select **$9.99**.

**5** Select **Accept and download**.

The app is downloaded to your tablet.

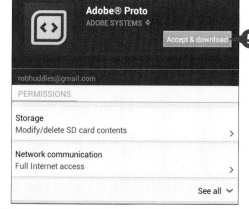

Proto finishes downloading and installing and launches for the first time.

**6** Select **Accept**.

The app is ready to use.

continued ▶

## TIPS

**How to I install Proto on my iPad?**

Proto for the iPad was not available as of the time of this writing, but it should be in the iTunes store by the time you read this. Purchasing and installing Proto on an iPad follows the same procedure as with any other app you purchase from Apple. Once installed, it works the same way on an iPad as it does on Android tablets.

**When I searched for Proto on my Android tablet, it returned no results. Why is this?**

Proto has a minimum screen resolution of 1280 × 800 for Android. All 7-inch tablets have a lower resolution, so they cannot run Proto. Additionally, some lower-end 10-inch tablets have the same issue. The Amazon Kindle Fire and the Barnes & Noble Nook Color Tablet both have too low of a resolution, and you can only download apps from the Amazon and Barnes & Noble app stores, respectively, to those devices. Because Adobe is selling the Touch Apps on Android only through Google Play, they are not available on those devices either.

Creating a comp in Proto is fairly intuitive. When you create a new project, Proto allows you to set the size of your page from a variety of templates. You can also set the number of columns to display. Then, you can draw boxes to represent sections of your layout, scribble to add placeholder text, and use the on-screen toolbar to add additional elements like menu bars, images, and video.

## Create a Layout Comp in Adobe Proto (continued)

**7** Select the plus sign at the bottom of the Proto window to create a new project.

**8** Set your desired layout properties.

**9** Select **Create**.

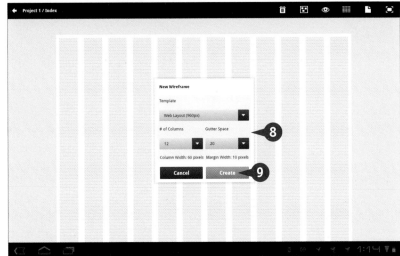

A new project is created.

⑩ Draw boxes on-screen to create containers.

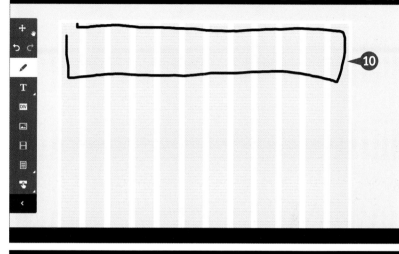

⑪ Draw a squiggle in a box to add placeholder text.

⑫ Use the tools on the left to add additional content.

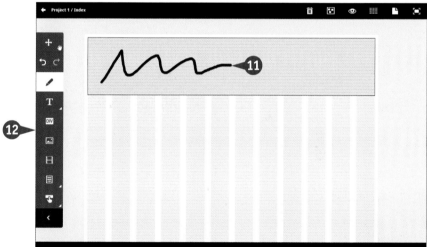

## TIPS

**How do I save my comp?**
Proto automatically saves your work as you create it. You can select the arrow in the top left corner of the screen to return to the project list to see other layouts you have created or to create a new layout.

**How can I use the layout comp I create in Muse?**
You cannot directly import the comp you create in Proto into Muse. Instead, you should use Proto as a way to quickly and easily explore layout possibilities to arrive at a design you will use when you create your site in Muse.

# CHAPTER 4

# Working with Content

Although making your site beautiful should always be an important consideration, your site will never succeed without good content. Content is why users visit your site. Presenting well-organized, compelling content is a far better strategy to getting users to return to your site than focusing solely on visual design.

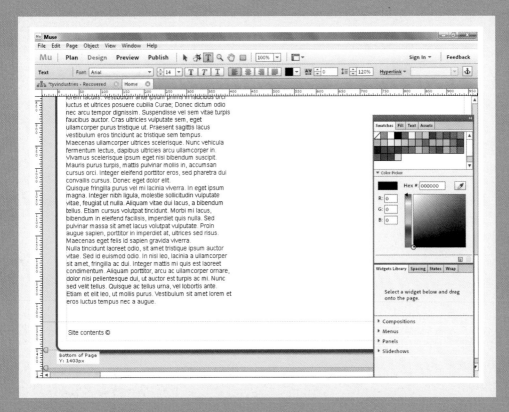

# Add Text to Pages

You can add text to your pages directly in Muse by creating a text box on the page and then typing. You can apply basic formatting as you would in most other programs, using the main toolbar in Muse. Text boxes can be resized as needed, but automatically expand to fit the content you put in them.

## Add Text to Pages

**1** Click the **Text** tool ( T ).

**2** Click and drag on the page to add a text block.

A text box is added.

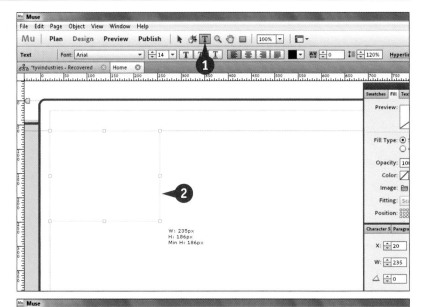

**3** From the toolbar, select a font.

**Note:** Be sure to select one of the "web-safe fonts."

**4** If necessary, change the size of the text.

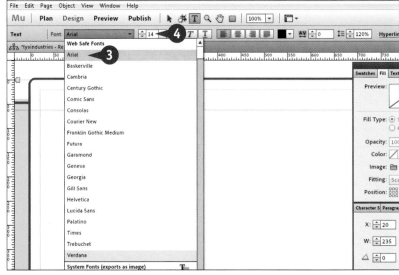

**5** Begin typing your content.

**Note:** If you type more than what will fit in the text box, it resizes.

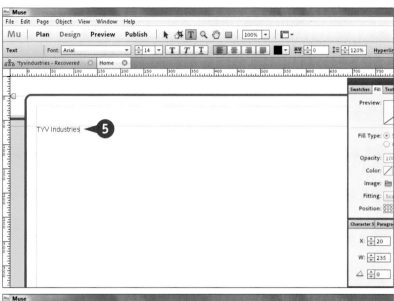

**A** The text is added to the page.

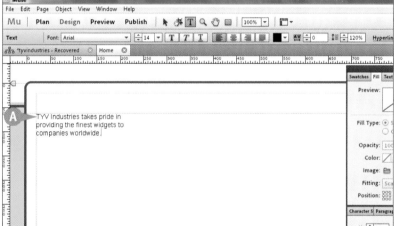

**What unit of measurement is being used for the font size? I do not see any listed, nor do I see a place to change it.**

Although several units of measurement are supported for fonts on the web, Muse only allows you to size text in pixels. On many computer screens, pixel sizes are roughly the same as point sizes, so in most cases 12-pixel text is the same size as 12-point text. Unfortunately, that is not always the case, but Muse provides no way to change the unit.

**Can I format only a portion of the text?**

Yes. While you type, you can change any of the font properties, which apply to any additional text you type. You can also select all or part of the text with the Text tool ( T ) and then change the font properties as desired, just as you would in other programs. You cannot change the properties by selecting the text frame with the Selection tool ( ꜛ ); you must use the Text tool ( T ).

# Import Text

If you have content that has already been created or that someone else is creating for you, you can import the text using the Place command. Unfortunately, however, you can at this time import only unformatted plain-text documents, so if your content is in Microsoft Word or something similar, you need to save it to a plain-text document with a .txt extension to place it. You can also copy and paste text. See the section "Paste Content" in this chapter for details.

## Import Text

1 Click **File**.

2 Click **Place**.

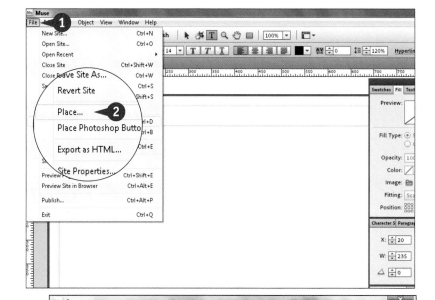

The Import dialog box opens.

3 Make sure Files of Type is set to either All Supported Formats or Text.

4 Select the file you want to import.

5 Click **Open** (**Select** on a Mac).

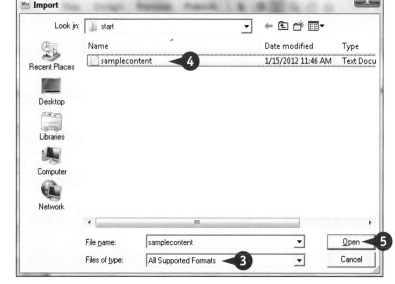

**A** The Loaded Text icon appears.

**6** Click to create a text frame.

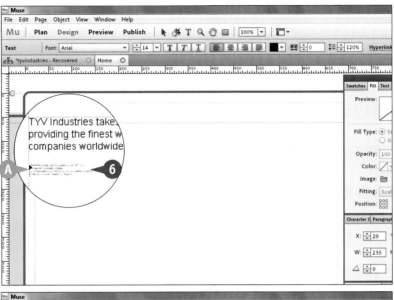

**B** The text is placed into the document.

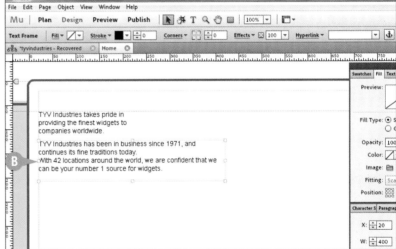

**Is there any way to preserve formatting when I import text?**

No. Muse imports only plain text, which by definition does not contain formatting. If you are importing formatted documents, you must re-create the formatting in Muse after you import.

**Is there a way to split imported text over multiple frames, the way I would in InDesign or other page layout programs?**

When you place the text, all of it drops into a single text box. After placing, you can select some of the text, cut it, and paste it into a new box, but it will not flow from one to the other the way text would in InDesign.

# Paste Content

In addition to typing content directly into Muse and placing text files, you can also copy and paste between Muse and Microsoft Word. You can paste only text, so images in your Word file will not paste. Also, any formatting you have applied to the Word document will be lost. You can either create a text box first and then paste the text into it, or you can simply paste the content onto the page, in which case Muse creates a text box for you.

## Paste Content

1 Open a Microsoft Word document.

2 Select the text you want to paste into Muse.

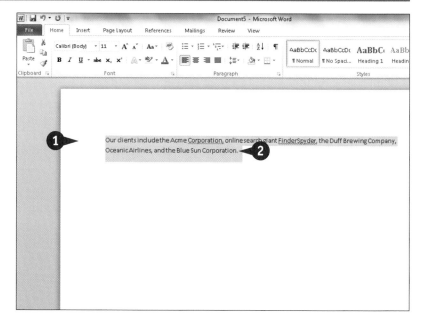

3 Click the **Copy** button ( ).

The text is added to the clipboard.

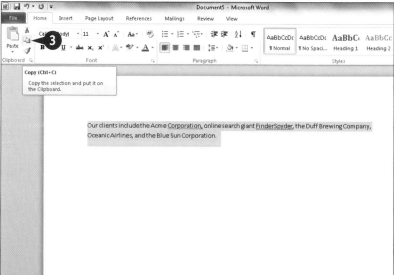

④ Return to Muse.

⑤ Either click in a text box or create a new one.

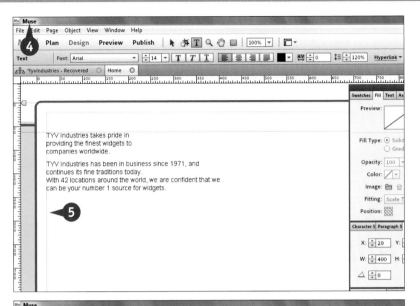

⑥ Click **Edit**.

⑦ Click **Paste**.

Ⓐ The text is pasted into the Muse file.

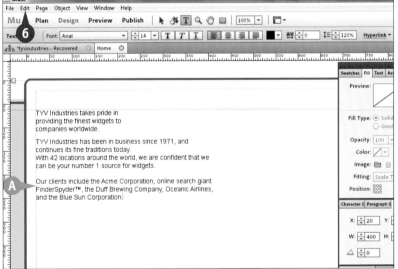

**Can I paste from programs other than Word?**

You can paste from any word processing or text-based program. You can paste data from Excel or from slides in PowerPoint, but you will get unformatted text. You can select text from a web page and paste it into your Muse document. You can also copy and paste images from image-editing programs such as Fireworks or Photoshop. See Chapter 7 for details.

# Using Placeholder Text

In a perfect world, all of your content would be created before you ever needed to sit down and start building a website, but in the real world that rarely happens. Often, you need to create the site either simultaneously with the content or possibly before the content. Therefore, you may need to create text boxes and fill them with placeholder text until you get the real content. As with print, web designers have long relied on Lorem Ipsum text, and although Muse cannot generate the text itself, you can easily copy and paste it from the web.

## Using Placeholder Text

1. In a web browser, go to www.lipsum.com.

2. Enter the desired number of paragraphs.

3. Click **Generate Lorem Ipsum**.

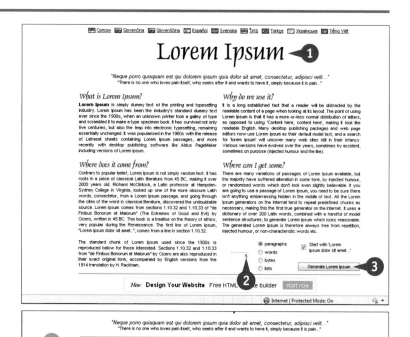

A. The placeholder text is created.

4. Click and drag to select the text.

5. Right-click the text.

6. Select **Copy**.

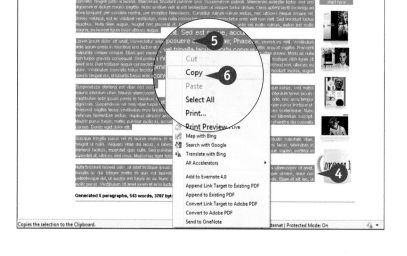

**7** In Muse, select the **Text** tool ( T ).

**8** Click and drag to create a text frame.

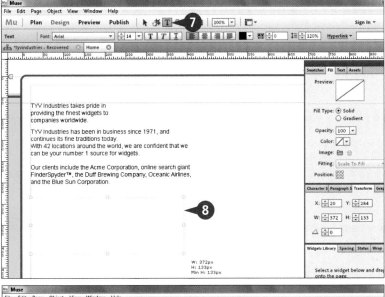

**9** Click **Edit**.

**10** Click **Paste**.

**B** The text is pasted into the document.

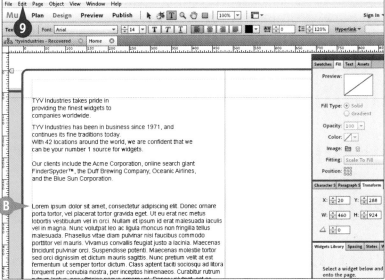

**Do alternatives to Lorem Ipsum exist?**
Yes. Over the last few years, quite a few enterprising individuals have played with the long-standard placeholder text. If you want something more fun than fake Latin, you can check out baconipsum.com, or its polar opposite veganipsum.com. Filler text from cupcakeipsum.com will likely make you crave dessert. The generator at www.malevole.com/mv/misc/text uses random TV show theme song lyrics, whereas fillerati.com generates filler text from famous novels such as *Moby Dick* and *The War of the Worlds*. A variety of pop-culture sources such as Monty Python, *The Simpsons*, and *Star Wars* are used to generate the text at http://chrisvalleskey.com/fillerama.

# Add Special Characters

Oftentimes you will need to add special characters to your document. Perhaps the most common of these is the copyright symbol, but you may also need the trademark symbol, non-U.S. currency symbols, the degree sign, or others. Unfortunately, Muse does not have a panel or dialog box to allow you to enter these directly, but you can either type them using special codes or copy them from another source such as Microsoft Word or your operating system.

## Add Special Characters

### Type a Special Character

**1** With the Text tool ( T ), click in a text frame.

**●** On a Mac, press and hold [Option] and press [G]. In Windows, press and hold [Alt], and then use the numeric keypad and type [0][1][6][9]. Release [Alt] and the symbol appears.

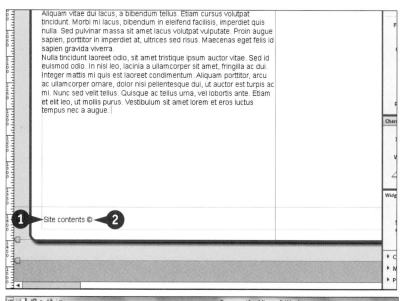

### Copy a Symbol from Word

**1** Open Word.

**●** Type **(tm)**.

The trademark symbol appears.

**●** Select the symbol.

**4** Click the **Copy** button ( 🗐 ).

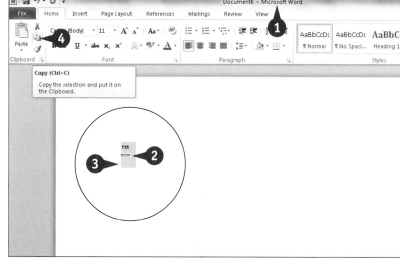

**5** Return to Muse.

**6** Click **Edit**.

**7** Click **Paste**.

Ⓐ The symbol is inserted into the page.

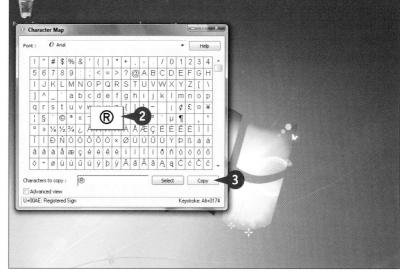

## Copy a Symbol from the Operating System

**1** In Windows, click **Start**, **All Programs**, **Accessories**, **System Tools**, and then **Character Map**. On a Mac, press ⌘+Option+T.

**2** Select the character you want.

**3** Click **Copy**.

The character is copied to the clipboard.

**4** Repeat steps **5** to **7** to paste the character into Muse.

## TIPS

**If I already have the symbol entered into a block of text I import or copy, will it be retained?**
Yes. Perhaps the easiest way to add the symbols is to insert them into your text when you create it in Word or another program. That way, they are there when you import the text and you do not have to worry about going through the steps outlined above. You could also copy the text from another text frame in Muse.

**Could I just create the symbol as an image and import it?**
Yes, but it will be much more difficult to manage. Muse does not support inline images; that is, images that flow with text. Therefore, if you have a symbol inserted as an image, you would need to constantly adjust its position as you edit the text. Inserting the symbol as text is far easier.

# Set a Minimum Height for the Page

In most cases, the amount of content on the page determines the height of the page. The page cannot be smaller than its content, but in certain situations you may want to force the page to always maintain a minimum height. This potentially results in empty space below the content on shorter pages, so you need to carefully consider its impact on your design.

## Set a Minimum Height for the Page

**1** If necessary, scroll to the bottom of the page.

**2** Click and drag the **Bottom of Page** guide to the desired location.

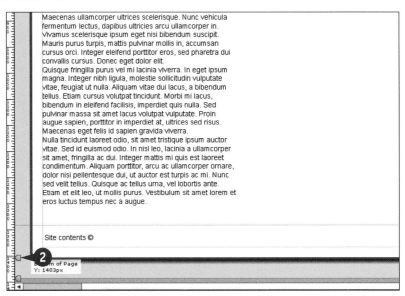

**A** The page has a minimum height set.

# Create Content with Flexible Widths

Sometimes, your design works best if your content is set to a predetermined width; this is the default setting. When you create a text frame, for example, its width is set to a number of pixels, based on how you dragged it. Other times, however, you may want to set content to be as wide as the browser window. You can do this by simply dragging the frame for the content to the edge of the screen.

## Create Content with Flexible Widths

**1** If it is not already selected, click the **Selection** tool ( ).

**2** Drag the left control handle to the edge of the window until you see a red guide.

The content's width is locked to the left edge of the browser.

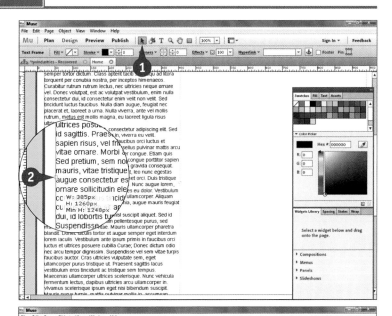

**3** Repeat step **2** for the right edge.

The content's width is locked to both edges of the browser window.

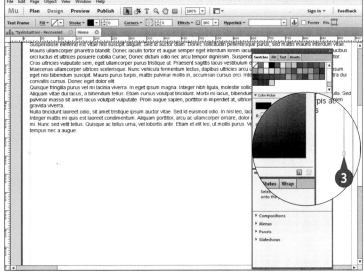

# Rearrange and Resize Content

You can freely move content on your page to redesign your layout. You can just as easily resize content. Both require that you use the Selection tool. You can move content by simply dragging it to a new location, and resize by dragging any of the resize handles. Content can overlap, so you need to be careful to avoid overlapping if it will make your content difficult to read.

## Rearrange and Resize Content

1 If necessary, click the **Selection** tool (↖).

2 Drag a content frame to a new location.

The frame is repositioned.

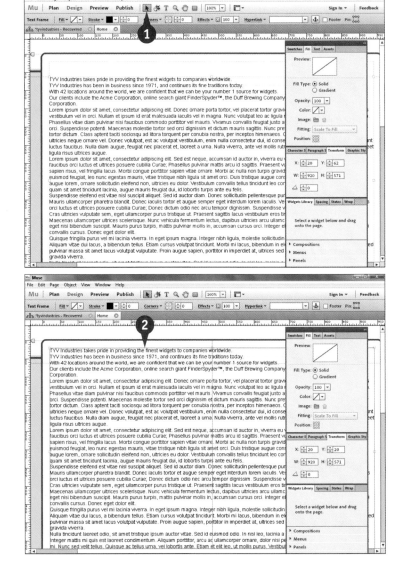

**3** Click and drag one of the control handles on a frame.

The frame resizes.

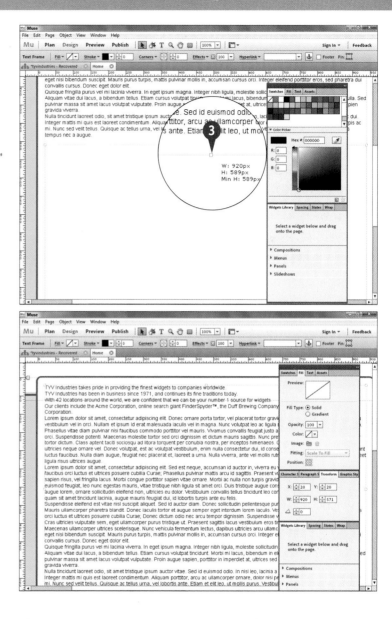

**4** Repeat steps **2** and **3** as needed to finish your layout.

**TIP**

**Does Muse include guides to help me lay out my page?**
Yes. Muse has Smart Guides that appear automatically as you drag objects, whether you are creating them, moving them, or resizing them. Smart Guides appear as you approach the centers and edges of the page or of other content.

# Add Non-Scrolling Content

Most of the time, your users expect that as they scroll down a page, all the content on the page will scroll as well. However, it may be helpful in some cases to have content that remains fixed as the page scrolls and so is always visible to the user. In Muse, this is known as *pinning* content. Achieving this effect used to be fairly difficult and required that developers learn and implement JavaScript, but Muse makes adding it to your page extremely simple.

## Add Non-Scrolling Content

**1** Add a text box.

**Note:** See the section "Add Text to Pages" for more information.

**2** Enter text.

**3** Click the **Selection** tool ( ).

**4** Select the content you want to pin.

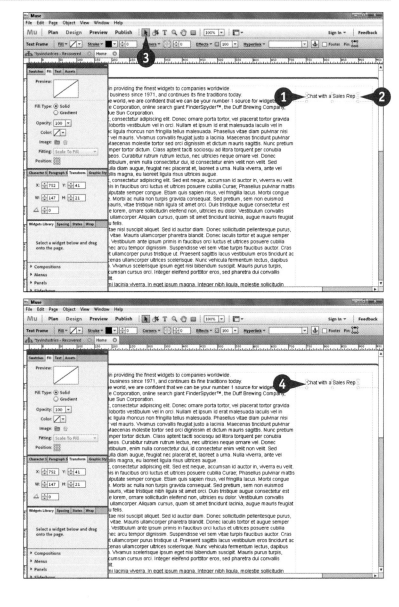

**5** On the Control bar, click one of the six options on the Pin tool.

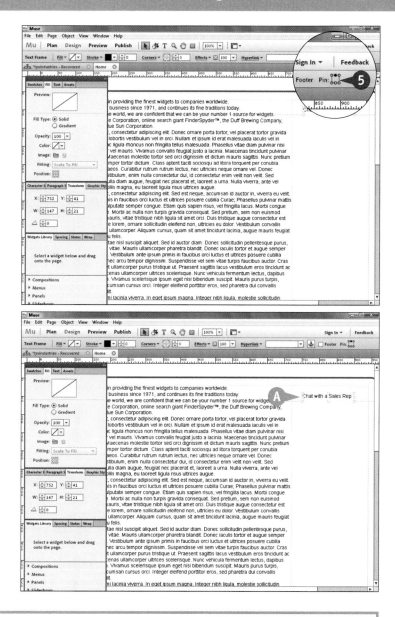

**A** The object is pinned to the browser window. When you preview the page, it does not scroll.

**Note:** Pinning does not work in Design view. To see the pinned text, preview the page, as explained in the next section.

**Can I pin an object to more than one edge?**

No. The Pin tool allows you to pin to only a single point. You also can pin only to the top or bottom edges of the screen. When you pin objects, Muse adds CSS code to your page to apply the effect, and CSS does not support pinning to multiple points or pinning to the right or left edges.

**Can I pin more than one object on a page?**

Yes. You can pin as many objects to the page as you want. Because the purpose of pinning is to keep objects on the screen and thus make them important enough so as to not scroll, you will likely want to minimize the number of objects you pin, but no technical limitation exists.

# Preview Your Page

While Muse is known as a WYSIWYG, or What You See Is What You Get, editor, its Design view does not always display the page exactly as a browser would. Two obvious differences are the presence of the margins and guides and the fact that the Browser Fill setting does not fill the entire screen. To see the page as it will look in a browser, you must periodically switch to Preview view.

## Preview Your Page

**1** Click **Preview**.

Preview view opens, displaying the page as it would appear in a browser.

**2** Scroll down the page.

Ⓐ Pinned content does not scroll off the page.

③ In Windows, click **Restore**.

④ Resize the Muse window.

Non-fixed-width content resizes with the browser window.

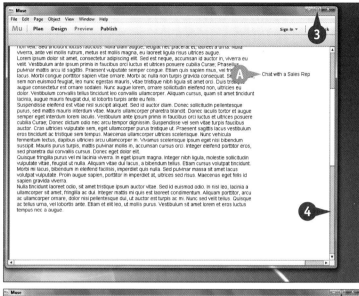

⑤ In Windows, click **Maximize**. On a Mac, expand the Muse window back to full size.

The window is maximized.

**TIP**

**I have heard that different browsers display pages differently. How can I preview in more than one browser?**
Muse previews your page using whatever browser your operating system sets to be the default. Although display differences between browsers are not as extreme as they once were, they still exist. Unfortunately, at this time Muse does not provide the ability to test in any other browser besides the default, so you either need to publish the page or generate HTML to see what your pages look like. See Chapter 13 for details.

# CHAPTER 5

# Formatting Text

The web is all about content. Making truly beautiful sites that stand out from the rest is ultimately about making that content look great.

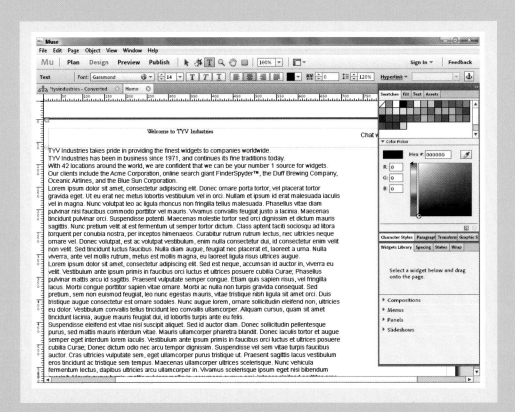

# Apply Web-Safe Fonts

Since the earliest days of the web, browsers have relied on what are known as *device fonts* to display text. This simply means that fonts are not embedded into your web page. Instead, your page contains a bit of code that tells the browser what font to use, but that font only be applied if installed on the user's machine. Muse refers to these fonts as *system fonts*.

## Apply Web-Safe Fonts

**1** Using the Text tool ( T ), select the text for which you want to change the font.

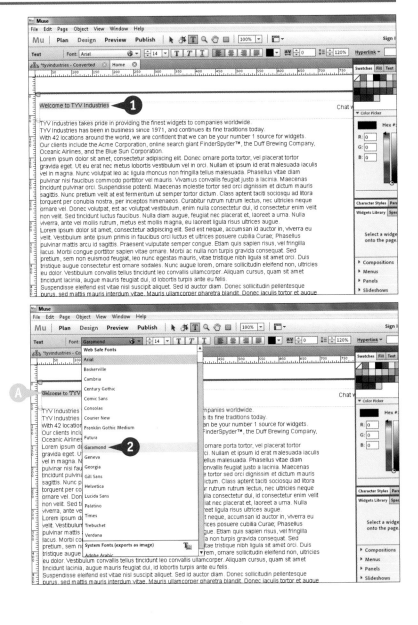

**2** Using the Control bar, select a font from those listed under the heading Web-Safe Fonts.

Ⓐ The font is applied to the text.

# Apply Other Fonts

You are not limited to the list of web-safe fonts in Muse. Instead, you can choose to format text using any font you want. If you select a non-web-safe font, Muse automatically creates an image out of the font and replaces your text with the image. Thankfully, this replacement happens only when you publish the site, so the text remains editable. You should limit your use of these fonts to headings, and never use them for body text because search engines will not be able to read your site.

## Apply Other Fonts

**1** Using the Text tool ( **T** ), select the text for which you want to change the font.

**2** Using the Control bar, select a font from those listed under the heading System Fonts.

The font is applied to the text.

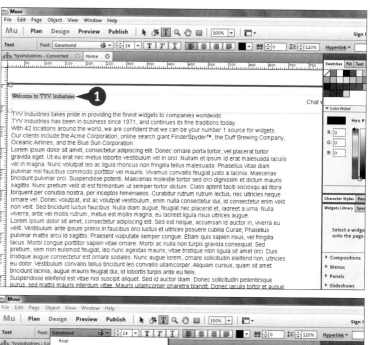

# Adjust Alignment and Spacing

You can adjust the alignment and spacing of the text. Alignment can be set to left, right, center, or justified. You have two options for spacing: letter spacing, which increases the space between individual characters, and line spacing or *leading*, the space between lines of text.

## Adjust Alignment and Spacing

### Adjust Alignment

**1** Using the Text tool ( **T** ), click within a paragraph of text.

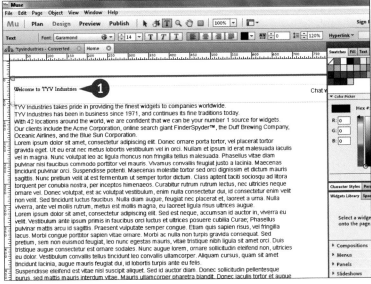

**2** Using the Control bar, click one of the Align buttons.

**A** The text aligns.

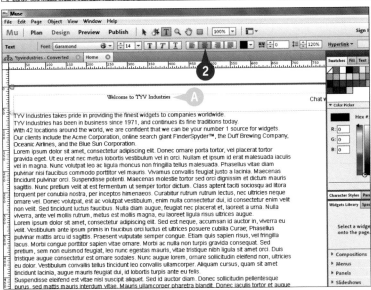

## Adjust Spacing

**1** Select the text you want to adjust.

**2** Using the Control bar, adjust the value in the Letter Space control.

**B** The text adjusts its spacing.

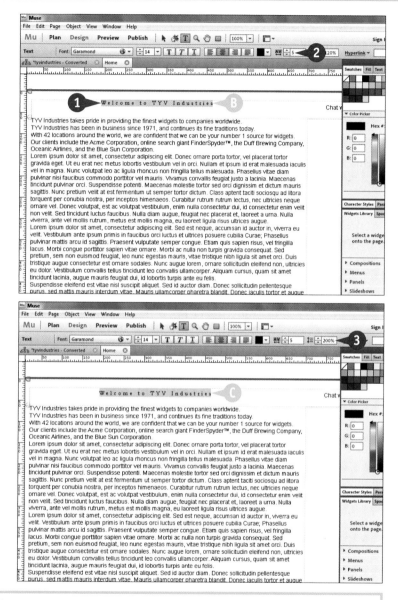

**3** Using the Control bar, change the value of the Leading control.

**C** More or less space is added to between lines of text.

**I am used to adjusting letter spacing in very small increments. In Muse, it seems like I can do only whole pixels, which is too much. Can I use a smaller unit?**

No. Print tools like the page layout program InDesign allow you to kern in very, very small increments because printers can print anywhere on the page. Computer screens simply cannot display things in fractions of a pixel, so you are limited in web design to adjusting in whole pixels. In a practical sense, this means that although kerning individual letter pairs is possible in Muse — you can click between any two letters instead of selecting a block of text — the minimum amount of adjusting you can do is too great and is unlikely to give you the look you want.

# Basic Text Formatting

You can format individual pieces of text using the Control bar. Select the text you want to format and then use the options on the Control bar to set the size, weight, style, and color. You can set these values to anything that works for your design. This formatting applies only to the selected text.

## Basic Text Formatting

1. Using the Text tool ( **T** ), select some of your text.

2. Select a size from the dropdown. You can also type your own value.

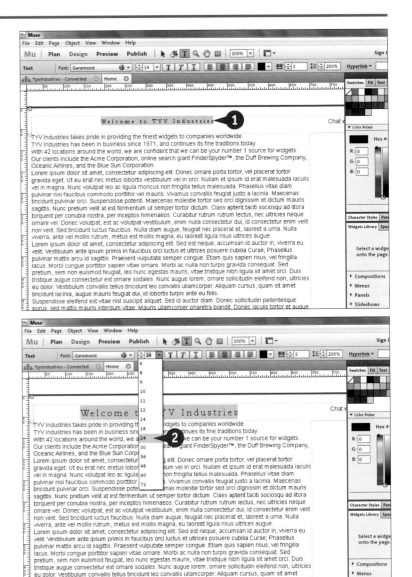

**3** If desired, apply other formatting, such as bold or italic.

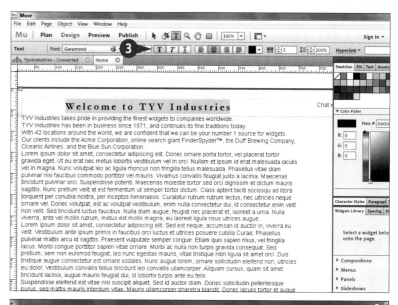

**4** Select a color from the color picker.

**A** The text is formatted.

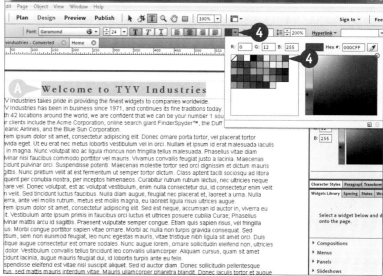

TIP

**I have heard that you should not underline text on a web page. Why is this?**

Hyperlinks are underlined by default on almost every web page, so people have become accustomed to the idea that if they see underlined text, they should be able to click it to go to another page. If you underline non-hyperlinked text on your pages, you will invariably confuse your users.

Another argument against underlining is that it is simply hard to read. Underlining became popular in the days of typewriters, which could not easily bold or italicize text. Computers have no such issue, so you should avoid underlines except for hyperlinks.

# Apply Formats with the Text Panel

Although most of the formatting options appear on the Control bar, a few additional attributes can be accessed with the Text panel. You can open the panel by clicking **Window** and then **Text**. The Text panel displays all the options from the Control bar, including font, size, color, weight, style, alignment, kerning, and leading. It adds options for spacing, including first-line indent, left indent, right indent, space before, and space after.

## Apply Formats with the Text Panel

1 Using the Text tool ( **T** ), select the text you want to format.

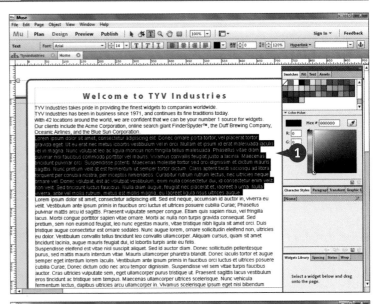

2 Click **Window**.

3 Click **Text**.

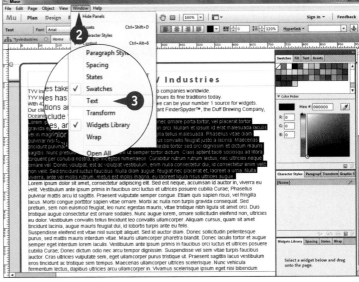

(A) The Text panel opens.

(4) Adjust any of the formatting options as needed.

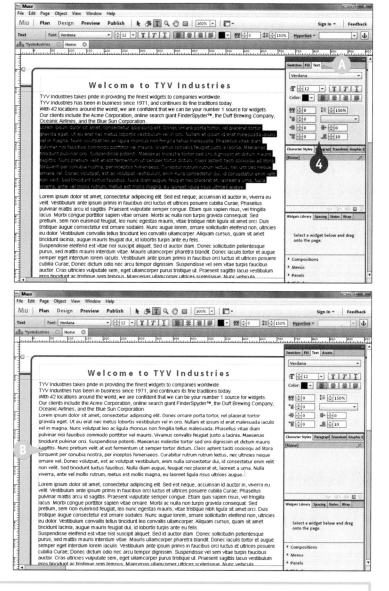

(B) The selected text is formatted.

**Is there any difference between using the Control bar and using the Text panel?**

For the options that appear on both, no. As with many other programs, Muse often gives you multiple ways to accomplish the same task. Which one you end up using on a regular basis is simple personal preference.

**InDesign provides many, many more formatting options. Why are so few here in Muse?**

When you work in InDesign, you have the freedom of formatting your text in almost any way you choose because your end result is print, which can handle extremely complex formatting. When creating a site in Muse, you work in a totally different medium — the web — which has much more limited formatting capabilities.

# Work with Character Styles

As your site expands, you should make sure that your design remains consistent. If you apply all of your formatting by manually adjusting settings on the Control bar, it can become increasingly difficult to remember exactly what formats you have applied to text, and you may end up with text that should look the same actually being different. Using styles in Muse solves this problem, by allowing you to save formatting instructions and reuse them later without having to remember the details of the format.

## Work with Character Styles

**1** Using the Text tool ( **T** ), select text that you want to format as the basis of your style.

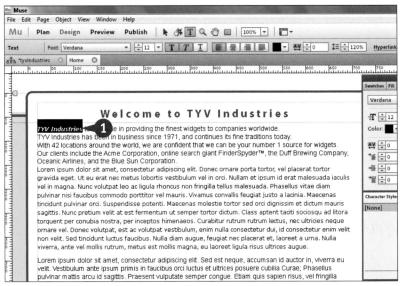

**2** Format the text as desired, using the Control bar or the Text panel.

**Note:** See the sections "Basic Text Formatting" and "Apply Formats with the Text Panel" in this chapter for details.

**3** Open the Character Styles panel.

**4** Click the **Create new style from the attributes applied** button (⊡).

A new style is created.

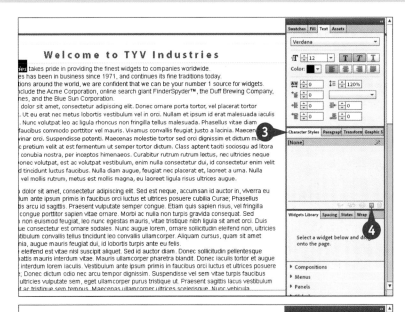

**5** Double-click the new style.

The Style Options dialog box opens.

**6** Give the style a descriptive name.

**7** Click **OK**.

The style is renamed.

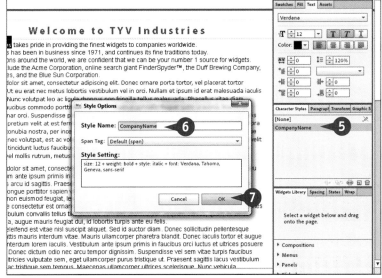

**Is there a limit as to how many character styles I can create?**

No. A complex site might have many dozens of styles. This is ultimately why giving the style a descriptive name is important, because you would not likely enjoy maintaining a site where everything was named Character Style 1, Character Style 2, and so on.

**Do I need a separate character style for each block of text I want to format?**

No. You only need a new style for each block of text that you want to style differently from other text. If you are formatting some text and you are relatively certain you will not need to reuse that format, then you do not need to create a style at all.

# Apply Character Styles

Once you have created a style, you can easily apply the style to any other text in your document by simply selecting the text and then selecting the style you want to apply in the Character Styles panel. You can apply only a single character style to any given block of text, but a single style can be reused as often as necessary.

## Apply Character Styles

**1** Using the Text tool ( T ), select the text to which you want to apply the style.

**2** Click the appropriate style in the Character Styles panel.

**A** The style is applied to the text.

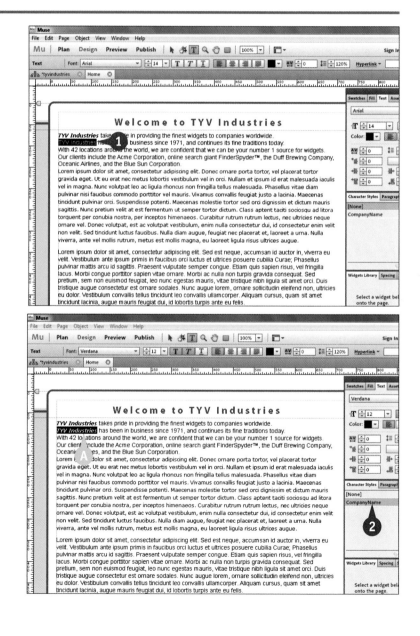

# Modify Character Styles

Occasionally, you may need to modify the appearance of a style. It may simply be that you changed your mind about how you want that style to look, or it might be that some other change in your design necessitates it. It could also be that your client or employer wants it changed. Whatever the reason, you can modify a style by manually editing the appearance of a piece of text that has the style applied, and then apply that change to the style. When you modify a style, all text that has the style applied automatically updates.

## Modify Character Styles

**1** Using the Text tool ( T ), select some text that has a character style applied to it.

**2** Using the Control bar or the Text panel, change the formatting of the text.

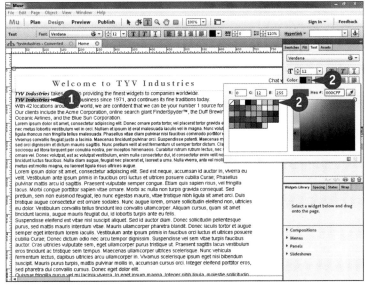

**3** On the Character Styles panel, click the **Refine selected style from the attributes applied** button ( ).

**Ⓐ** The style, and any text using the style, updates.

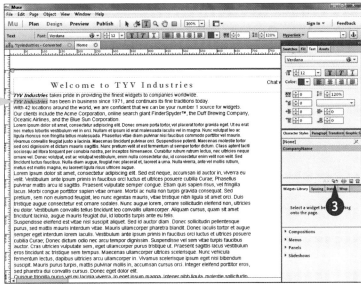

# Understanding How Character Styles Apply to Text

Although Muse does its best to hide code from you and make it possible to create pages without writing code directly, you should understand certain aspects of the underlying HTML in order to make sure that your styles are applied correctly. When you apply a character style, Muse adds some code around the text in question. In most cases, the default code, called a `span` tag, works when applying the style, but in some situations it might help to apply the style using a different tag.

## Span and Footer

The `span` tag has existed in HTML for decades as a generic way of adding a style to text. The newer `footer` tag is intended, as its name implies, to mark up the footer of a section or document.

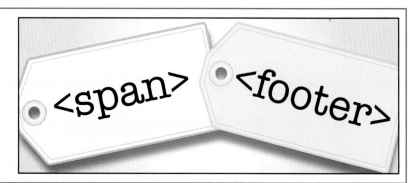

## Abbr, Q, Cite, and Mark

The `abbr` tag, short for abbreviation, and the `q` tag, short for quotation, are intended to allow designers to designate text as quotes from other sources. The `cite` tag should be used to designate a citation, whereas the `mark` tag is intended for designating portions of quotes.

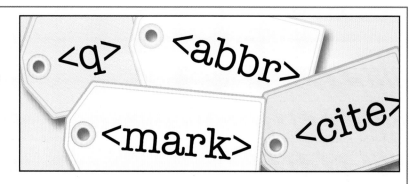

## Samp and Code

The `samp` tag is short for sample. Both it and the `code` tag exist to designate blocks of code within a page, used frequently in technical tutorial sites and blogs.

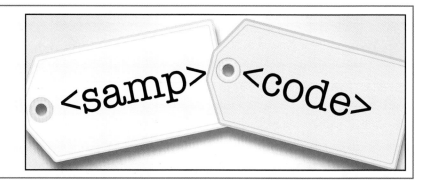

## Sup and Sub

The `sup` tag is for superscript, whereas the `sub` tag stands for subscript. Both are intended to mark text as being either superscript, where the text lies above the normal line, and subscript, where it lies below.

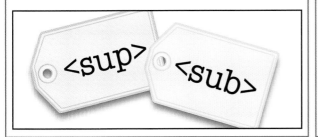

## No Default Appearances

Although many of these tags have defaults if used alone, Muse overrides them. For example, if you were to write HTML and include a `cite` tag, the browser would italicize the text, but if you apply that tag to a character style in Muse, the text will not be italic unless you specifically add that format.

## Applying the Tags

You can change the tag applied to a character style by double-clicking the style name in the Character Styles panel (Ⓐ) and then selecting the appropriate style from the dialog box.

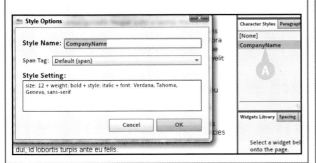

## Why They Matter

Applying the tag that makes the most sense logically in the context of how the text is being used benefits you in several ways. It helps search engines better index your page and helps those with disabilities better understand your page.

# Manage Local Overrides on Styles

If you apply a character style to a block of text, you can still directly format that text using the Control bar or the Text panel. You can apply any formatting you want to the text without affecting the style, unless your formatting specifically changes a property controlled by the style. In this case, you are creating a local override to the style. For example, if your style made the text bold, you could locally change the font; but if you unbold the text, you create a local override. Using the Character Styles panel, you can clear these overrides to reapply the properties as defined in the style.

## Manage Local Overrides on Styles

**1** Select some text to which you have applied a character style.

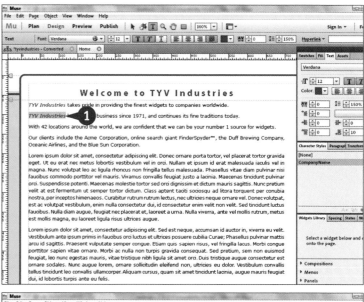

**2** Apply formatting that overrides a property of the style.

**A** The Character Styles panel updates to display a plus sign next to the style name, denoting a local override.

**3** On the Character Styles panel, click the **Clear Style Overrides** button ( A ).

**B** The style is reapplied and the formatting from step **2** is removed.

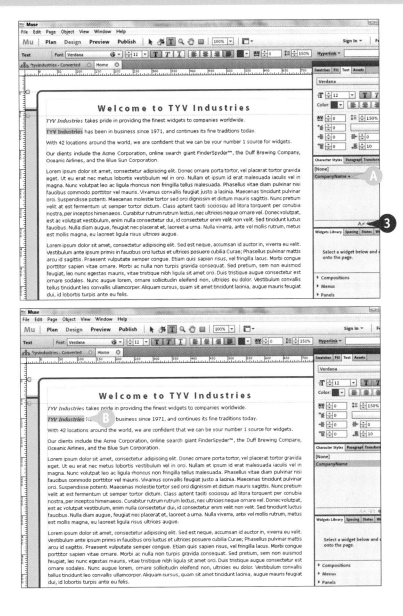

**Can I apply local overrides to paragraph and graphic styles?**
Yes. If you apply a style to a paragraph or to a graphic and then apply formatting changes, you can clear those overrides as well. The key difference is that with character styles, only properties that you change that are part of the style register as an override. With paragraph and graphic styles, any changes are considered overrides, including adding new formatting properties.

# Work with Paragraph Styles

Character styles are intended to apply to individual words within a larger text block. Paragraph styles are intended, as their name implies, to apply to entire paragraphs. Any block of text on a page is considered a paragraph, so every time you press `Enter` while typing, you are creating a new paragraph. You create paragraph styles in the same way you create character styles: by applying the desired formats to a paragraph, and then using that as the basis for a new style. Paragraph styles can, and often do, contain character formatting.

## Work with Paragraph Styles

**1** Using the Text tool ( T ), select the text of a paragraph.

**2** Use the Control bar or Text panel to apply formats to the paragraph.

**Note:** See the section "Basic Text Formatting" in this chapter for details.

**3** Open the Paragraph Styles panel.

**4** Click the **Create new style from the attributes applied** button (■).

A new style is created.

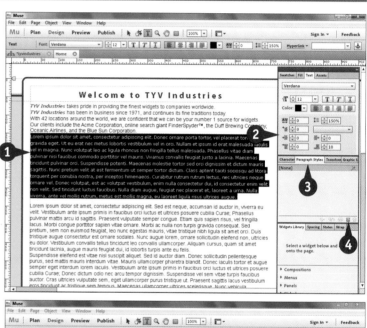

**5** Double-click the new style.

The Style Options dialog box opens.

**6** Give the style a descriptive name.

**7** Click **OK**.

The style is renamed.

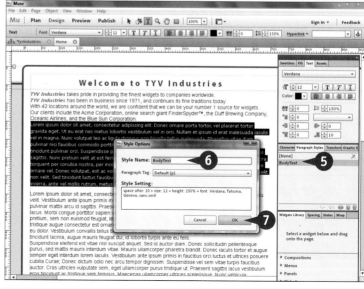

# Apply Paragraph Styles

A pplying an existing paragraph style to your text is even easier than applying an existing character style to text: Simply use the Text tool to click into a paragraph and then select the style from the panel. As with most other programs, you only need to select text when applying paragraph styles if you plan to apply the style to more than one paragraph. You can also select an entire text box using the Selection tool and then apply the style to all paragraphs within the box.

## Apply Paragraph Styles

**1** Use the Text tool ( **T** ) to click within a paragraph of text or to select multiple paragraphs, or use the Selection tool to select a text box.

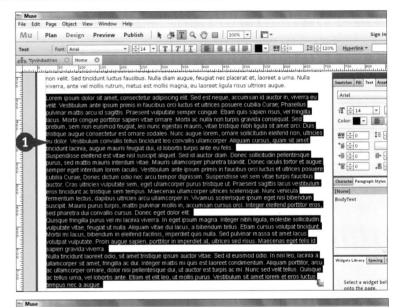

**2** From the Paragraph Styles panel, select the style you want to apply.

**A** The style is applied to the paragraph or paragraphs of text.

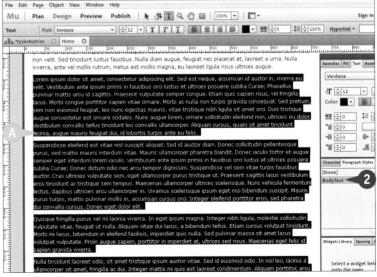

# Modify Paragraph Styles

You can modify paragraph styles in the same way you modify character styles: Make changes to the formatting of text that already has the style, and then apply those changes to the style. As with character styles, any changes to a paragraph style automatically affect all paragraphs with that style throughout your site. This allows you to leverage one of the most powerful aspects of using styles: the ability to change the appearance of your text throughout your site by making a change in one place.

## Modify Paragraph Styles

1 Using the Text tool ( T ), select some text that has a paragraph style applied to it.

2 Using the Control bar or the Text panel, change the formatting of the text.

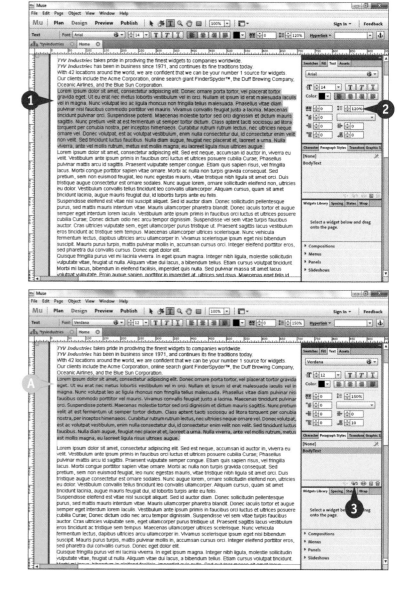

3 On the Paragraph Styles panel, click the **Refine selected style from the attributes applied** button ( ).

Ⓐ The style, and any text using the style, update.

J ust as you have the ability to control which HTML tag is used in applying a character style, you can do the same with paragraph styles. Proper application of paragraph styles is perhaps even more important than with character styles, however. When you change a paragraph style from being applied with the paragraph tag to being applied with a heading tag, you can make the text you designate stand out more to search engines.

## Paragraph

The basic building block of the content of almost every web page, the paragraph tag should be used for most of your content.

## Headline and Subheads

Ideally, every page should have at least one headline, or h1. Main topics below that should be set off with the first subhead, h2. Topics below that should use h3, and so on.

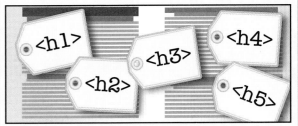

## Marquee

Perhaps the biggest feature in Muse that no one would recommend you use, the marquee produces scrolling text. Professional web designers long ago abandoned marquee because of its amateur look.

## Apply the Tags

You can change the tag applied to a character style by double-clicking the style name in the Paragraph Styles panel (Ⓐ) and then selecting the appropriate style from the dialog box.

# CHAPTER 6

# Creating Graphics for Your Site

The web is of course a visual medium, and the careful application of graphics on your site can greatly enhance its overall appearance.

# Understanding Image Formats

Hundreds of graphics formats exist, but the web supports only three: GIF, JPEG, and PNG. Before you can begin working with images on your pages, you need to understand these formats so that you can choose the one that works best. Each format has specific advantages and disadvantages, and you must evaluate each image to determine the format that works best for it.

## The Formats for the Web

Browsers can natively display images saved in the JPEG, GIF, and PNG formats. Any other format requires that the browser use a plug-in, so these three are commonly thought of as the formats the web supports. If you have an image in any other format, you must convert it to one of these.

## JPEG

JPEG is short of Joint Photographic Experts Group, the organization that originally developed the format. The JPEG format supports millions of colors and is thus best for photographic images. Most of today's digital cameras save images as JPEGs by default.

## GIF

Originally developed in the 1980s by CompuServe, the Graphics Interchange Format has long been a standard on the Internet, even before the web. GIFs support a maximum of 256 colors, and today are primarily used for logos, line art, and buttons. Unlike JPEG, GIF supports transparency and animation.

## PNG

Developed as an alternative to GIF, the Portable Network Graphics format combines the best features of the JPEG and GIF formats. Like JPEG, PNG can have millions of colors, and like GIF, PNG can support transparency.

# Legally Acquiring Stock Images

Any creative work is protected by copyright. This applies to written works such as this book as well as artistic works such as photographs. You are of course free to use any image that you create yourself. If you work for a large company, they may have already acquired sets of images that are again safe to use on the company's websites. Before you can use an image that you or your company did not create, you need to be sure that you have the legal right to use it.

## Royalty-Free Images

If you want to use someone else's work, you must pay them for that work through royalties every time you use it. However, you may be able to pay for an image once and then freely use that image from then on. Such images are known as *royalty-free* images. Note that you may have to pay a fee upfront, so royalty free does not necessarily mean free.

## Stock Images

Stock images are generally royalty-free images made available for use by companies and organizations. Stock images tend to be somewhat general in their subject matter: Groups of people, animals, and scenery are common subjects for stock images.

## When in Doubt, Do Not Use It

The penalties for using someone else's copyrighted material can be severe. The simplest way to protect yourself from getting sued for illegally using images is to never use something unless you are absolutely certain doing so is okay. Do not use an image off a site unless you can find text on the page from which you are getting the image that clearly states that it is okay.

# Understanding Image Optimization

Every image you add to a page increases the overall size of the page, which can result in your page loading slower, using more of your user's bandwidth. Optimizing your image is the process of reducing its file size while minimizing the impact of that reduction on the quality of the image. Every major graphics program offers tools to optimize images, but these generally provide an array of options that can be highly confusing, so you should gain a basic understanding of the various ways in which graphics can be optimized to better understand the process.

## JPEG Optimization

JPEGs are optimized by compressing the image. Unfortunately, this uses a technique known as *lossy compression*, where data is removed from the image. Therefore, the more you optimize an image, the worse it looks. The compression is often expressed as a percentage, with 100% retaining all the original data and thus applying no compression.

## GIF Optimization

You can optimize a GIF by removing unnecessary colors from it. GIFs can contain up to 256 colors, but they do not need to use all of those. A simple logo may be made up of only one or two colors, so saving the GIF with additional embedded colors in the file is nothing more than a waste of space. However, more complex images may start to lose quality if you remove needed colors.

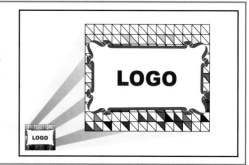

## PNG Optimization

PNG files can be compressed via lossy compression, just like JPEGs, or via removing colors, like GIFs. PNGs can also contain additional embedded data that describes the image to editing software but is unnecessary when used on web pages, so removing this data can be seen as a form of optimizing for the format.

## GIF and PNG Features

GIF supports optional features such as animation and transparency. PNG supports transparency. Adding these can make your image look better, but also adds to the file size. Therefore, choosing to not use these features reduces the size of the images.

## Choose the Right Format

Because the JPEG and GIF formats were specifically designed for a particular image type, each is inherently more efficient when used on the correct type of image. Therefore, an image that should be saved as a JPEG will be larger if you attempt to save it as a GIF, and vice versa.

## Scale and Crop Images

Images with needlessly large pixel dimensions will also be needlessly large files. Using a good image-editing tool to reduce the dimensions of the image dramatically reduces its file size. You can also crop unneeded portions out of the image to reduce its size.

## Resolution

Image resolution describes the number of pixels per inch in an image. Whereas images for print need to have a high resolution, images for the web should be no more the 72 dots or pixels per inch. Many computer screens are incapable of displaying higher-resolution images, so keeping the image at a higher resolution simply wastes file size.

# Download a Stock Image from the Web

The website at www.istockphoto.com is an excellent resource for finding royalty-free images. Although you need to pay for most of the images, the site provides a single image each week that you can freely download and use. You begin the process of getting images at the site by creating a free account. You can use this account to search the site and download the free image of the week. As with other sites that you have accounts with, you should pick a strong password that is easy for you to remember but hard for others to guess.

## Download a Stock Image from the Web

### Sign Up for a Free Account

① Open a web browser and go to www.istockphoto.com.

② Click **Sign Up**.

A sign-up form appears.

③ Fill in the requested information on the form.

④ Click **I agree to the Membership Agreement** (☐ changes to ☑).

⑤ Click **Next Step**.

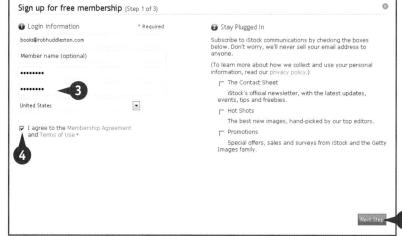

**6** Complete the second screen.

**7** Click **Sign me up!**.

A confirmation screen appears.

**8** Double-check that the information is correct.

**9** Click **Confirm**.

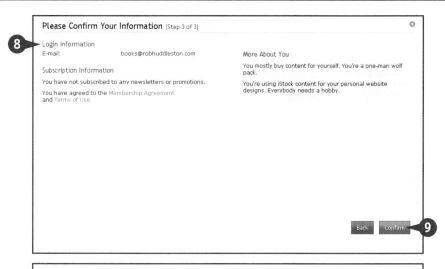

The You're In! screen appears.

**10** Click **Continue**.

The sign-up process is complete, and you are returned to the home page.

---

## TIPS

**What other stock image sites exist online?**
There are too many to count, but SpiderPic, at www.spiderpic.com, is a good place to start. Unlike other sites, SpiderPic does not sell its own images; instead, it allows you to comparison-shop across many other stock sites, and you can often find the same image for less.

**What about using Google Images or Flickr?**
Just because you can easily find an image online does not mean it is not protected by copyright, so using images you find on Google Images, Flickr, or other image sharing sites is almost certainly illegal. Flickr does provide the ability to search for images licensed for reuse; look up their Creative Commons search for more details.

continued ▶

Once you have signed up for a free account at iStockphoto, you can either purchase credits to buy images or visit the site every week to download their free image of the week. Credits are about $1 each, but as with many other sites, the price per credit drops if you purchase more at one time. However, plan carefully, because credits expire one year after you purchase them. You should therefore try to plan ahead so that you can purchase enough credits for the year to take advantage of discounts, while not buying so many that you end up losing some.

## Download a Stock Image from the Web (continued)

### Download the Free Image of the Week

**1** On the iStockphoto home page, click the image below the heading Download Free Image Now.

The free photo page loads.

**2** Select the image size you want to download.

**3** Click **Download this Photo**.

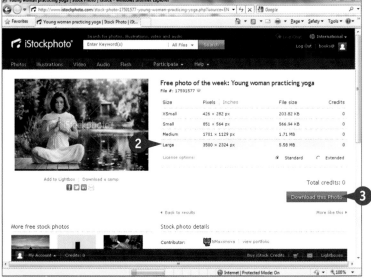

The Download free file of the week page appears.

**④** Click **Accept Agreement & Start Download**.

**Note:** If a page appears asking you to complete your membership profile, fill out the form and click **Update Profile**.

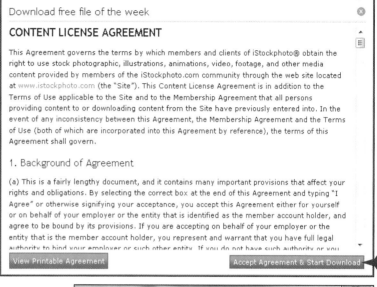

## What size image should I choose?

For the free image of the week, you should download the largest size available, because this gives you the most flexibility in working with the image later. Images can be easily scaled down, but not up, so for images you are purchasing, you should get the largest size you think you might need.

are either
just
ll likely be
r on your

# Introducing the Fireworks Interface

Adobe currently develops three graphics tools: Fireworks, Photoshop, and Illustrator. Although print designers are almost certainly familiar with the latter two, Fireworks is the only one of the three created specifically with web graphics in mind. A complete overview of Fireworks is beyond the scope of this book, but a basic introduction will help you get familiar with its tools.

**ⓐ Menu bar**

Most of the commands in the program are accessed from these menus.

**ⓑ View options**

Zoom in and out and move around on the document with these tools.

**ⓒ Workspace switcher**

Change the layout of panels by selecting a different workspace.

**ⓓ Panels**

Most of your work in Fireworks is done through panels.

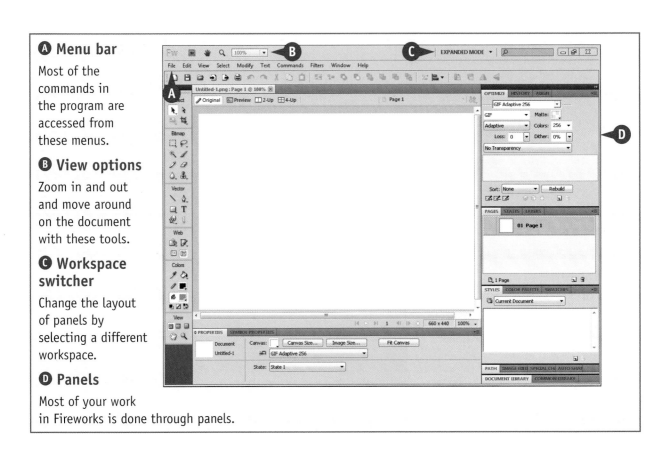

se

## ⓔ Toolbox

The drawing tools in Fireworks are found here.

## ⓕ Document tabs

You switch between open documents by selecting the document's tab.

## ⓖ Preview options

Choose to view your document in Original, Preview, 2-Up, or 4-Up mode.

## ⓗ Properties

This panel is dynamic, and presents different options depending on the tool or object currently selected.

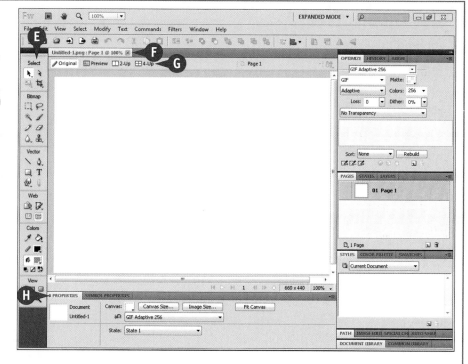

# Create a Simple Graphic in Fireworks

One of the things that make Fireworks unique is that it contains a set of powerful vector tools, similar to Illustrator, along with equally powerful bitmap editing tools, similar to Photoshop. Because it was designed specifically for the web, the New Document settings in Fireworks have web-appropriate defaults, such as RGB color, pixel-based measurements, and a 72-pixel-per-inch resolution. Although these can be changed, you will rarely need to.

## Creating a Simple Graphic in Fireworks

**1** From the Start screen, click **Fireworks Document (PNG)**.

The New Document dialog box opens.

**2** Select your desired width, height, resolution, and canvas color settings.

**3** Click **OK**.

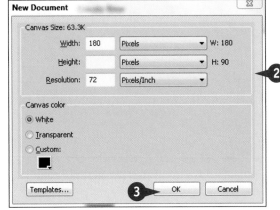

Ⓐ The new document is created and opens in Fireworks.

④ Click the **Rectangle** tool (▭).

⑤ Click the **Fill Color Picker** (△).

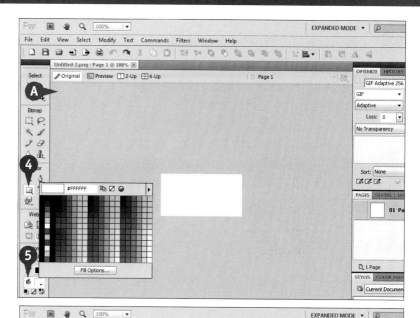

⑥ Select a color to use as the fill.

The tool is ready to use.

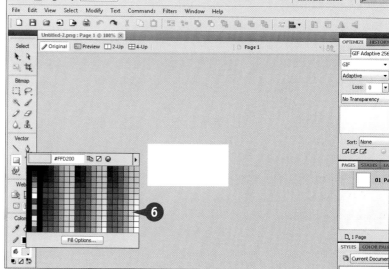

continued ▶

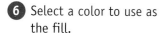

## TIPS

**Can I modify existing images as well as create new ones in Fireworks?**

Yes. Fireworks provides tools not only for creating new images, but also for manipulating existing images. In fact, most of the things you can do to images in Photoshop can be done in Fireworks.

**When I click the Color Picker, I do not see many colors to choose from. Are more available?**

Yes. Fireworks displays a limited color palette at first, but you can click the small color wheel (●) in the top right corner of the Color Picker to open a dialog box from which you can select almost any color.

**D**rawing simple shapes such as rectangles, ellipses, and polygons in Fireworks is very similar to drawing them in other graphics tools. Basically, you select the tool, set your colors, and click and drag to draw. Fireworks, however, offers a host of other preset shapes, and includes some nice hidden features to modify shapes as you draw them, minimizing the need to spend a lot of time modifying the shape later.

## Create a Simple Graphic in Fireworks (continued)

**7** Position your mouse pointer over the canvas.

**8** Press and hold your mouse button and begin to draw the rectangle.

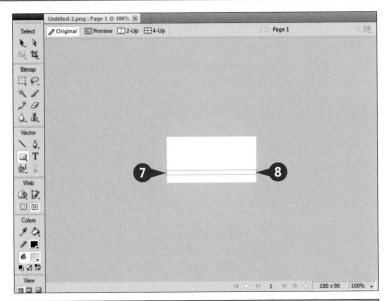

**9** While still holding the mouse button, press ⬆ or ➡ repeatedly.

The shape acquires rounded corners.

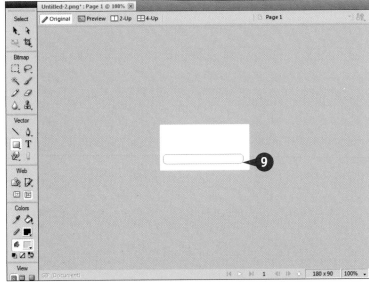

**10** While still holding the mouse button, press 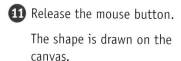 or 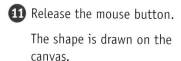 repeatedly to reduce the radius of the rounded corners.

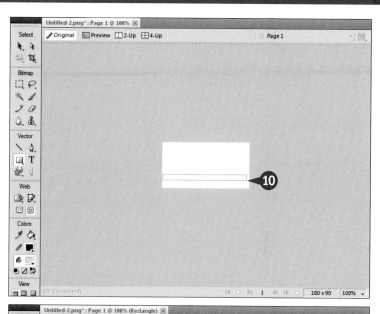

**11** Release the mouse button.

The shape is drawn on the canvas.

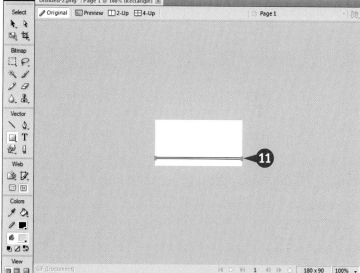

## TIPS

**Can I change the fill or stroke colors after I have drawn the shape?**

Yes. Simply select the shape with the Selection tool ( ), and then pick a new Fill or Stroke color from either the color pickers on the Toolbox or the Properties panel, or from the Color Palette or Swatches panels. If using the panels, be sure that you select either the Stroke or the Fill button ( or ) on the Toolbox to change the appropriate attribute.

**How can I make a thicker stroke?**

With the shape selected, you can adjust the size of the stroke, the brush used to draw the stroke, and other attributes from the Properties panel. You can also use the Properties panel to change the fill, set transparency, and add filters such as drop shadows.

# Using Text in Fireworks

Ideally, you will enter most of the text on your page directly into Muse. However, sometimes you may want to add text directly to a graphic, for example as a part of a button. Fireworks allows you to add text to your document using any font you want, and provides a wide variety of settings to allow you to control your type.

## Using Text in Fireworks

**1** Click the **Text** tool ( **T** ).

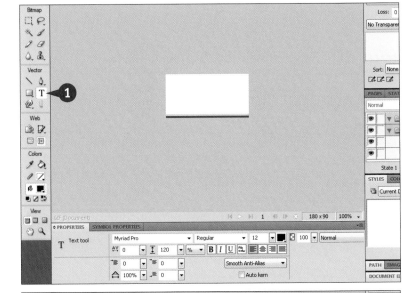

**2** From the Properties panel, select the font you want to use.

**3** Select a font style.

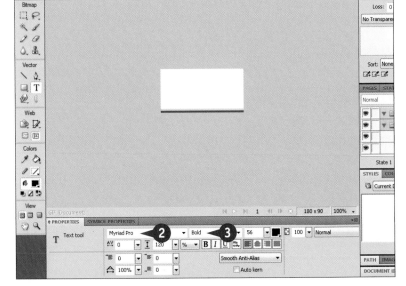

**4** Select a font color.

**5** Select a font size.

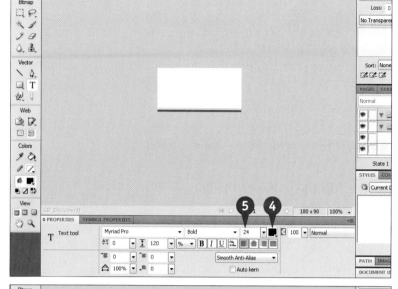

**6** Click the canvas at the point you want to enter your text.

**7** Type your text.

The text is inserted into the document.

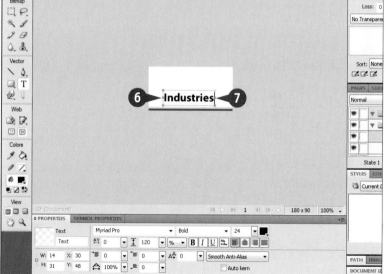

## TIPS

**Can I modify text properties such as the font, style, color, and size after I type?**

Yes. Simply select the text block on the canvas and use the Properties panel to make any needed changes. You can also click and drag the text to reposition it within your artwork.

**Do I need to create a new layer before I create text?**

No. Just like Illustrator, Fireworks automatically creates a new layer when you click the canvas with the Text tool or any drawing tool. You can change the stacking order of the layers and rename them using the Layers panel.

# Optimize Graphics in Fireworks

Once you have completed your artwork, you need to optimize your graphic before you can export it to Muse. When you optimize the graphic, you need to set your desired output format and then, based on which format you chose, apply optimization settings. A key difference between Fireworks and other programs is that Fireworks has integrated optimization directly into the toolset with its own panel, which makes optimizing the graphic and seeing the results much easier.

## Optimize Graphics in Fireworks

### Access the Optimize Panel

**1** Open the Optimize panel.

**2** Select a desired export format.

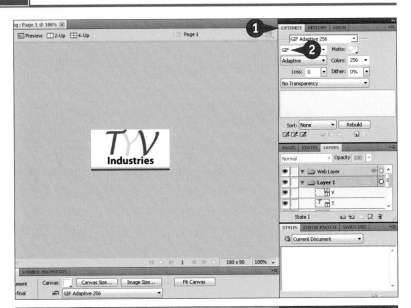

### Optimize a GIF

**1** For a GIF, select the desired number of colors. Use the fewest colors possible.

**2** If your image is not rectangular, select transparency.

The image is optimized.

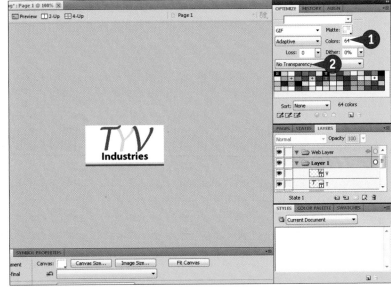

## Optimize a JPEG

**1** Select the desired quality percentage. Lower percentages result in smaller images but more quality loss.

The image is optimized.

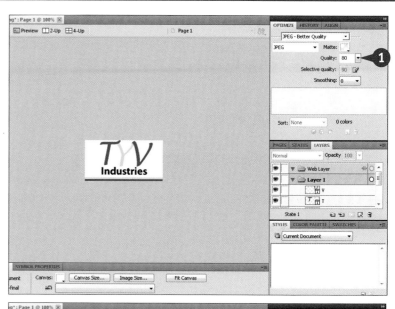

## Optimize a PNG

**1** Select whether you want an 8-bit PNG, which is similar to a GIF, or a 24- or 32-bit PNG, similar to a JPEG.

**2** If you choose 8-bit, select the number of colors to retain.

**3** Select whether or not to use transparency.

The image is optimized.

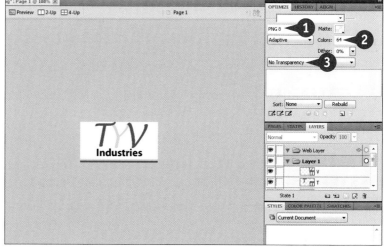

## TIPS

**How can I compare different optimization settings?**
You can use the 2-Up and 4-Up views. Click the appropriate button in the top left corner of the document window. If you click 2-Up, you see two copies of your image side by side. Whichever side is selected has the optimization options applied to it. The 4-Up displays your document in a grid and lets you compare four sets of settings. Once complete, leave the window with the settings you want to preserve selected.

**What do the PNG bit numbers mean?**
PNG files have three supported *bit depths*, representing the number of colors that can exist in the image. Take the number as a power of two to calculate the possible colors, so an 8-bit PNG has $2^8$ colors, or 256, while a 24-bit PNG has $2^{24}$, or 16,777,216 colors. Simple images such as line art that do not contain many colors can use 8-bit, whereas photographs require the millions of colors offered by 24-bit PNG.

# Save and Export an Image from Fireworks

As with any work you do on your computer, you should save your work in Fireworks on a regular basis to prevent loss in case the program or your computer crashes. Fireworks does not include an autosave feature, so you need to be sure to manually save your work.

Although Fireworks does use PNG as its native file format, a Fireworks PNG contains a lot of information not needed on a web page. Therefore, to use your graphic on your site, you must export it.

## Save and Export an Image from Fireworks

### Save the Image

1 Click **File**.

2 Click **Save**.

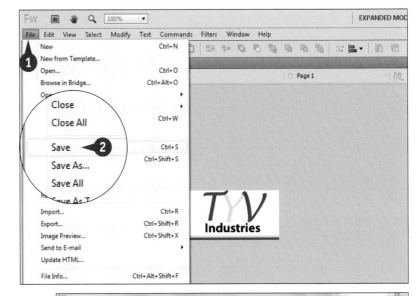

The Save As dialog box opens.

3 Navigate to the folder into which you want to save the image.

4 Give the file a descriptive name.

5 Click **Save**.

The image is saved.

## Export the Image

**Note:** Be sure to optimize the image before export.

① Click **File**.

② Click **Export**.

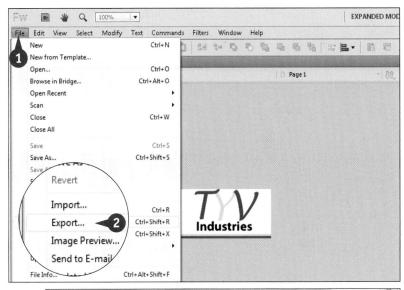

③ Navigate to the folder into which you want to save the exported image.

④ Select **Images Only**.

⑤ Click **Save**.

The image is exported.

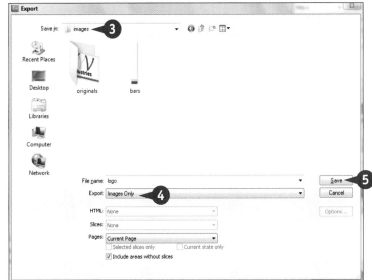

## TIPS

**I was expecting to be able to select a file format on export. Why can I not do this?**
Fireworks exports images as the file format selected in the Optimize panel, which is why optimizing your images before you export them is important. If you are using the 2-Up or 4-Up view, the file is exported using the settings in the Optimize panel for the currently selected view.

**Do I need to save my images anywhere specific?**
No. Images imported into Muse become part of the Muse file, so while you are creating the images, you can save them anywhere you want. That said, you should probably keep all of your site's assets organized in a central location.

# CHAPTER 7

# Using Images

Once you have created your images, you need to bring them into your pages. Although placing images into pages is quite simple, a number of other factors must be considered.

# Place Images

You can add images to your pages with the Place command. You can place JPEG, GIF, and PNG images that you have already optimized for the web. See Chapter 6 for details on optimizing images to prepare them for import. Regardless of the format, you are given a place gun, and you can either click to place the image at its native size, or click and drag to place it in a custom size.

## Place Images

### Place an Image at Full Size

1 Click **File**.

2 Click **Place**.

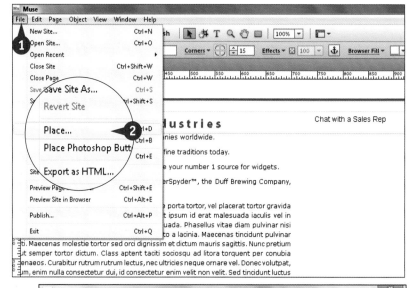

The Import dialog box opens.

3 Select the file to import.

4 Click **Open**.

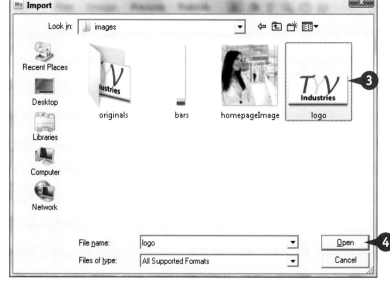

The place gun appears.

**5** Click on the canvas at the point you want your image to appear.

**A** The image is placed on the canvas.

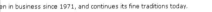

## Place an Image at a Custom Size

**1** Repeat steps **1** and **2**.

**2** Click and drag on the canvas to define the size of the image.

The image is placed at the desired size.

**Can I import more than one image at a time?**
Yes. You can select multiple images in the Import dialog box. Each time you click and drag to place the image, the next image loads and is ready to place with your next click and drag.

**What resolution should the images be?**
You can import images at any resolution. Muse automatically converts any image you import to 72 dpi, the standard screen resolution most appropriate for web graphics.

# Place Photoshop Images

I f you create your images in Fireworks or Illustrator or another similar program, you must be sure
to convert the image to JPEG, GIF, or PNG first. If on the other hand you use Photoshop, you can
place the native PSD file into your Muse document. You can then have Muse merge the image's layers
or import selected layers. Once placed, the Photoshop image looks and acts just like any other image
you have on your page.

## Place Photoshop Images

**1** Click **File**.

**2** Click **Place**.

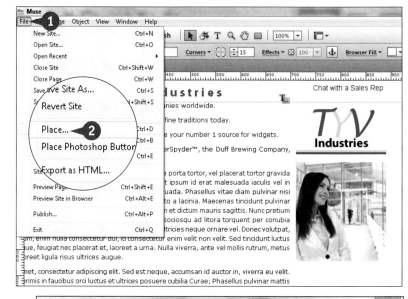

The Import dialog box opens.

**3** Select the PSD file you want
to import.

**4** Click **Open**.

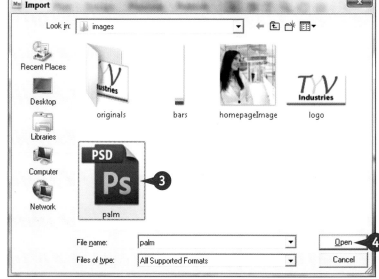

The Image Import Options dialog box appears.

**5** Choose either to import a composite image or select one or more layers to import (○ changes to ⦿).

**Note:** Press and hold Shift to select multiple adjacent layers, or Ctrl (⌘ on a Mac) for multiple non-adjacent layers.

**6** Click **OK**.

The place gun appears.

**7** Either click to place the image at its native size, or click and drag to set a size for the image.

The image is placed in the document.

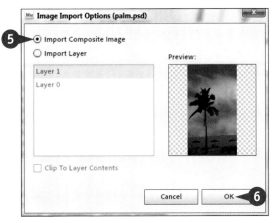

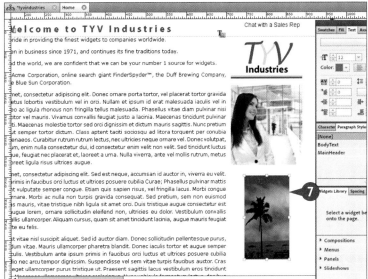

# Copy and Paste Images

In addition to placing images, you can also copy and paste image data from graphics programs directly into Muse. To do this, simply select the elements you want to copy in the graphics program, copy them to the clipboard, and then paste them into Muse. While you work in Muse, you can treat the copied data just as you would any other image. When you publish or export the site, Muse converts the image to a JPEG.

## Copy and Paste Images

**Note:** The steps that follow show copying from Fireworks, but the process is the same from Illustrator or Photoshop.

**1** Open Fireworks.

**2** Open a Fireworks image and select the elements you want to copy.

**3** Click **Edit**.

**4** Click **Copy**.

The elements are placed on the clipboard.

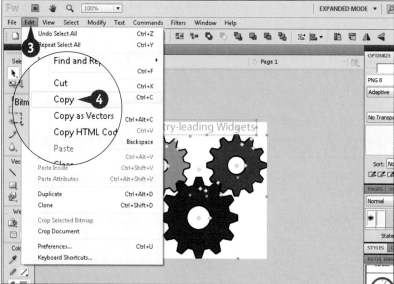

**5** Return to Muse.

**6** Click **Edit**.

**7** Click **Paste**.

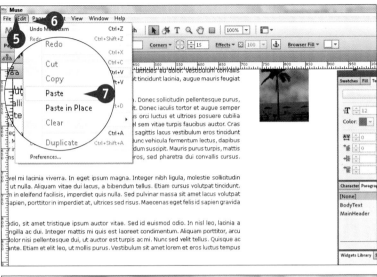

**A** The copied elements are placed as an image in Muse.

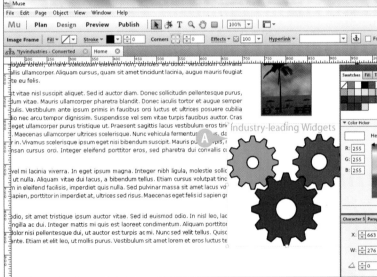

**If I select elements from multiple layers in my graphics program, will they copy correctly?**

As long as the elements are placed on the clipboard together, they will paste as a single merged image into Muse. In Fireworks and Illustrator, you can simply select elements directly on the canvas, regardless of their layers. In Photoshop, you generally need to use the Layers panel to select elements on more than one layer.

**I see from the Assets panel that all items I paste are called Clipboard. Can I rename them to make that less confusing?**

At this time, you cannot rename elements using the Assets panel. Also, as of this writing a bug exists in Muse that causes it to display all pasted items as black boxes on the panel, and causes them to disappear from the canvas when they are resized. Hopefully, a future update of Muse will fix these issues.

# Resize Images

You may decide that an image is the wrong size after you place it on your page. You can freely resize images on the page, using techniques that will be familiar if you have used InDesign. You can resize images proportionally, or you can distort them. You can either resize the frame that contains the image or resize the image itself. You can also resize by either dragging on the canvas or using the Transform panel or Control bar.

## Resize Images

### Resize the Frame

1 Using the Selection tool ( ▸ ), click an image.

2 Click and drag a control handle on the image to resize.

Ⓐ Both the image and the frame resize.

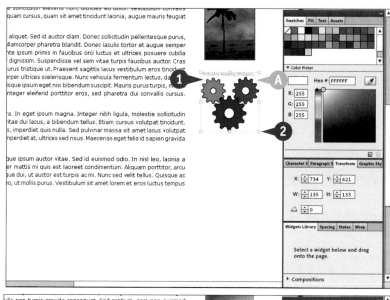

Ⓑ On either the Transform panel or the Control bar, you can enter new values for the width or height to resize the image and frame proportionally.

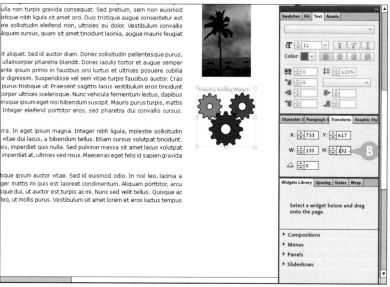

## Resize the Image

**1** Double-click the image.

**C** The control handles turn brown, showing that the image and not the frame is selected.

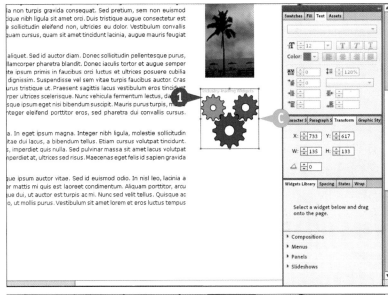

**2** Click and drag to resize. If you drag the side control handles, the image resizes nonproportionally. If you drag the corner handles, it resizes proportionally.

**Note:** You can also use the Transform panel or Control bar.

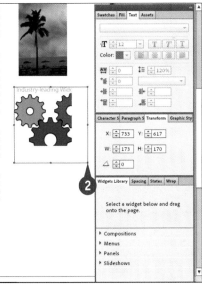

**Can I make the image larger than its original size?**
Yes, but you should be careful. Although Muse does a lot to maintain the image's quality, an image made significantly larger than the original will begin to pixelate and lose quality. In general, you should try to make images only smaller in Muse and not larger.

**When I resize, am I affecting the original image?**
No. When you place an image into Muse, you are creating a copy of the image. Any changes you make to it directly in Muse impacts only the copy in Muse; the original file is unaffected.

# Manage Image Sizes

When you place a large image in Muse and then resize it to something smaller than the original, Muse optimizes the image to try to save file space, both within its own MUSE file and on the web when you publish the file. This may cause problems if you later need to make the image larger because it may appear pixelated. You can solve this issue by telling Muse to import additional data from the original image.

## Manage Image Sizes

**1** Click **File**.

**2** Click **Place**.

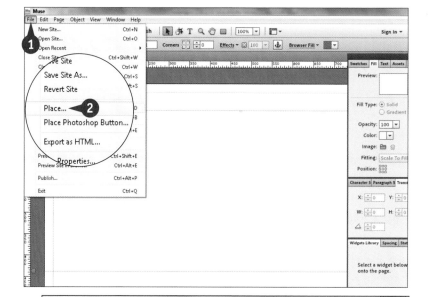

The Import dialog box opens.

**3** Navigate to the folder that contains your images.

**4** Select the image you want to import.

**5** Click **Open**.

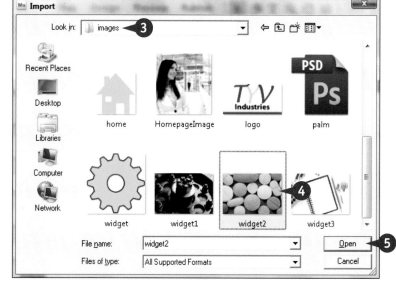

The place gun appears.

**6** Click and drag to place the image at a set size.

**7** On the Assets panel, right-click the image.

**8** Select **Optimize asset size**.

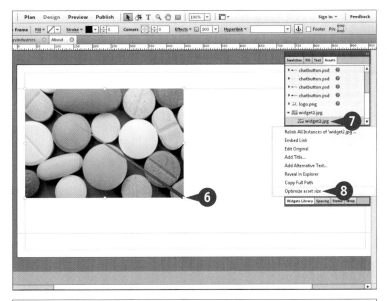

**9** Click and drag a corner handle to make the image larger.

**10** On the Assets panel, right-click the image.

**11** Select **Import larger size**.

Muse imports additional image data and cleans up the image.

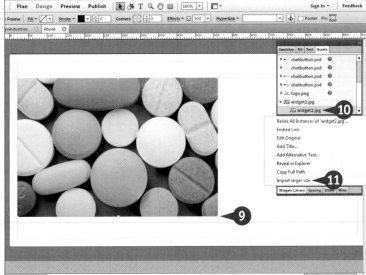

TIP

**I have tried the steps outlined above, but when I resize the image it looks fine and the Import Larger Size option is not available on the Assets panel. What am I doing wrong?**

Nothing. When optimizing images, Muse causes this pixelation only on very large images — according to the documentation, those with a width or height greater than 2048 pixels. If you are importing smaller images to begin with, Muse retains all the original image data, making this process unnecessary.

# Rotate Images

You can rotate images on your page to create more dramatic effects. Muse does not have a specific rotate tool, and instead just uses the Selection tool. You can also rotate images when using either the Transform panel or the Control bar, both of which are nice when you want to rotate by a specific percentage. When you rotate, Muse creates a new copy of your image, so your original is unaffected.

## Rotate Images

### Use the Selection Tool

1 With the Selection tool (▶), click an image.

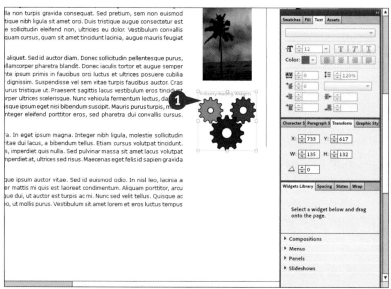

2 Position your mouse pointer just above one of the top corner control handles, or just below one of the bottom corner handles.

The mouse pointer changes to a rotate icon.

3 Click and drag to rotate the image.

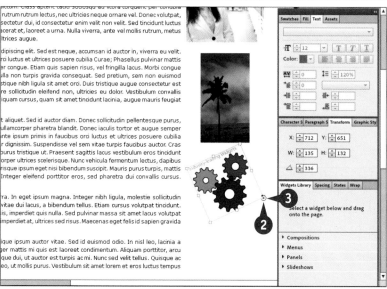

## Use the Transform Panel

**1** Click an image with the Selection tool ( ▶ ).

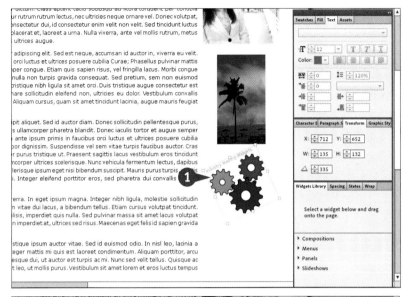

**2** On the Transform panel, enter a value between 0 and 360 in the Rotation Angle box to rotate the image.

**Note:** You can also use the Control bar.

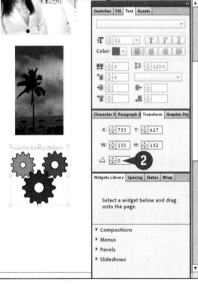

**How does Muse export rotated images?**

Because the JPEG format does not support transparency, but rotated images likely need transparent regions on their corners, any JPEG image that you rotate converts to the PNG format, but retains the original name. Oddly, even though the GIF format supports transparency, rotated GIFs also convert to PNGs on export. In both cases, you should not see any difference in quality.

# Crop Images

If you need to use only a portion of an image in Muse, you can crop it in Muse. In effect, when you place an image, Muse creates both an image and a frame. The frame can act as a sort of mask over the image, so making the frame smaller has the appearance of cropping the image. You can reposition the image within the frame to control exactly what portion is visible. You can crop using the Crop tool or the Selection tool.

## Crop Images

### Use the Crop Tool

1. Select the **Crop** tool ( ).

2. Click the image you want to crop.

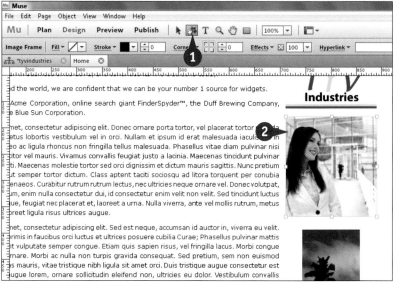

3. Click and drag one of the control handles from the edges of the image toward the middle.

   The image is cropped.

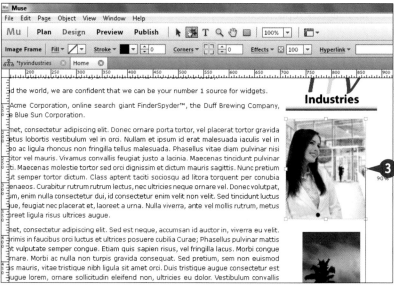

## Use the Selection Tool

**1** Click the **Selection** tool ( ).

**2** While pressing `Ctrl` ( on a Mac), click and drag one of the control handles.

The image is cropped.

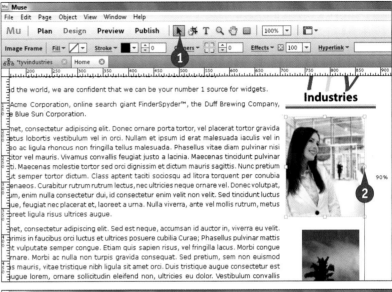

## Reposition the Cropped Image

**1** Click the image with the **Crop** tool ( ).

**2** Click the content grabber in the center of the image.

A hand tool appears.

**3** Drag to reposition the image within the cropped frame.

The image is repositioned.

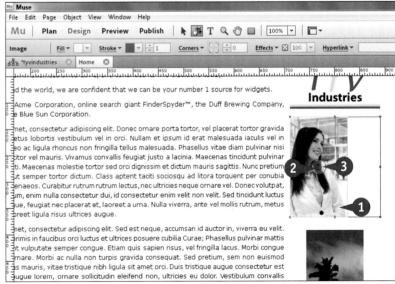

### When I crop an image, am I changing the original?

No. Just as with resizing images, cropping images in Muse does not affect the original. When you publish or export the site, a new copy of the cropped image is created in the site folder, leaving the original untouched.

### Can I rotate an image within a cropped frame?

Yes. Once you have cropped the frame, you can use the content grabber to select the image. Then, position your cursor just beyond one of the corner control handles to get the rotate icon and click and drag. You can also enter a rotation value in either the Transform panel or Control bar.

# Apply Effects to Image Frames

The images you place on your website do not need to be rectangular. Of course, you could always bring the picture into Fireworks or Photoshop and apply curved edges and drop shadows to it, but you can also achieve the same effect directly in Muse. An image in Muse is placed within an invisible frame, and you can use the Control bar to give that frame a stroke, round its corners, and apply effects such as drop shadows, bevels, and glows. You can also make an image semitransparent.

## Apply Effects to Image Frames

**1** With the Selection tool (►), select an image on the page.

**2** Adjust the thickness and color of the stroke.

**Ⓐ** A stroke is added around the image.

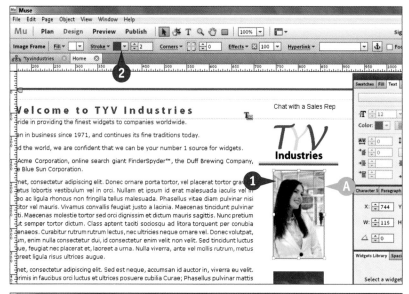

**3** Click one or more of the corner radius buttons to apply rounded corners.

**4** Adjust the radius.

The corners of the image appear to be rounded.

**⑤** Click **Effects**.

**⑥** Apply any desired effects.

**Ⓑ** The effects are applied.

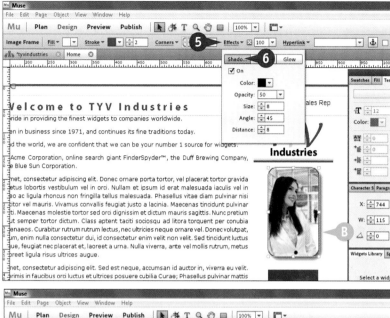

**⑦** Adjust the transparency of the image.

**Ⓒ** The image becomes semitransparent.

**How are these effects actually applied to the image?**

Although the most recent version of CSS can do most of these effects, Muse takes a simpler approach: It creates a new copy of the image. The new image is saved as a PNG, which has the advantage of preserving the appearance of a JPEG while supporting effects such as drop shadows and transparency. As with other image-related changes in Muse, your original image remains unaffected.

# Add Graphic Styles

Once you have added borders and effects to your images, you can save those settings as a graphic style and easily apply them to other images in your site. Graphic styles function the same way as character and paragraph styles, allowing you to save a set of formatting instructions, apply them to a variety of objects in your site, and then ensure that when they are edited, the formatting is applied to every object with the style.

## Add Graphic Styles

**1** Click an image to which you have applied borders or effects.

**2** Open the Graphic Styles panel.

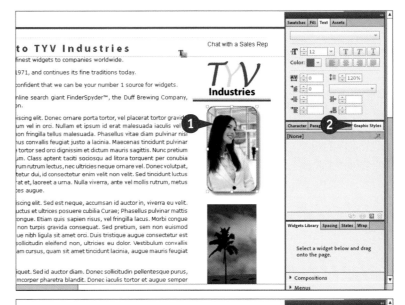

**3** Click the **Create a new style from attributes applied** button (◫).

A new style is created.

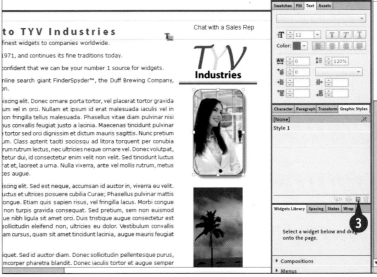

**4** Double-click the new style.

The Style Options dialog box opens.

**5** Give the style a descriptive name.

**6** Click **OK**.

The style is renamed.

**7** Select another image.

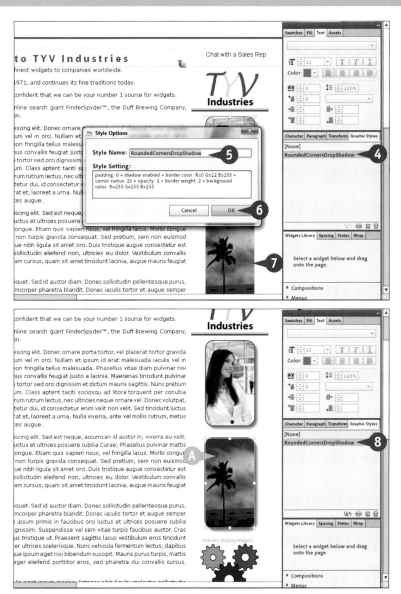

**8** Click the style.

**A** The style is applied to the other image.

**Can I apply graphic styles to anything other than images?**

Yes. You can apply a graphic style to almost any object on the page, including text frames, media such as video or Flash animation, buttons, and widgets. See Chapters 10 and 11 for details on adding media, animation, and buttons.

**How do I edit a graphic style?**

Graphic styles can be edited in the same way you edit character and paragraph styles: Select an object that has the style applied, edit its appearance as needed, and then click the **Refine selected style from the attributes applied** button ( ).

# Edit Images in a Graphics Tool

I f you need to make changes to an image that are beyond the limited capabilities of Muse, you can open images you have imported into Muse in a graphics program such as Fireworks. From there, you can perform any editing tasks you want. Once you save the image, Muse automatically updates all instances of the image used in your site to reflect the changes.

## Edit Images in a Graphics Tool

**1** Open the Assets panel.

**2** Right-click the image reference in the panel.

**3** Select **Edit Original**.

The image opens in your image-editing tool.

④ Make any desired changes to the image.

⑤ Save the image.

The image is saved.

⑥ Return to Muse.

Ⓐ The image is automatically updated with the changes.

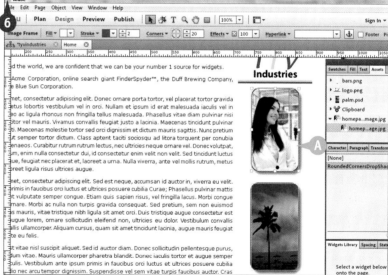

---

**TIP**

**How can I choose in which program the image opens?**

Unfortunately, Muse relies on the operating system to determine which program is used to open a file. If you want to use a different tool, right-click the image in the Assets panel and select **Reveal in Explorer** (**Reveal in Finder** if you are on a Mac). From there, you can open the image in any tool you want, and when you save the image the changes are automatically applied in Muse, just as before.

# Add Alternate Text and a Title

Although the web is of course primarily a visual medium, many of your users may have a disability that limits their eyesight. Whether they are completely blind or merely have extremely impaired vision, they may rely on software known as a *screen reader*, which as its name implies reads the contents on-screen to them. When you add images to your site, you should designate alternate text, which provides a description of the image for the screen reader to present to your user. You can also add a title to your image, which appears as a tool tip when your user mouses over the image.

## Add Alternate Text and a Title

1. If necessary, open the Assets panel.

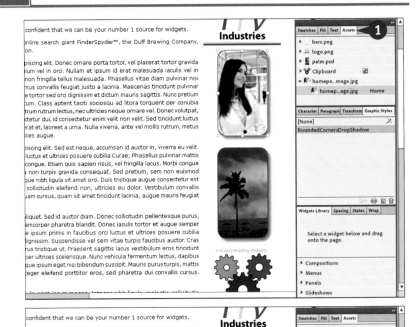

2. Right-click an image in the panel.

3. Select either **Add Title** or **Add Alternative Text**.

The Image Properties dialog box opens.

④ Enter a descriptive title for the image.

⑤ Enter a description as the alternative text.

⑥ Click **OK**.

⑦ Click **File**.

⑧ Click **Preview Page in Browser**.

The page opens in a web browser.

⑨ Position your mouse pointer over the image.

Ⓐ The title appears.

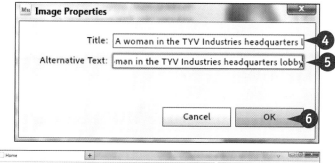

TIPS

**How can I check that my alternate text is correct?**
Muse does not provide an easy way to check alternate text, other than to right-click the image in the Assets panel and view it there. Otherwise, you must wait until you publish the site to check it.

**Do I have to provide alternate text for every image?**
You should provide a good alternate description for every image that could be considered part of your content. For example, your logo is important content and needs alternate text. If you are creating a photo gallery, the photos are your content and should have alternate text. Images that exist merely to make your site more visually interesting but do not add to the content do not need alternate text.

# Wrap Text around an Image

You can wrap text around an image in Muse. First, you need to have the image inline with your content, which requires that you first place the image and then cut and paste it into the text. Once you have done that, you can use the Wrap panel to set how the text wraps around the image and adjust the offset, or space between the image and the text, on each side. Muse allows you to decide to have the text appear above and below the image, or wrap to the left or to the right.

## Wrap Text around an Image

**1** Place an image on the canvas.

**2** Select the image.

**3** Click **Edit**.

**4** Click **Cut**.

The image is placed on the clipboard.

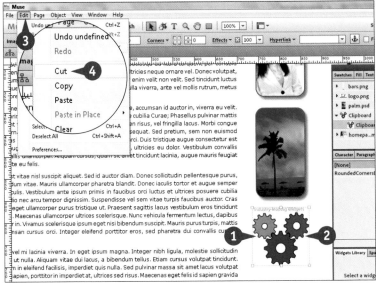

**5** With the Text tool ( T ), click in the text where you want the image to appear.

**6** Click **Edit**.

**7** Click **Paste**.

**A** The image is pasted into the text.

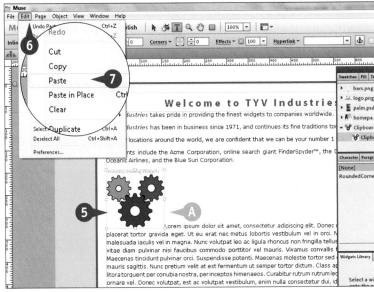

8. With the Selection tool (), select the image.
9. Open the Wrap panel.
10. Select a wrap option.
    - B The text wraps around the image.

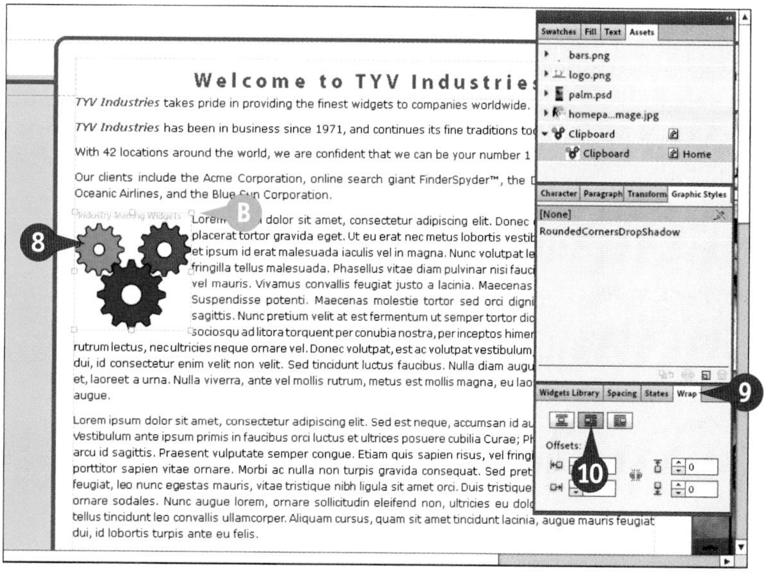


11. Adjust the offsets as needed.
    - C The text moves away from or closer to the image.

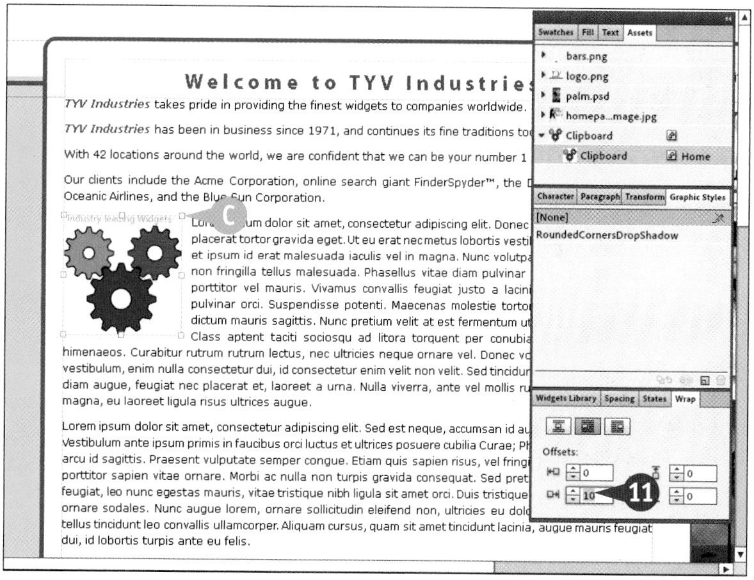


## TIP

**Can I wrap text around the shape of an image, rather than its frame, as I can in InDesign?**

No. This is again a limitation of the underlying technologies, and not just a limitation of Muse. HTML and CSS do not have a way to wrap text around irregular shapes, so the only way Muse could do it would be to rasterize all of the text, which creates problems for the site's ability to be indexed on search engines and read by people with disabilities. Therefore, the program does not support the feature.

# Fix Broken Asset Links

When you place an image in a page in Muse, the program retains a reference back to the original. If you rename or move the original file, the Assets panel displays a warning that the link is no longer valid. This does not affect the appearance of your page, but it prevents you from being able to edit the original file and have Muse update the image. You can fix these broken links from the Assets panel, or you can embed the link to remove the warning message.

## Fix Broken Asset Links

**1** In Windows Explorer and Mac Finder, move or rename a file that you have placed in Muse.

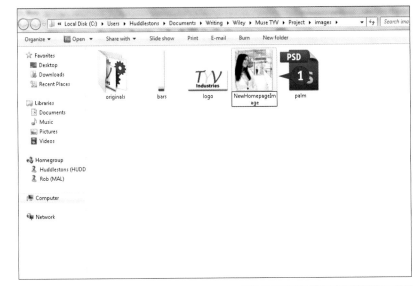

**2** In Muse, open the Assets panel.

**Ⓐ** The panel displays a warning that the asset link is missing.

**3** Right-click the asset.

**4** Click **Relink**.

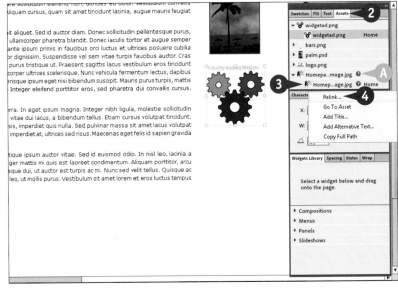

The Relink dialog box opens.

**5** Navigate to the file you changed in step **1**.

**6** Click **Open**.

The file is relinked and the warning disappears.

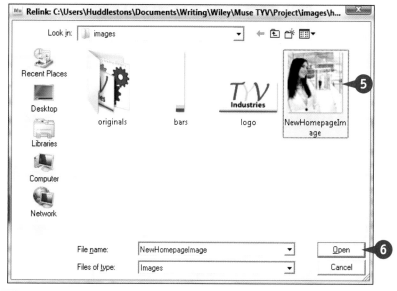

**7** Repeat step **1** to break the link again.

**B** The warning reappears.

**8** Right-click the image in the Assets panel.

**9** Click **Embed Link**.

The warning is removed.

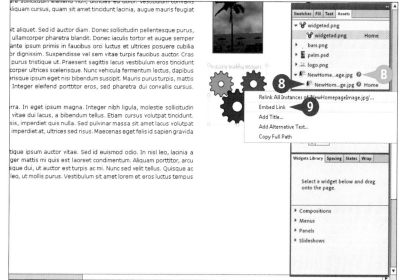

**If I change my mind about the image I want to use, can I swap it with another image?**
Yes. Simply right-click the old image in the Assets panel and then choose **Relink**. Instead of selecting the correct location of the old image, select a different image. The new image replaces the old, in the old image's frame, so you may need to move the image within the frame.

**I have a lot of broken image links, but my page seems to display just fine. Can I just ignore the warnings?**
Yes. When you place an image in Muse, a copy of the image is included in the Muse file, and this copy is used when you export the site, so you can safely ignore the warning. It only becomes a problem if you want to edit the original.

# Create a Favicon for Your Site

A *favicon* is a small graphic that browsers display to help your users further identify your site. Most modern browsers display the favicon on the browser tab and in the address bar next to your site's URL. Users also see it when they save your page to their favorites or bookmarks. Creating a favicon is fairly straightforward: Just make a square image 32 pixels on a side. The name is not important, and the image can be a JPEG, GIF, or PNG. Muse automatically converts the image to the proper format when you use it.

## Create a Favicon for Your Site

1 In an image-editing tool such as Fireworks, create the image you want to use for the favicon.

2 Save the image.

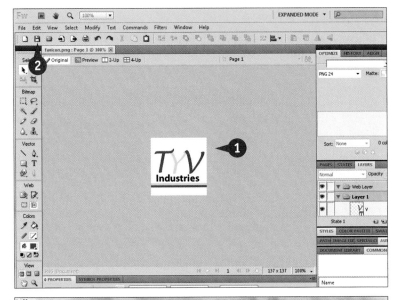

3 In Muse, click **File**.

4 Click **Site Properties**.

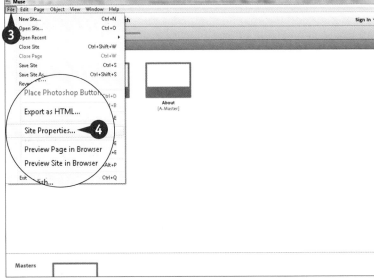

The Site Properties dialog box opens.

**5** Click the **Choose a new image file to use as a favicon** button ( ).

The Choose a Favicon Image dialog box opens.

**6** Select the image to use.

**7** Click **Open**.

**8** Click **OK**.

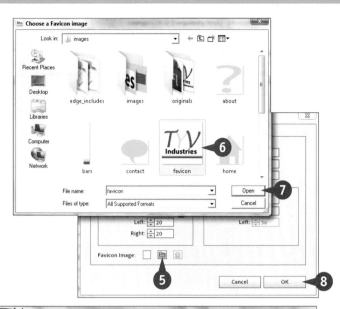

**9** Click **File**.

**10** Click **Preview Page in Browser**.

 The page opens in a browser. The favicon appears on the browser tab and the address bar.

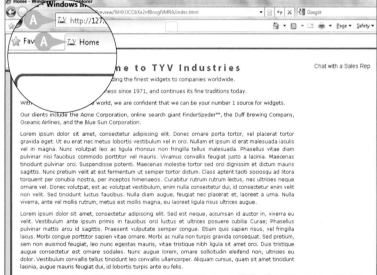

## TIPS

**Can I have different favicons for different pages in my site?**

Yes. Instead of selecting Site Properties from the File menu, you can open an individual page and choose **Page Properties** from the Page menu and then select the favicon you want to use for that page. Once you click OK, the favicon is set on that page alone.

**Can I have an animated icon?**

Officially, browsers are supposed to allow favicons to be animated, but actual browser support for this feature is very limited. If you create the icon as an animated GIF, Muse correctly imports it. However, many of your users will not see the animation depending on their browser.

# CHAPTER 8

# Adding Navigation

Your website is of course nothing more than a collection of linked pages. A key component to the success of your site is building a good navigation system.

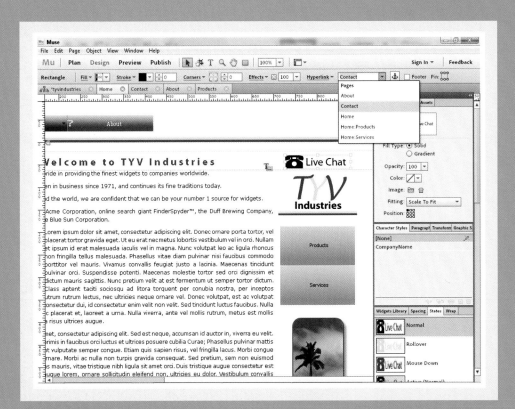

# Insert a Menu Bar

Clear, intuitive navigation is vital to the success of your site. You never want your users to have to hunt for links to your other pages. Creating good navigation has long been a challenge for web designers, but thankfully Muse simplifies this. The Plan view forces you to think about how your pages relate to one another, which naturally leads to improved navigation. Once you have your pages laid out in Plan view, Muse can automatically generate menu bars to add to your pages.

## Insert a Menu Bar

**1** Click **Plan**.

Plan view opens.

**2** Ensure your pages are organized correctly.

**Note:** See Chapter 2 for more details on using Plan view.

**3** Click **Design**.

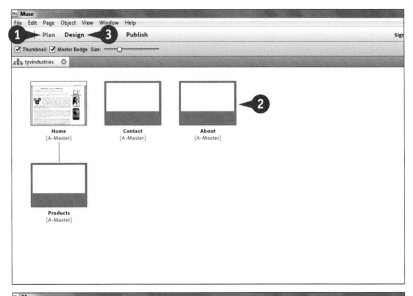

Design view opens.

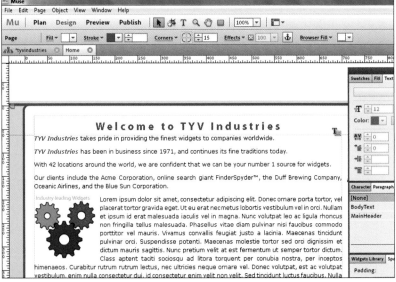

④ Click **Object**.

⑤ Click **Insert Menu**.

⑥ Click **Bar**.

The place gun appears.

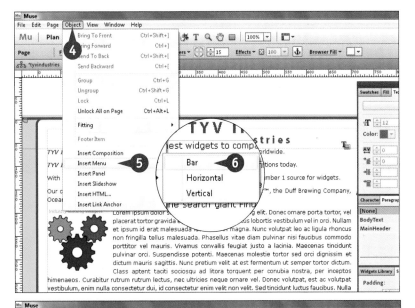

⑦ Click the page at the point at which you want the menu bar to be placed.

Ⓐ The menu bar is added to the page.

**TIP**

**How can I change the name of the page as it appears on the menu bar?**
You cannot edit the names of the pages on the menu bar directly. Instead, you need to rename the pages in Plan view. Simply click **Plan**, and then double-click the name of the page you want to change. Type a new name and press Enter or click another portion of the page. When you switch back to Design view on the page with the menu bar, the page updates with the new name.

# Insert a Vertical Menu Bar

The default menu bar in Muse is a horizontal group of buttons. You can instead insert a vertical group of buttons if that fits your design better. The functionality of the vertical bar is the same as that of the horizontal bar. In both cases, the pages from your Plan view automatically appear on the bar, and in both cases the appearance of the buttons can be changed to fit your design.

## Insert a Vertical Menu Bar

① Open a page onto which you want to add a vertical menu bar.

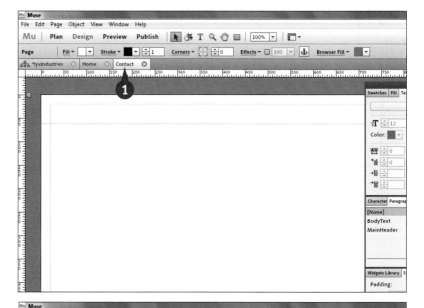

② Click **Object**.

③ Click **Insert Menu**.

④ Click **Vertical**.

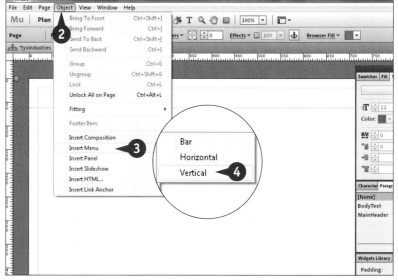

**5** Click the page at the point at which you want to insert the menu bar.

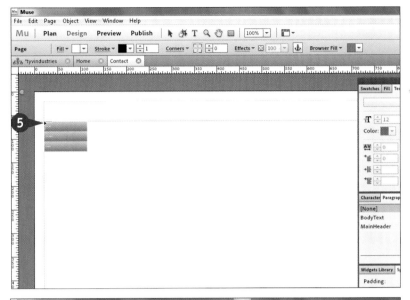

**Ⓐ** The menu bar is inserted into the page.

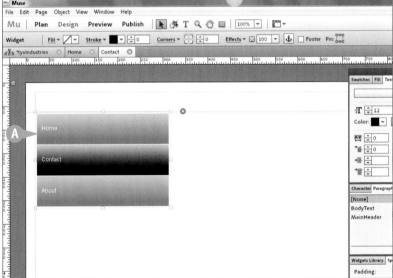

**Can I move the menu bar after I insert it?**
Yes, the menu bar is inserted as a single object on the page. You can use the Selection tool (▶) to move it to a new location if you need to. As with other objects, you will see guides appear as you move the menu to help you line it up with other objects on the page.

**Can I have both a vertical and a horizontal menu bar on the same page?**
Yes. Many pages use both: Often, a horizontal bar at the top of the page is used for site-wide navigation, whereas a vertical bar, usually positioned in a right or left sidebar, is used for page-specific navigation.

# Add a Horizontal Menu

The menu bars in Muse, whether vertical or horizontal, are made up of visual buttons. Although you can change the appearance of the buttons, as is covered elsewhere in this chapter, sometimes your site design may call for a simpler look to your navigation. Muse therefore also includes the ability to add a horizontal menu with a much simpler look: a basic set of text links that nonetheless still include a rollover effect.

## Add a Horizontal Menu

① Open a page onto which you want to add a menu.

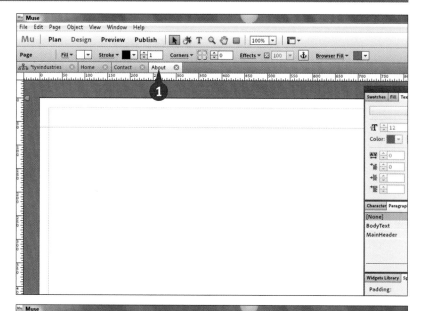

② Click **Object**.

③ Click **Insert Menu**.

④ Click **Horizontal**.

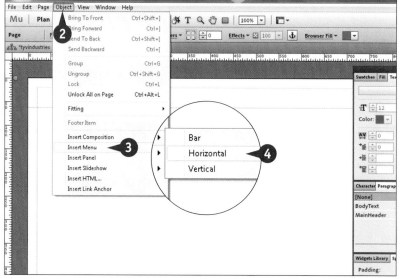

**5** Click the page at the point at which you want to insert the menu.

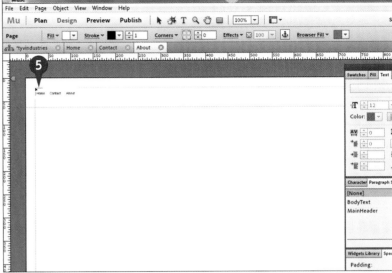

**A** The menu is inserted into the page.

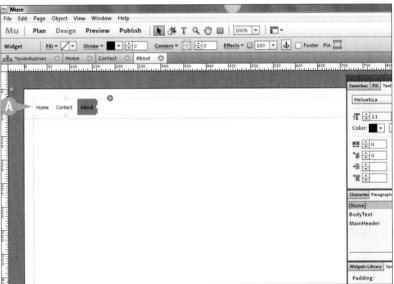

**Can I change the look of the text in the menu?**
Yes. The horizontal menu is made up of simple text frames. You can use the Text tool ( T ) to select the text frame, and then use the Control bar to adjust font properties. You can also apply a character or paragraph style. See Chapter 4 for details on using styles. You cannot change the wording of the links — that must be done by changing the relevant page name in Plan view — and you cannot format individual words or characters.

# Create a Multilevel Menu

Most sites contain more than one level of pages. For example, your site might have a set of top-level pages such as Home and About Us, and then a set of second-level pages off the home page. Muse makes creating multilevel menus quite easy, because you can take any menu that you create and change its settings so that it displays all pages in the site in a cascading menu.

## Create a Multilevel Menu

**1** Click **Plan**.

Plan view opens.

**2** If necessary, add second-level pages.

**Note:** See Chapter 2 for details on adding pages in Plan view.

**3** Double-click the page on which you want to add the menu.

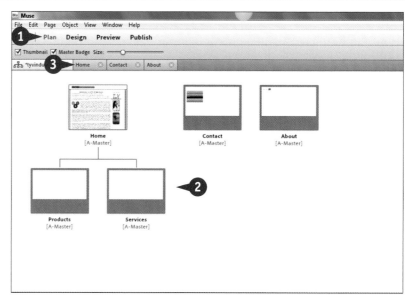

Design view opens.

**4** Insert a menu.

**Note:** See the first three sections in this chapter for details on inserting menus.

**5** With the Selection tool ( ▶ ), click the menu.

**6** Click the editing options icon ( ◉ ) to open the menu options.

A menu opens.

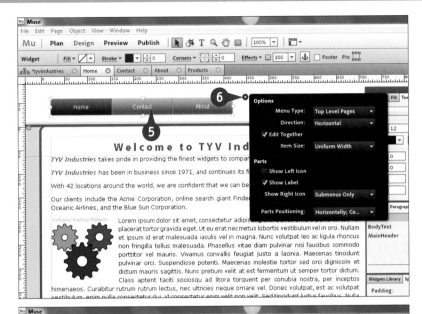

**7** Click the Menu Type dropdown.

**8** Select **All Pages**.

Ⓐ The menu updates to display additional levels for the subpages.

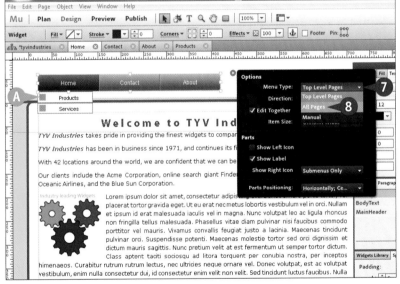

**TIP**

**If I have multiple levels of pages, will I get multiple levels of menus? How many levels can I have?**
Yes, you get menu levels for each level of pages you have in your Plan view. So, if you have a page that contains a subpage, and then that subpage contains subpages, you will have three levels on your menu. In theory, you can add as many levels as you need, but in practice after you get beyond two or three levels, your menu is going to become extremely difficult to use.

# Change a Menu's Orientation and Size

egardless of the type of menu you add to your page, Muse provides a set of additional options that allows you to customize the menu. One such option allows you to change the menu from horizontal to vertical or from vertical to horizontal. Once you change the orientation, you can resize the menu and control whether the items remain the same size or if they can be sized individually.

## Change a Menu's Orientation and Size

**1** Insert a menu.

**Note:** See the first three sections in this chapter for details on inserting menus.

**2** If necessary, use the Selection tool ( ) to select the menu.

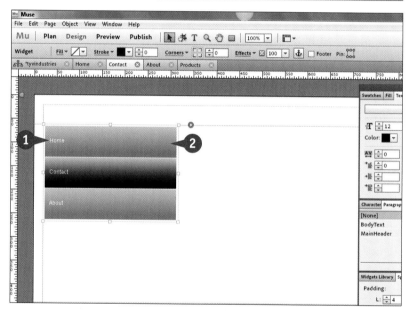

**3** Click the editing options icon ( ).

The editing options menu opens.

**4** Select a direction.

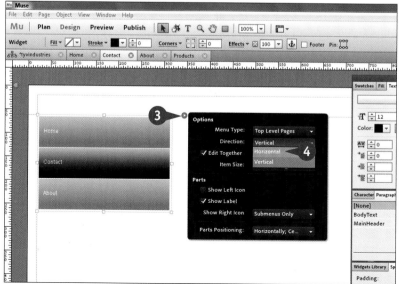

🅐 The menu changes from horizontal to vertical, or from vertical to horizontal.

**5** Click the Item Size dropdown.

**6** Select **Fit Width**.

🅑 The menu resizes so that each button is only as large as the text on that button.

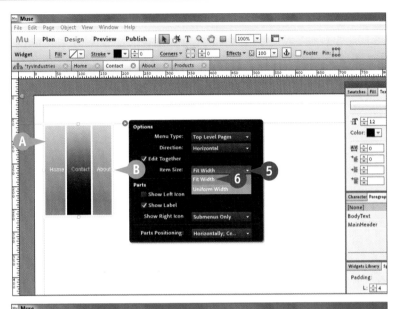

**7** Click the Item Size dropdown.

**8** Select **Uniform Width**.

**9** Click and drag the control handles to resize the menu.

The menu resizes.

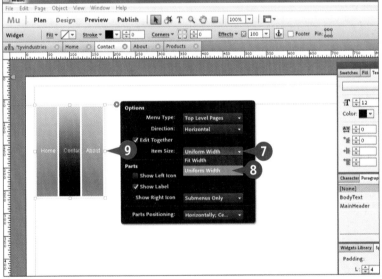

## TIPS

**I cannot seem to resize a menu. What is wrong?**

You can only manually resize a menu if the Item Size option is set to Uniform Width. If it is set to Fit Width, you cannot resize because by definition that option sets each menu item to exactly the width of the link text.

**If I manually resize a menu and then later add or delete pages from my site, does the menu size change?**

No. If you add additional pages to your site or remove pages from it, Muse adjusts the width of each item in the menu to make room for the new page, while leaving the size of the overall menu the same. Ultimately, this behavior is quite helpful because it means that adding or removing pages does not mess up your page designs.

# Add Icons to Menus

When using menus, you can add an icon in addition to, or instead of, a text label. The icon itself can be any image you choose, although of course it needs to be small and needs to make its function clear. You can set a menu to the left or right of the label, and set the right icons to appear only on submenus.

## Add Icons to Menus

### Add an Icon to a Menu

**1** Insert a menu.

**Note:** See the first three sections in this chapter for details on inserting menus.

**2** If necessary, use the Selection tool () to select the menu.

**3** Click the editing options icon ().

The editing options menu opens.

**4** Click **Show Left Icon** ( changes to ).

**Ⓐ** A small grey box appears to the left of the menu labels.

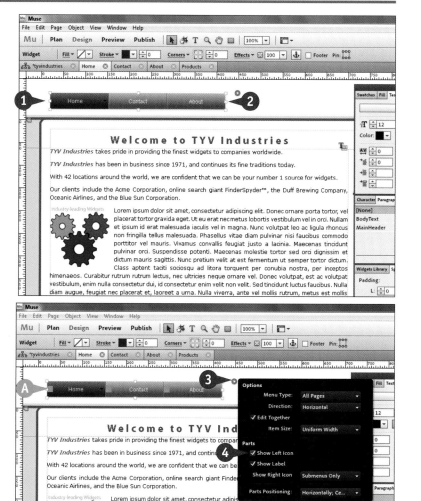

**5** Click one of the boxes.

**6** Use the Fill panel to change the color or set a background image; make any other formatting changes you need.

**7** Repeat steps **4** to **6** to set a right icon.

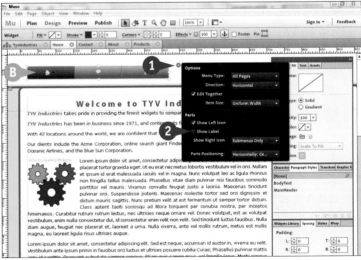

## Show Only Icons

**1** On the menu, click the editing options icon ( ⊙ ).

**2** Click **Show Label** ( ☑ changes to ■).

**Ⓑ** The option is deselected.

**3** Resize the icon as needed by selecting it and dragging its control handles.

**One of my menu's buttons seems to disappear when I test the page. Why is this happening?**

Buttons contain multiple states. Adding an icon to the Normal state adds it to the rest of the states. However, if the button is on the Active (Normal) state — which it will be for the button referencing the current page — then the icon is added only to that state. You need to use the States panel to select the Normal state for that button and add the icon to that state to prevent it from disappearing.

**Where can I get icons to use?**

The icon can be a GIF, JPEG, PNG, or even PSD file, so you can use any image you already have on your computer, or you can create your own. There are also resources online that offer free website icons. Search for "web site icons" on your favorite search engine to find links. Just be sure that any icons you download are legal to use on your site.

# Change a Menu's Appearance

The menus that Muse creates have four states: Normal, Rollover, Mouse Down, and Active (Normal). The Normal state shows the button when the user is not interacting with it. The Rollover state changes the button to provide users with feedback when they position their mouse pointer over it; the Mouse Down state is how the button will look when the user clicks it. The Active (Normal) state is what the button that links to the current page will look like. By default, each has a gradient with varying shades of gray. You can change the colors on each of these states so that the menu better matches the color scheme of your site. You can also change properties of the gradient such as its center or focal point and its direction.

## Change a Menu's Appearance

**1** Insert a menu.

**Note:** See the first three sections in this chapter for details on inserting menus.

**2** If necessary, use the Selection (▶) tool to select the menu.

**3** With the Selection tool (▶), click one of the buttons on the menu.

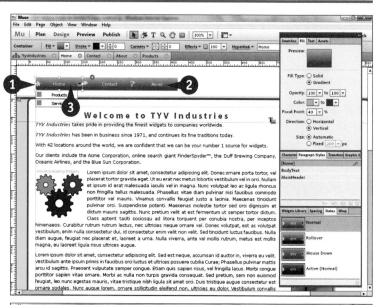

**4** Open the States panel.

**5** Click **Normal**.

**6** Use the Control bar or the Fill panel to change the appearance of the button.

Ⓐ This example applies a new color fill to the button.

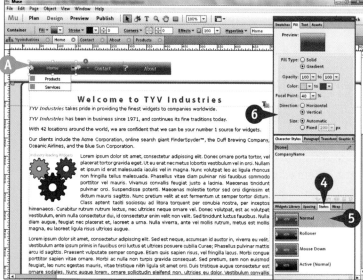

**7** On the States panel, click **Rollover**.

**8** Use the Control bar or the Fill panel to change the appearance of the button.

**B** This example reverses the fill colors.

**9** Repeat steps **7** and **8** for each of the other states.

The menu's appearance is changed.

**Do the changes I make to the button apply to all the buttons on the menu?**

Yes. When you edit a single button, all the rest of the buttons are updated as well. You can make changes to an individual button if you want by clicking the editing options icon ( ◉ ) for the menu and deselecting **Edit Together** ( ☑ changes to ■ ).

**I made a change to the Rollover state, but when I deselect the menu it seems to go away. Why?**

The states of the button are triggered by your user's actions. Muse displays a selected button in a selected state to allow you to edit, but once you deselect the menu it reverts all the buttons to Normal except the button for the current page, which is set to Active (Normal). You can preview the page to test how the states work.

# Control Which Pages Appear in Menus

Menus in Muse automatically contain links to the pages in your site, based on the page layout you have defined in Plan view. Sometimes, however, there may be pages in Plan view that you do not want to appear in the navigation. For example, you might have pages that show a project you are working on for a client, and you do not want that appearing as a link on all your pages. Using Plan view, you can designate certain pages to not appear in menus.

## Control Which Pages Appear in Menus

**①** Click **Plan**.

Plan view opens.

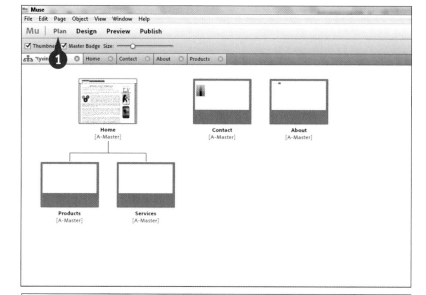

**②** Right-click (⌘+click on a Mac) a page that you do not want to show on menus.

The context menu appears.

**③** Select **Include Page In Navigation**.

The option is deselected.

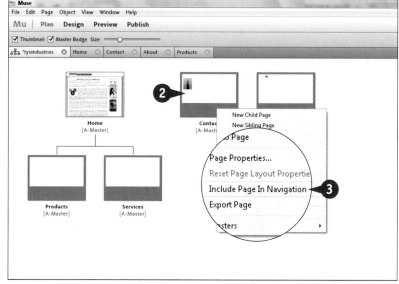

④ Double-click a page that contains a menu.

Design view opens.

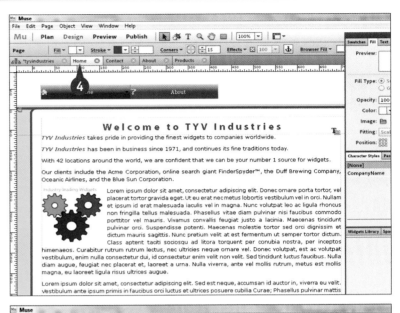

Ⓐ The menu no longer displays a link to the page selected in step **2**.

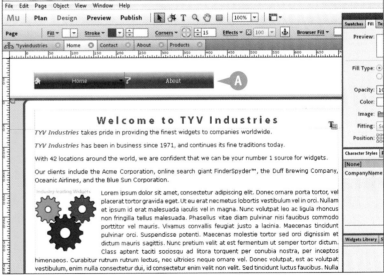

## TIPS

**If I remove a page from the navigation and then later change my mind, can I add it back in?**

Yes. You can always repeat the steps in this section to include a page in the navigation again. Just as with adding pages, the menus add the page back in and resize the other items appropriately to fit.

**Can I remove an item from a menu on a single page but leave it on the menu for other pages?**

Not directly. Menus are controlled site-wide, so removing a page from the navigation removes it from every menu in the site. However, you can create a menu on a page manually, and add whatever links you want to it. See the sections "Add a Manual Menu" and "Manually Create Hyperlinks" for details.

# Add a Manual Menu

Although Muse's menus are helpful for quickly building site navigation, they have a few limitations. Many sites, for example, have two sets of navigation per page: one menu bar for global or site-wide links, and a second for page-specific links. Muse does not have the ability to limit the links on a menu to only second-level pages, so you need to build a manual menu if you want this kind of navigation. The first step in creating a manual menu is converting a normal menu.

## Add a Manual Menu

**1** Insert a menu.

**Note:** See the first three sections in this chapter for details on inserting menus.

**2** If necessary, use the Selection tool (▶) to select the menu.

**3** Click the editing options icon (◉) for the menu.

The editing options menu opens.

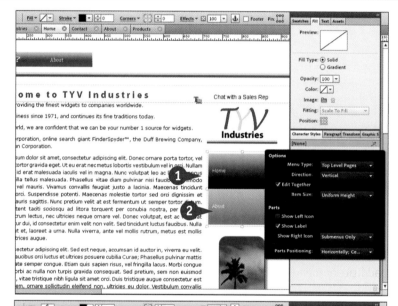

**4** Click the Menu Type dropdown.

**5** Click **Manual**.

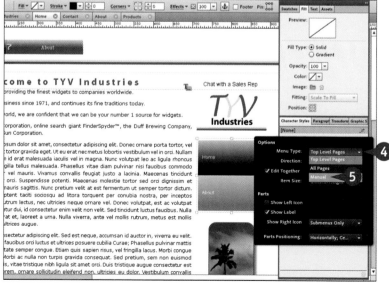

The menu changes to a manual menu, with only a single button labeled [Name].

**6** With the Text tool, select **[Name]** and type the name of the page you want to link to.

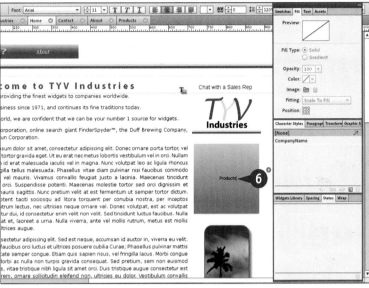

**7** With the Selection tool (⬀), click the menu.

**8** Click the menu a second time.

**9** Click the plus sign to add a new menu item.

**10** Repeat steps **6** to **9** to add additional menu items.

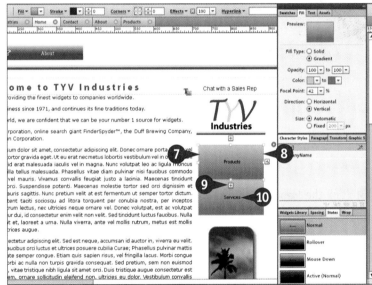

TIP

**Other than setting up the links manually, are there any other differences between manual menus and automatic menus?**

No. Everything else covered in this chapter on menus can be applied to manual menus. For example, you can switch manual menus between the Bar, Vertical, and Horizontal styles. You can add icons. You can change the appearance of the menus by formatting their states. The only difference is that with the automatic menus, if you change the name of a page in Plan view, the menus with that page update, whereas manual menus do not update based on changes in Plan view.

continued ▶

# Add a Manual Menu (continued)

Once you have added the necessary pages to the manual menu, you need to create the necessary hyperlinks so that users are taken to the correct page when they click an item on the menu. After selecting the menu item you want to edit, you can use the Hyperlink dropdown on the Control bar to select the page to which the item will be linked. You can also add a title to the link, which appears as a tool tip when your user positions her mouse pointer over it.

## Add a Manual Menu (continued)

⑪ With the Selection tool (➤), click one of the buttons on the menu.

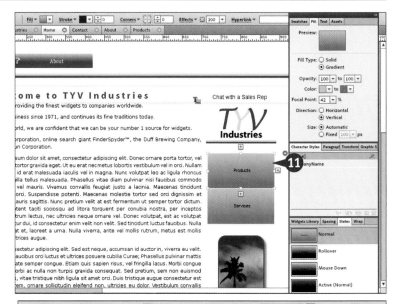

⑫ Click the Hyperlink dropdown.

⑬ Select the page to which you want to link.

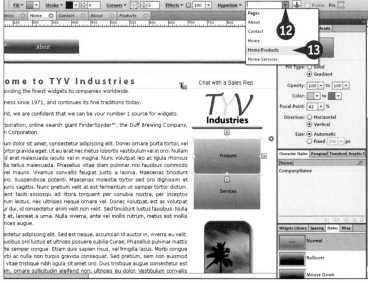

**14** Click **Hyperlink** on the Control bar.

**15** Enter a descriptive title for the page to which you are linking.

**16** Repeat steps **11** to **15** for each additional link.

**Can I have one of the buttons in the menu link to another website?**
Yes. You can enter the address to the site in the menu that appears when you click **Hyperlink** on the Control bar. However, a link to an external website in the same menu bar as links to pages within your site will likely confuse your users, so you should either make sure the link is clearly stated as external or group your external links in a different section of the page.

# Insert a Photoshop Button

Instead of setting up the states of the button individually, you can create an image in Photoshop that contains four layers, one for each state of the button. When you import the button into Muse, you can designate which layer applies to which state. Once you place the button, you can link it to any page in your site or on the web. A big advantage of creating a Photoshop button is that Muse menus do not allow you to use images as backgrounds for buttons, an effect that can obviously be achieved in Photoshop.

## Insert a Photoshop Button

### Create the Button in Photoshop

1 Open Photoshop.

2 Click **File**.

3 Click **New**.

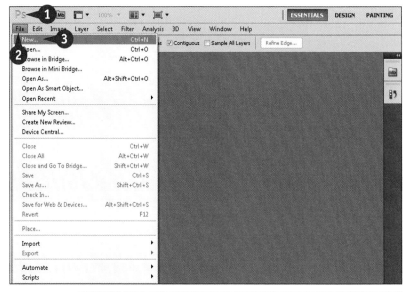

The New dialog box opens.

4 Enter the desired dimensions of the button.

5 Click **OK**.

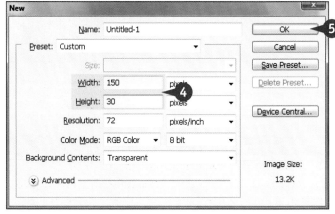

A new Photoshop document is created.

**6** Draw the button.

**Note:** For more information on using Photoshop, see *Teach Yourself VISUALLY Photoshop CS6* (John Wiley & Sons, 2012).

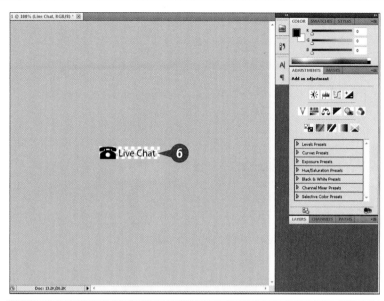

**7** On the Layers panel, click the **Create a New Layer** button () three times.

**8** Add artwork to the new layers.

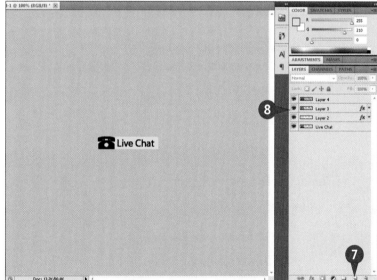

**TIP**

**Can I use a tool other than Photoshop?**
Muse can import only Photoshop PSD files for this feature. However, Fireworks does have the ability to create new images and then export them as PSD, so it is possible to use Fireworks rather than Photoshop. The only caveats are that you need to be sure to name your layers in Fireworks, because Muse does not correctly assign the correct layer to the correct state if all the layers have the same name. If you would like to see a demonstration of using Fireworks to create a Photoshop button for Muse, visit www. robhuddleston.com/books/tyvmuse.

continued ▶

# Insert a Photoshop Button (continued)

Although Muse allows you to insert a button with any layer data, you can assign a state only to a single layer. So if you are using multiple layers to achieve a look, such as applying an adjustment layer, you must be sure to merge the layers in Photoshop. You will also have an easier time placing the button if you name the layers based on the Muse states. Once you have placed the button, you can add a link to it from the Control bar.

## Insert a Photoshop Button (continued)

**9** Double-click the name of the layer you plan to use for the Normal state.

**10** Type **Normal**.

**11** Repeat steps **9** and **10** to name the remaining layers to match the state names in Muse.

The layers are renamed.

**12** Save the button.

## Place the Button in Muse

**1** Return to Muse.

**2** Click **File**.

**3** Click **Place Photoshop Button**.

The Place Photoshop Button dialog box opens.

**4** Navigate to the location where you saved the button.

**5** Select the button.

**6** Click **Open**.

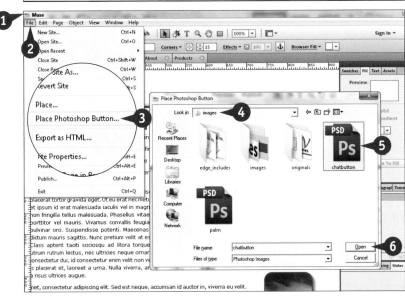

The Photoshop Import Options dialog box opens.

**7** Ensure that the proper layers are associated with the proper states.

**8** Click **OK**.

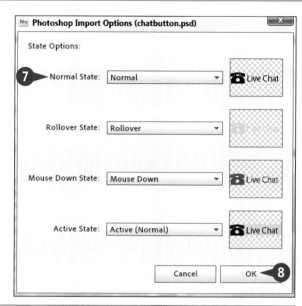

**9** Click the canvas where you want to place the button.

The button is placed on the canvas.

**10** Click the dropdown next to Hyperlink on the Control bar.

**11** Select a page to link to.

The button is linked to the page.

**When I placed the button, I accidentally selected the wrong layer to go with a state. Is there a way to change this association?**

Unfortunately, no. You need to delete the button from the canvas, click **File**, and then **Place Photoshop Button** to place the button again, which gives you the option to choose the layer-state association again.

**When I place my Photoshop button, the image becomes blurry. How can I fix this?**

When you place your image, Muse needs to convert each layer into a web-safe JPEG or PNG file. Although it does an excellent job of optimizing images, it still does not do as good a job as Photoshop. Therefore, you should do as much work as you can in Photoshop. Make sure the image size is what you need for Muse, and make sure the resolution is set to 72 dpi.

# Manually Create Hyperlinks

Menus are fine for the primary navigation areas of your site, but other times you may simply need a hyperlink, such as when you want to link a word or words in your text to another website or other page in your site. To create a link to an external website, you need to type the website's address, such as www.google.com, into the Hyperlink box on the Control bar. To link to a page within your own site, you can simply select the page from the Hyperlink dropdown.

## Manually Create Hyperlinks

### Create a Link to an External Website

1 Click the **Text** tool ( T ).

2 Select the text you want to use for the link.

3 In the Hyperlink text box on the Control bar, type the address you want to link to.

The link is created.

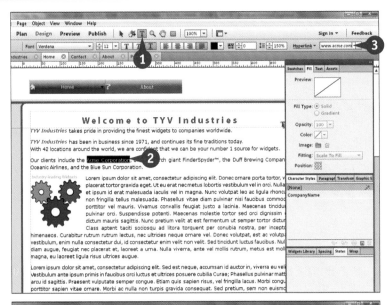

### Create a Link to a Page within Your Site

1 Select the text you want to use for the link.

2 Click the Hyperlink dropdown.

3 Select the page you want to link to.

The link is created.

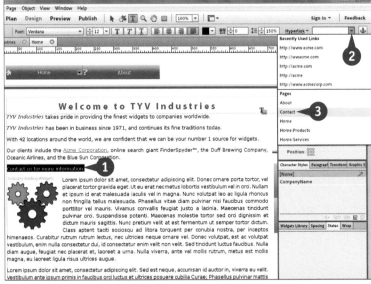

## Test Your Links

**1** Click **File**.

**2** Click **Preview Page in Browser**.

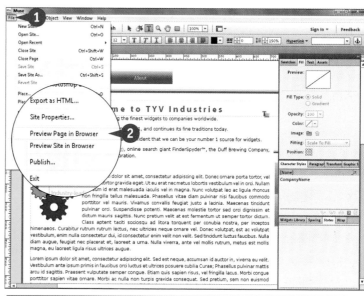

The page opens in a web browser.

**3** Click the links.

**4** Use the browser's Back button to return to your page.

**Can I have the link open in a new browser window?**

Yes. When you create the link, click **Hyperlink** on the Control bar, and then select **Open the link in a new window or tab**. Be aware, however, that this behavior can be confusing or undesirable to some users, so you should use it sparingly, and only when you can be reasonably sure that users would want the link in a new tab or window.

**Can I use an image as a link?**

Yes. Simply select the image with the Selection tool ( ), and then follow the steps in this section to create the link. Unlike text links, images do not automatically offer a visual clue that they are a link, so you need to be sure that the image's context makes it clear it is serving as a link.

# Add Links to PDF, Word, or Other Files to Your Site

Although keeping the majority of your content as text on your web page is best, sometimes you may want to link to other document types, such as a PDF file or a Microsoft Word document. You can create the link just as you would any other manual hyperlink, but you need to go through a few additional steps to make the page available online. See Chapter 13 for details on these final steps.

## Add Links to PDF, Word, or Other Files to Your Site

**1** Click the **Text** tool ( T ).

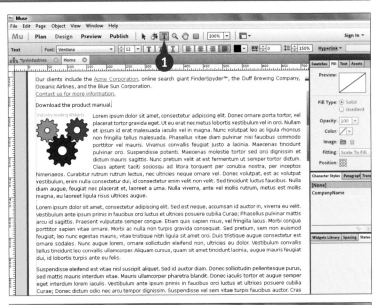

**2** Select the text you want to use for the link.

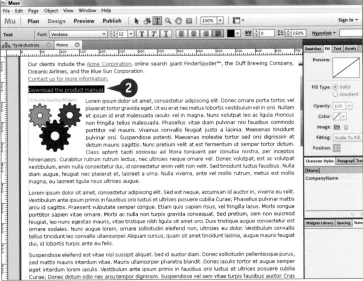

**③** In the Hyperlink box on the Control bar, type the filename of the document to which you want to link. For example, type **manual.pdf**.

**Note:** You must include the file extension.

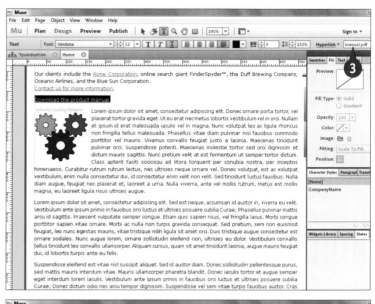

**Ⓐ** The link is created.

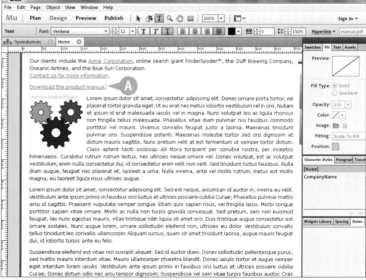

**What other file types can I link to?**
Technically, you can link to any file you want. The most common are probably .pdf and .zip, followed by Word and Excel files, but you are free to link to absolutely any file. Be aware, however, that you cannot control how the user's browser handles the files. Sometimes, it may open the file directly, as most browsers do with .pdf, and other times it may force the user to download the file, as most do with .zip. You cannot force a particular behavior in any way.

# Edit Link Styles

Links need to be visually different from the surrounding text, or your users will never know that they can click that text. The original design of the web called for link text to be blue, because blue is the darkest color that is obviously not black. Links to pages you have already visited are purple by default. If your page background or site color scheme does not work with these, you can change them. You can also remove the underline if you want. Always ensure, however, that you have sufficient contrast between your text and link colors to make the links stand out.

## Edit Link Styles

**1** With the Text tool ( **T** ), select text that you have turned into a hyperlink.

**2** Click **Hyperlink**.

**3** Click **Edit Link Styles**.

The Site Properties dialog box opens.

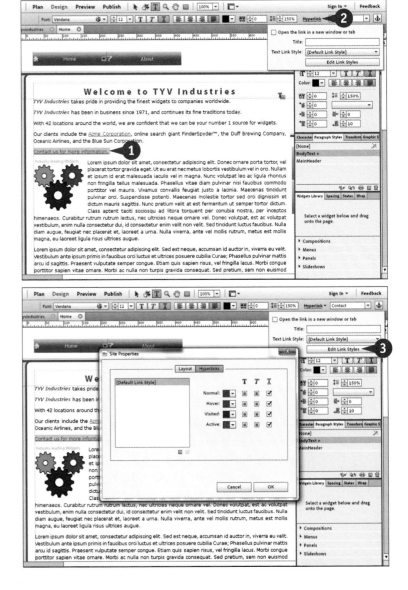

**4** Select a new color for the link styles.

**5** If desired, click to make the styles bold or italic, or to remove the underline (☐ changes to ☑ ).

**6** Click **OK**.

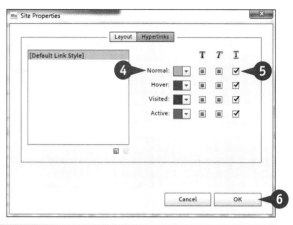

**Ⓐ** The appearance of the links changes.

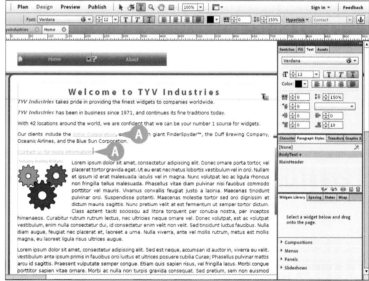

**What are the Hover and Active settings for?**

Hover is the appearance of the link when your user positions the mouse pointer over the link. By default, hover is set to look like Normal, but many sites leverage hover effects to make links stand out even more. Active is, in theory, the appearance of the link when the user is in the act of clicking it. Today, very few browsers display the Active state at all.

**Why can I not change text properties such as fonts?**

Links inherit basic text properties from the paragraph they are in. Muse only allows you to set the color, bold, italic, and underline settings for links. If you really need to change other properties, you could apply a character style to the text instead, but it overrides your link styles.

# Create Custom Link Styles

Although you should establish an overall style for your links to maintain visual consistency through your site, you may have times when you need links in a particular section to be visually different from links in another section. The simplest example of this would be a page that used a color for links, but then had a sidebar that had that same color as a background, forcing the links in the sidebar to be a different color. You can define and use custom link styles in the same way that you define and use character styles.

## Create Custom Link Styles

**1** With the Text tool ( T ), select text that you have turned into a hyperlink.

**2** Click **Hyperlink**.

**3** Click **Edit Link Styles**.

The Site Properties dialog box opens.

**4** Click the **New Link Style** button ( ).

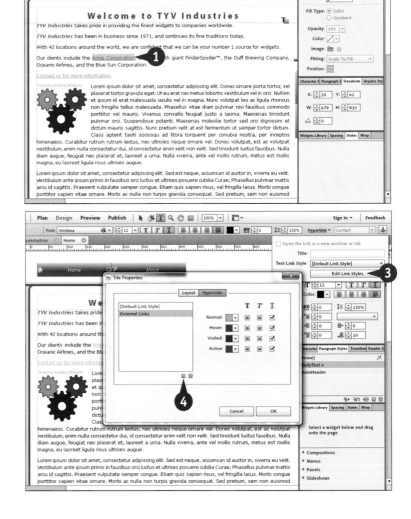

**⑤** Double-click the style name and enter a new, descriptive name.

**⑥** Set the desired appearance of the style.

**⑦** Click **OK**.

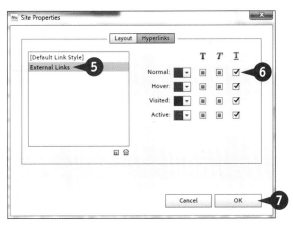

**⑧** From the Text Link Style dropdown, select the style you created in steps **5** and **6**.

**Ⓐ** The style is applied to the link.

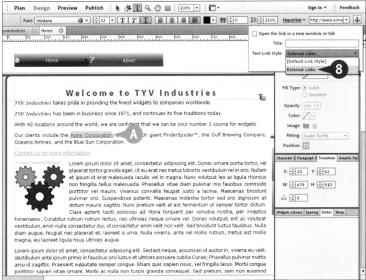

**Can I base my link styles on other styles, such as a character style?**

No. Unlike programs like InDesign, Muse does not allow you to create styles based on other styles. You must re-create the styles when you create new ones.

**Can I remove a link style I no longer plan to use?**

Yes. Click **Hyperlink** on the Control bar, and then click **Edit Link Styles**. Select the style you want to delete and click the trash can icon at the bottom of the dialog box. If you have any links using this style, they automatically revert to the default link style.

# Using Anchor Links

Sometimes, you may need to link not between pages, but rather from one place on a page to another place on the same page. In this case, you need to create the point to which you plan to link as a link anchor. Then, you can use that anchor as the target of any other link, whether on a menu or in a hyperlink. Anchor links can be placed anywhere on the page. Although they show with an icon in Design view, anchor links are invisible in the browser.

## Using Anchor Links

**1** Scroll to the point on the page to which you want to link.

**2** Click the **Link Anchor** button (⚓) on the Control bar.

**Ⓐ** The place gun appears.

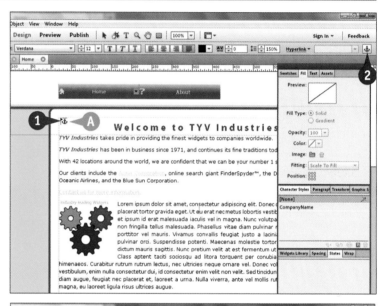

**3** Click the page at the point at which you want to set the anchor.

The Create an Anchor dialog box opens.

④ Enter a descriptive name for the anchor.

⑤ Click **OK**.

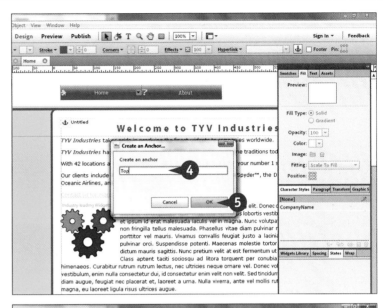

⑥ Create a hyperlink.

⑦ From the Hyperlink dropdown, choose the anchor you created in step **4**.

The anchor link is created.

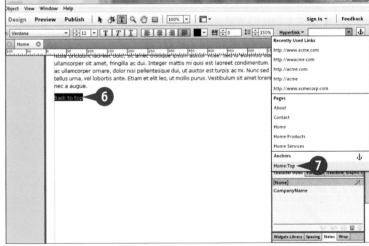

**When I test the page with an anchor in the browser and click the link to the anchor, the browser does not scroll all the way to the anchor. Why is this?**

Browsers attempt to place the anchor location at the top of the screen when they follow the link, but they can only scroll down to the bottom of the page. Therefore, if your anchor is too close to the bottom, the browser cannot scroll all the way down to the anchor.

**Is it preferable to have long pages with anchor links, or divide the content into individual pages?**

This issue has no right or wrong answer. Personal preference and the site content dictate which method to use. You need to assess each page you create and decide if it would be easier for your users to consume your content on one page, or on separate pages.

# CHAPTER 9

# Using Master Pages

The web is of course a visual medium, and the careful application of graphics on your site can greatly enhance its overall appearance.

# Understanding Master Pages

Almost all websites will have elements common to all pages. At a minimum, you will likely want a header with your logo and company name and a footer with copyright and contact information to appear on all pages. You may also want common design elements such as a shared background. All of these can be managed using Master pages, which allow you to add content that will appear on all pages created from the Master.

## Shared Design

If you design the overall look of your site in a Master, that design automatically applies to the pages in your site. You can set the browser fill color or background image, the width of the page, and the background color or image of the page in a Master and not have to keep redoing those steps as you create pages.

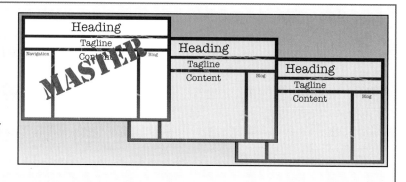

## Content on Masters

Although most of your content will be page-specific, some may be appropriate for the Master. For example, you might have a corporate motto or tagline that you want to appear on all pages. You might also have legal text you need for every page. This content can be placed on the Master so that you do not need to worry about forgetting to put it on the pages later.

## Global Updates

Whenever you edit the design of or content on a Master, those changes instantly apply to all pages. This allows you to update the look and feel of all the pages in your site very easily, and without having to worry that you might apply changes to some pages but not others.

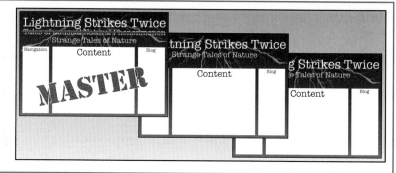

# Open a Master

Before you can begin designing and using a Master, you need to open it for editing. All of the Masters in your site appear at the bottom of Plan view. You can open a Master just as you would any other page: by double-clicking it in Plan view. You can edit elements on a Master only when it is open; the contents of the Master are locked while editing any other pages.

## Open a Master

**1** Click **Plan**.

Plan view opens.

**2** Double-click **A-Master**.

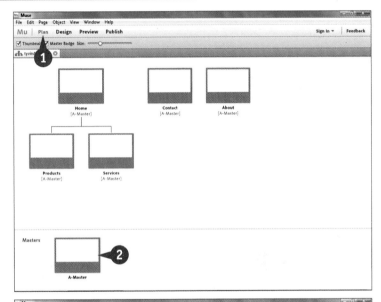

The Master page opens for editing.

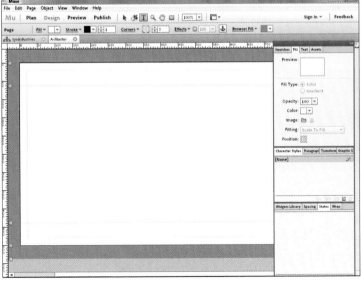

# Design the Background for the Site

reating the background of your site is one of the more important tasks that you can simplify with a Master. The actual process of applying background images or colors and setting the size of elements on the page is the same on a Master as it is on a regular page; however, you do need to be sure that your design allows for the type of content you want on all the pages you plan to base on this Master.

## Design the Background for the Site

**1** Open the A-Master page.

**Note:** See the previous section, "Open a Master."

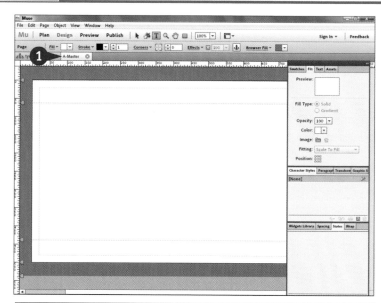

**2** From the Control bar, click the color picker next to Browser Fill.

**3** Select a color to use as the background on your site.

**A** The color applies to the page.

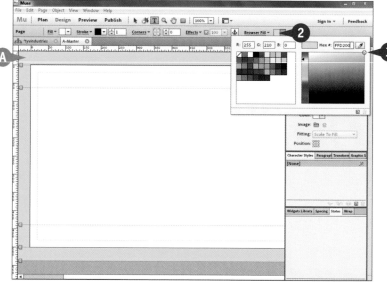

④ Click **Browser Fill**.

⑤ Click the **Choose background image** button ( ▤ ).

⑥ Navigate to the image you want to use.

⑦ Click **Open**.

The image is added to the background.

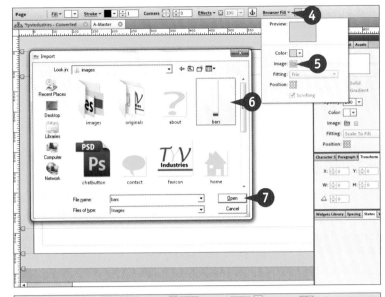

⑧ Select the tiling option you want for your image.

Ⓑ The image tiles appropriately, completing the background design.

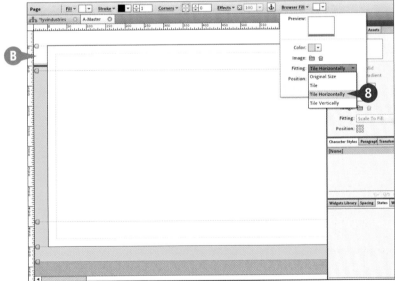

## TIP

**I know that I am going to need several different backgrounds in my site. If I set up the background on the Master, will I be able to change it on individual pages?**

Yes. When you create a page based on a Master, the page will have any design elements you placed on the Master. However, items such as browser fill remain editable on individual pages. Be aware, however, that if you later change the background on the Master, those changes do not affect pages where you overrode the Master's design.

# Set the Appearance of the Content Area

Most of the content in your site will need to be placed within the boundaries of the Page element. Although you should add the actual content to individual documents, you can set up the design of the Page in the Master to ensure consistency through your site. These design elements might include a background color or image for the Page, whether or not it contains a border, and the shape and size of its corners.

## Set the Appearance of the Content Area

**1** On the Master, use the Selection tool (⬉) to click in a blank area to deselect any elements.

**A** The Control bar displays Page.

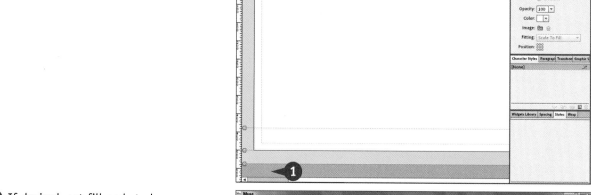

**2** If desired, set fill and stroke properties for the page.

**Note:** See Chapter 3 for details on setting the fill and stroke.

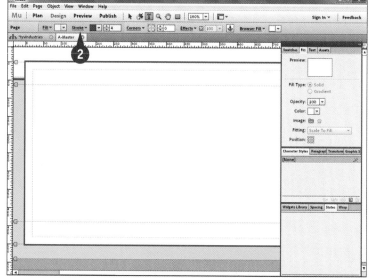

**3** If desired, set corner rounding properties.

**Note:** See Chapter 3 for details on setting corner rounding.

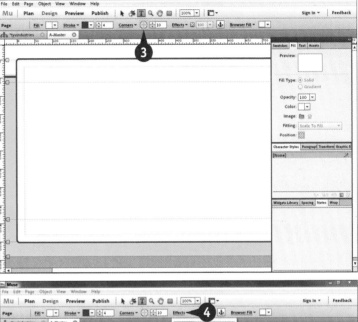

**4** If desired, add effects.

**Note:** See Chapter 3 for details on effects.

The Page area is designed.

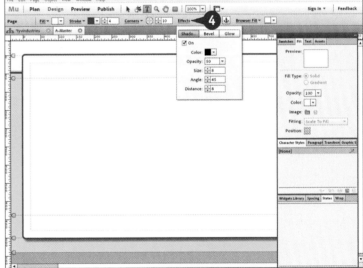

**Are there limits to what I can design on the Master?**
From a technical standpoint, no. You can design the page however you need to. The important thing to consider is that the Master is setting up the design for the site, so you want to make sure that you add only those things that you want on every page. Any page-specific elements should be on the pages, not the Master.

# Create a Site Header

The header appears at the top of every page, above your content. Most often, your header will at a minimum contain your site's logo, company or organization name, and a tagline. You might also decide to place your main site navigation here. In most cases, this content is placed above the page, so when creating your site header you may need to move the Page element down to allow sufficient space.

## Create a Site Header

### Import a Logo

1 Click **File**.

2 Click **Place**.

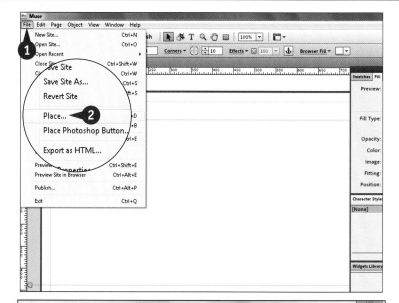

The Import dialog box opens.

3 Navigate to the directory that contains your logo.

4 Select the logo.

5 Click **Open**.

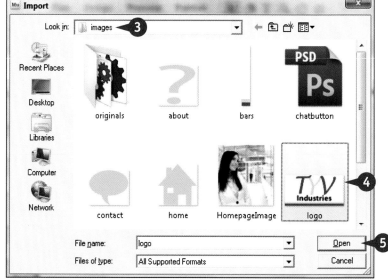

The place gun appears.

**6** Click in the Master window where you want to place the image.

The image is placed.

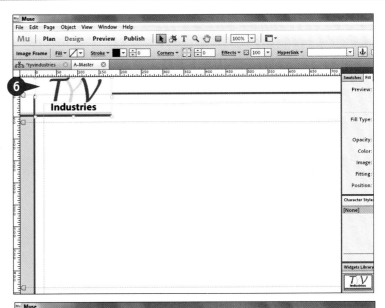

## Create Space for the Header

**1** Drag the Top of Page guide down to create space for your logo.

The header is created.

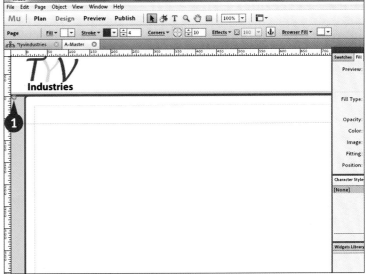

---

**TIP**

**If I want a slightly different header on some pages, will I be able to edit it?**
No. The site header can be edited only on the Master. You cannot change any aspect of the site header on individual pages. In this situation, you must create a different Master for those pages. See section "Create Additional Master Pages," later in this chapter, for more information.

# Design a Site Footer

You can add elements between the Bottom of Page guide and the Bottom of the Browser indicator to act as a site footer. The footer area is often used to provide links to lesser-used pages, legal verbiage, and copyright notices. When designing the footer, keep in mind that many users will ignore it, so you should avoid placing critical items in the footer.

## Design a Site Footer

**1** Drag the Bottom of Browser guide down to create enough space for your footer.

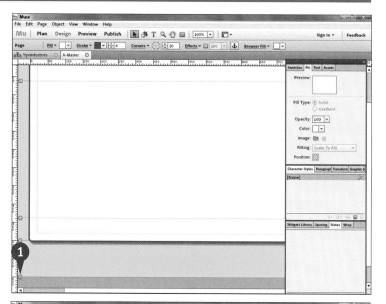

**2** Use the Rectangle tool ( ▭ ) to draw a box to hold your footer content.

**3** Make any desired visual changes to the rectangle, such as adding a border.

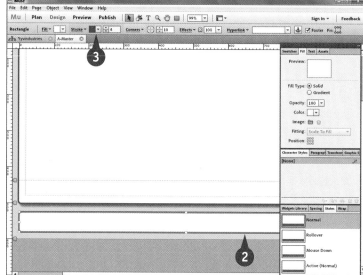

④ Use the Text tool ( T ) to add content to the footer.

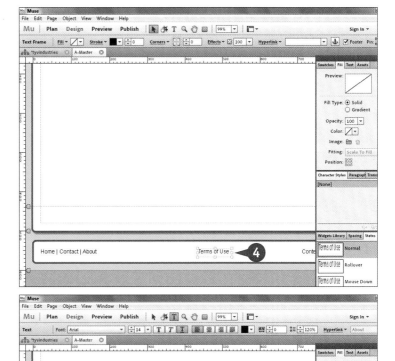

⑤ Add hyperlinks as needed.

**Note:** See Chapter 8 for details on adding hyperlinks.

The footer is designed.

## TIPS

**Will the footer remain below my page no matter how long my content gets?**

Yes. The Bottom of Page guide remains above your footer. As you build pages and add more content to them, that guide pushes down, forcing your footer and the Bottom of Browser guide down with it.

**How can I create space between my footer and the bottom edge of the browser window?**

The Bottom of Browser guide represents the bottom edge of the browser window. You can drag this guide down to create more space between your footer content and that bottom edge, or drag it up to reduce the space.

# Create Headers and Footers that Stretch

The page content area in your Muse site is a fixed width. Your header and footer can either also be a fixed width or be set to stretch so that they are as wide as the browser window. Keep in mind that you cannot know or control the size of your user's browser window, so you need to consider both very small screens such as those on smartphones and very large screens such as widescreen monitors.

## Create Headers and Footers that Stretch

**1** With the Selection tool (▶), click your footer.

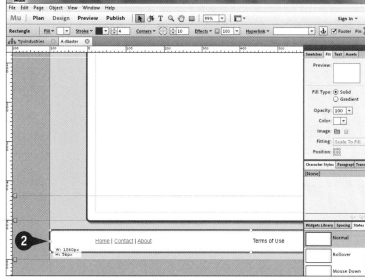

**2** Drag the left side control handle to the edge of the browser display area until you see a red line.

The left edge is anchored to the left edge of the browser.

**3** Repeat step **2** for the right edge.

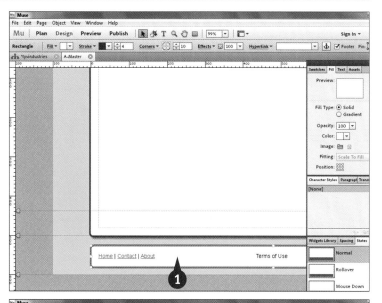

④ Click **File**.

⑤ Click **Preview Page in Browser**.

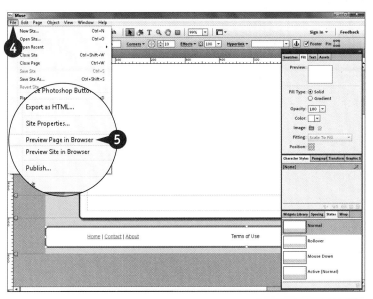

The file opens in a browser.

⑥ In Windows, click **Restore**.

⑦ Resize the browser window.

The footer edges remain locked to the edges of the browser window.

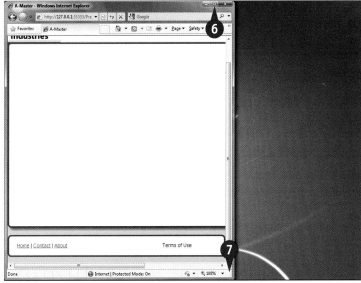

# Define Space for Page Headers and Footers

**Y**our site header and footer should be designed in the Master. You may also want to have headers and footers on individual pages. Your page header will likely contain the main heading for your document, but it might also contain other elements such as page-specific navigation or images. The page footer may contain additional links or references relevant to the page. Although you create the content for the page header and footer on the pages themselves, you need to define how much space will be allocated to each in the Master.

## Define Space for Page Headers and Footers

**①** Drag the Header guide up or down to define the space for the header.

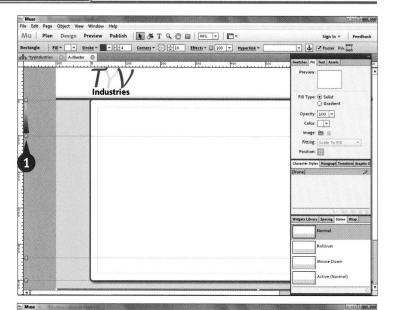

**②** Drag the Footer guide up or down to define space for the footer.

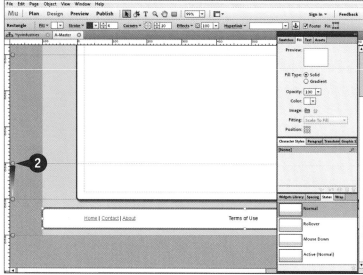

# Create Additional Master Pages

When you create a site in Muse, the program automatically creates one Master. You can, however, have as many Master pages as you need. Because you cannot change content on a Master from the pages, you must create a Master for each layout you will use in your site. You might create additional Masters for pages that require a different layout, or for pages that need different visual design.

## Create Additional Master Pages

**1** Click **Plan**.

Plan view opens.

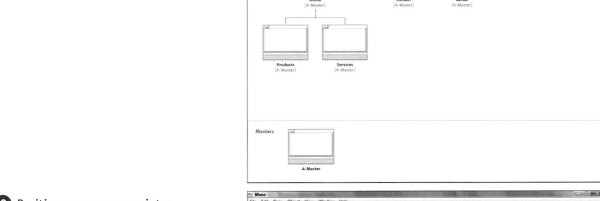

**2** Position your mouse pointer over an existing Master.

**3** Click the plus sign to create a new Master.

**4** Type a name for the new Master.

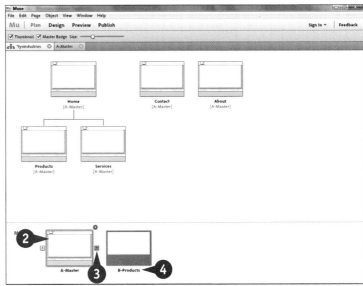

# Duplicate and Delete Masters

New Masters are by default empty. If you want to create a new Master using some or all of the content from a prior Master, you must duplicate the Master, which creates an exact copy of the first Master. You can then make any changes you need to the new one. You can also delete a Master you are not using. Deleting a Master does not change the content added directly to any existing pages that use it.

## Duplicate and Delete Masters

### Duplicate a Master

**1** In Plan view, position your mouse pointer over an existing Master.

**2** Right-click the Master.

**3** Select **Duplicate Page**.

**A** A copy of the Master is created.

**4** Type a new name for the Master.

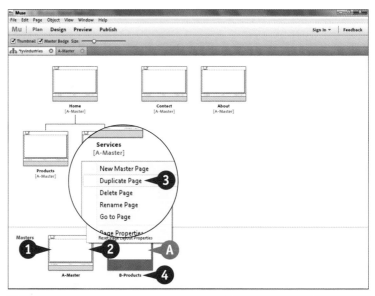

### Delete a Master

**1** Right-click a Master you no longer need.

**2** Select **Delete Page**.

The Master is deleted.

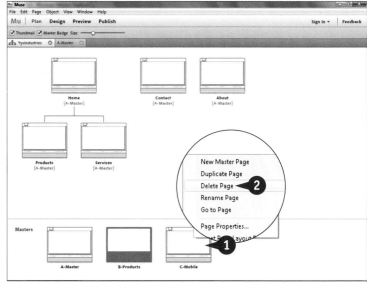

# Associate Masters with Pages

You create new pages in Plan view by adding them as a child or sibling of an existing page. These new pages automatically use the same Master as the page you created the new page from, but you can easily apply a different Master to a page. You can either drag a Master from the Masters section of Plan view to the page, or you can right-click a page and select the Master you want to use. You can also choose to have no Master associated with a page.

## Associate Masters with Pages

**1** In Plan view, drag a Master onto a page.

The Master is assigned to the page.

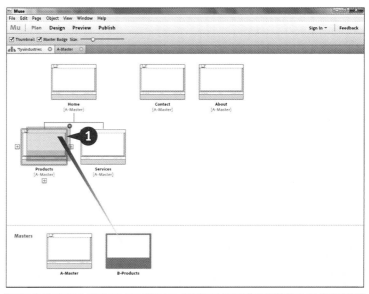

**2** Right-click a page.

**3** Select **Masters**.

**4** Select a Master.

The Master is assigned to the page.

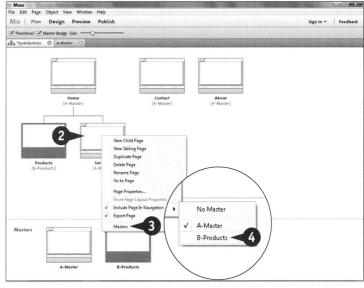

# CHAPTER 10

# Adding Widgets

Adobe Muse comes with a variety of widgets that add advanced functionality to your pages but still do not require you to write any code.

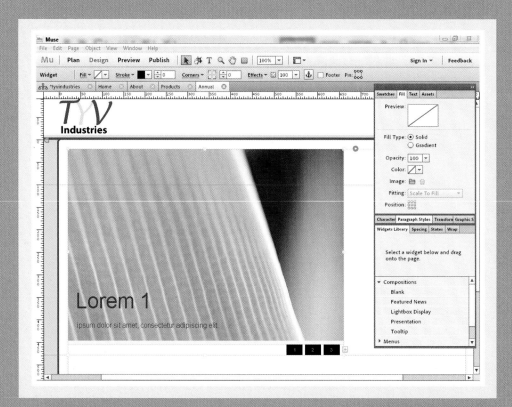

# Add a Featured News Widget

Composition widgets display pieces of content in a large window, with a set of smaller containers that allow the user to navigate through the content. Muse includes five Composition widgets. The Featured News widget includes by default a vertical menu and a stacked set of content. Once you add the widget, you can change the labels and content and add additional content.

## Add a Featured News Widget

**1** Open a page onto which you want to add a widget.

**2** Open the Widgets Library panel.

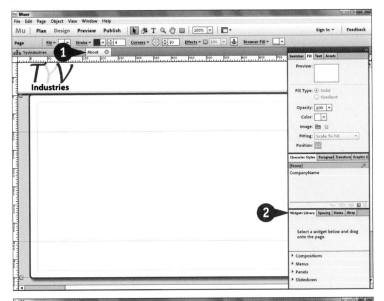

**3** Expand the Compositions section.

**4** Drag a Featured News widget onto the canvas.

The widget is added to the page.

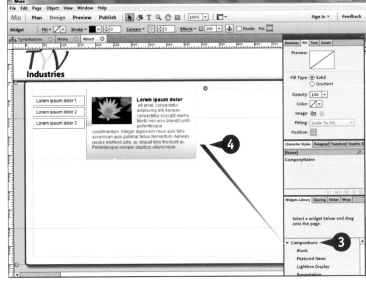

# Resize the Widget

Even though a widget displays resizing handles when selected, you cannot resize the widget as a whole. Instead, you need to select the individual components of the widget and resize them, which expands the overall size of the widget itself. In order to select the components, you need to click the widget once with the Selection tool, and then click the component you want to resize.

## Resize the Widget

1 With the Selection tool ( ), click the widget.

2 Click the component of the widget you want to resize.

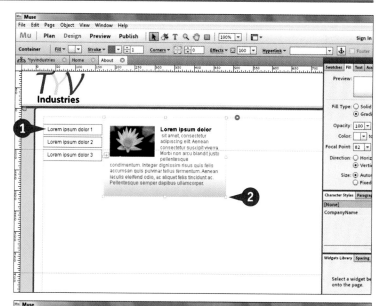

3 Click and drag one of the control handles to resize the component.

The component and the widget resize.

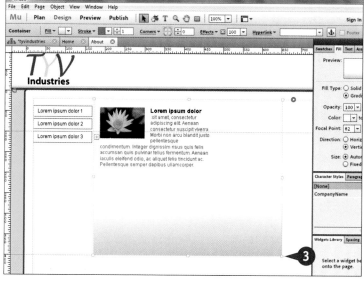

# Understanding Composition Widget Options

The Composition widgets are highly customizable. You can change how the elements in the widget appear on the page, the event that changes the item to display, the transition and speed, and whether the widget plays automatically. You can also ensure that the triggers, or buttons, remain on top of the content should they overlap; hide all the content initially; add next, previous, or close buttons; and choose which elements should appear while you design the widget.

## Position

The widget has three position options: stacked, staggered, and lightbox. The stacked option, which is the default, places each content piece directly on top of the others. This arrangement takes up the least amount of space and so is good for times when you need to present a lot of information in a small space. Staggered allows you to position each content piece independently on the page, even though only one appears at a time. Lightbox displays the content piece as an overlay on the page.

## Event

The event is used to trigger the change in content. If you choose On Click, your user must click the button to view the next piece of content, whereas selecting On Rollover allows your user to trigger the event by just moving his mouse pointer over the button. If you believe you may have users on mobile devices, be sure to choose On Click, because On Rollover does not work on smartphones and tablets. On Click is the only option if position is set to Lightbox.

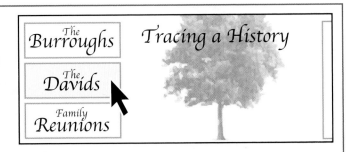

## Transition

If position is set to Stacked or Lightbox, you can choose between Fading, Horizontal, or Vertical transitions. Fading creates a crossfade where each content box becomes transparent while the next simultaneously becomes opaque. Horizontal and Vertical slide each box in either from left to right or from bottom to top. The Scattered position only supports Fading.

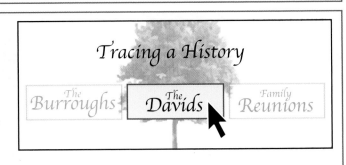

## Speed and Auto Play

You can choose to set the speed of the transition to fast, medium, or slow, depending on your preference. You can also set it to None, which disables the transition. You can also set the widget to play automatically, without user interaction, and choose to have it play fast, medium, or slow. You cannot fine-tune the speed.

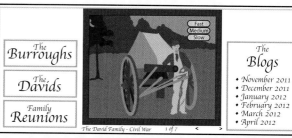

## Triggers On Top and Hide Initially

The Triggers On Top option allows you to determine whether the buttons remain on top of the content or fall behind it, should they overlap. You can also choose to have the content boxes invisible initially, and appear only when the user interacts with the triggers. Neither setting has any practical effect when the position is set to Lightbox.

## Parts

You can use the Parts settings to add up to three additional triggers: a back or previous button, a next or forward button, and a close button. The next and previous buttons can be particularly helpful when using the Lightbox, and the close button has no effect except when used with Lightbox.

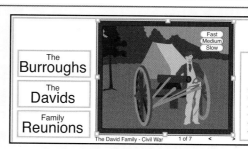

## Editing

The final two customization options have no effect when your users view the widget, and exist solely to help you when working with the widget in Design view. If you are using the Lightbox position, you can choose whether to show the content box on-screen or hide it. Showing it is useful when editing the content, but hiding it helps when laying out the page as a whole. If you use the Scattered position, you can select to show all of the content boxes to help place them correctly.

# Customize the Featured News Widget

Once you have added a Featured News widget to the page, you can customize its appearance and behavior. All the customization options are accessible from the editing options icon — the small white arrow in the blue circle that appears when you select the widget. The widget updates in real time as you select options, so feel free to experiment with the settings to decide on the one that works best for your site.

## Customize the Featured News Widget

**1** Click the widget you want to customize.

**2** Click the editing options icon ( ● ).

A menu of options appears.

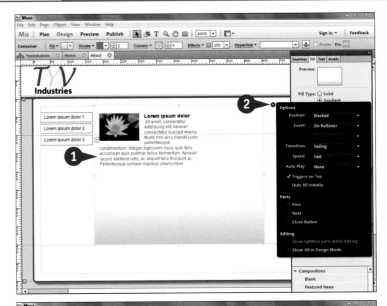

**3** Choose a position for the components.

**4** Choose an event to trigger changing the content.

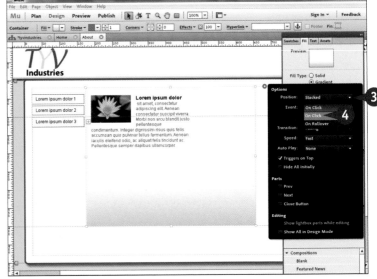

**5** Choose a speed and, if you want, a speed for auto play.

**6** Select whether to keep triggers on top (■ changes to ✓).

**7** Select whether to initially hide the content (■ changes to ✓).

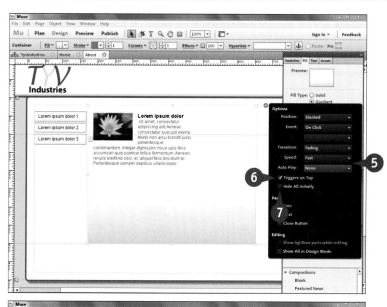

**8** If desired, show additional parts (■ changes to ✓).

**9** Choose editing options (■ changes to ✓).

The widget is customized.

---

## TIPS

**When I select the widget and click the editing options icon, I notice that some of the options are not available. Why is this?**

The editing options display a standard set of options for all the Composition widgets, but not all apply to every widget. Also, some of the options are dependent on your selection of other options. See the previous section, "Understanding Composition Widget Options," for more details.

**Can I save the configuration I selected for one widget so that I can easily apply the same settings to another widget?**

Unfortunately, no. Muse does not allow you to save the configuration of the widget to apply it to others. If you need to add another similar widget to a page and use the same settings, you must look up the settings from the first widget and manually re-create it. You could also copy and paste the first widget and then simply change the content.

# Change the Content in the Widget

All widgets come preloaded with filler content so that you can see how they should look and how they work when you place them on the page. You must replace this filler content with your own. The Featured News widget contains a single text frame, so you can simply select the text and replace it with your own content. You can either delete the inline picture in the filler content or replace it with your own image.

## Change the Content in the Widget

1 Click the **Text** tool ( T ).

2 Click in the content area in the widget.

3 Select all the filler text.

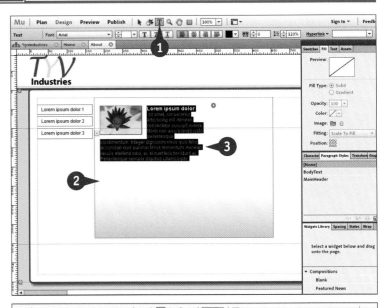

4 Enter your own content.

**Note:** See Chapter 7 for details on inserting images and wrapping text around them if you want an image in the content.

5 Change the text on the trigger button.

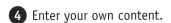

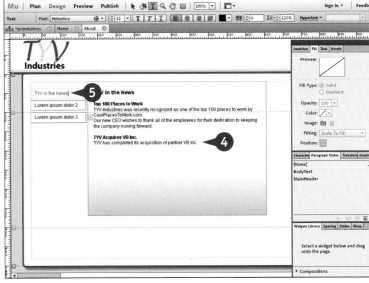

**6** Click the next trigger button.

**7** Repeat steps **2** to **5** to replace the content.

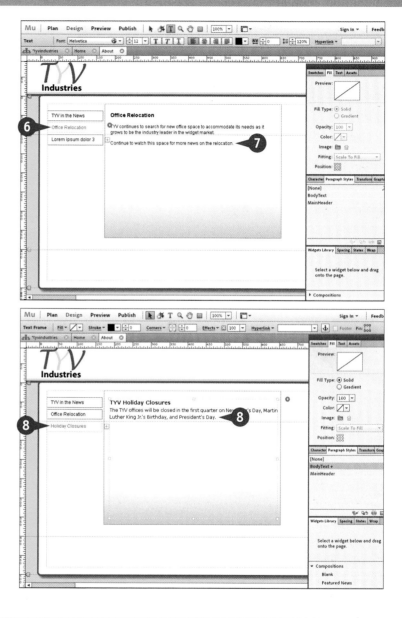

**8** Repeat step **7** for each additional content area.

The widget's content is updated.

**I cannot seem to view more than one content area, no matter how many times I click the trigger buttons. Why is this?**

If you are using the Stacked or Lightbox positions, all the content boxes appear on-screen in Design view at the same time, stacked on top of one another. You need to turn this option off to switch between content pieces while editing. If you are using the Scattered position, you must drag each content area to different locations on-screen to see and edit the pieces.

# Add Additional Content to the Widget

You can add as many content areas to the widget as you need. Each content area has an associated trigger button. You can add additional content by positioning your mouse pointer over the last trigger button and clicking the small plus sign that appears. Simply repeat this for as many content areas as you need, and then add labels to the buttons and new content to the content area.

## Add Additional Content to the Widget

① Click the plus sign.

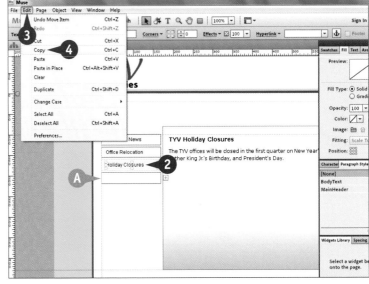

Ⓐ A new trigger button and content area are added.

② Select the label of the third button.

③ Click **Edit**.

④ Click **Copy**.

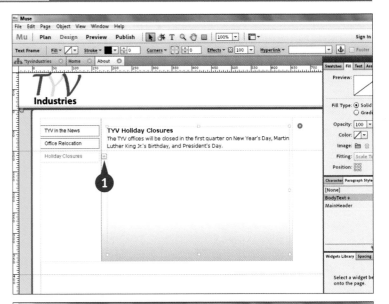

**5** Select the new button.

**6** Click **Edit**.

**7** Click **Paste**.

**Ⓑ** The label is pasted into the button.

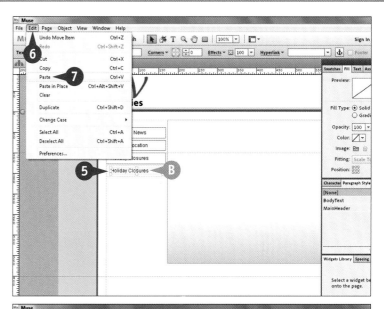

**8** Change the text on the new label.

**9** Add content to the widget's content area.

The widget updates with the new content.

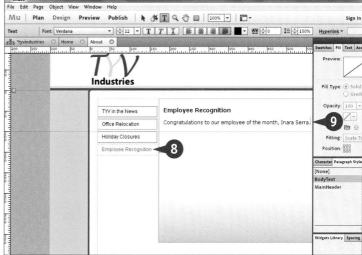

**How can I make sure that the formatting of the text in the button labels and the text in the content areas remain consistent?**

You should use character and paragraph styles to maintain consistency. At a minimum, you should create a paragraph style for the button labels and a paragraph style for the content, but depending on the complexity of your design you may need more. See Chapter 5 for details on creating and applying styles.

**Can I change the appearance of the buttons?**

Yes. The buttons can be formatted just like any other object on the canvas, so you can use the options on the Control bar to apply fill colors, strokes, rounded corners, and effects. You can do the same to the content area of the widget and to the widget as a whole.

# Add a Lightbox Display Widget

nother Composition widget available in Muse is the Lightbox Display. This widget automatically hides all of its content areas when the page opens in the browser. When a user clicks a trigger button, the content area appears in an overlay on the page, graying out the rest of the page. Most of the options on the Lightbox Display are the same as those found on the Featured News widget.

## Add a Lightbox Display Widget

① Open the Widgets Library panel.

② Expand the Compositions section.

③ Drag the Lightbox Display widget to the canvas.

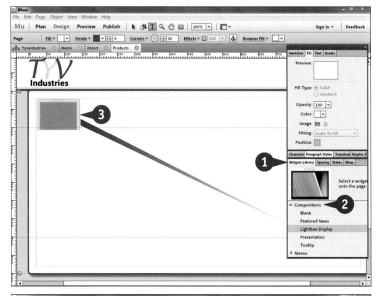

Ⓐ The widget is added to the page.

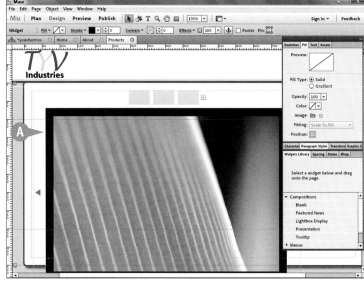

When your user browses the content from the Lightbox Display widget, the content appears centered on the browser window. The rest of the window fills with a partially transparent solid color. By default, this fill color is black, but you can change it to be any color you want. You can also adjust the level of opacity for the fill.

## Change the Browser Fill Color for the Lightbox Display Widget

**1** Click the Lightbox Display widget.

**2** Click the black background of the widget.

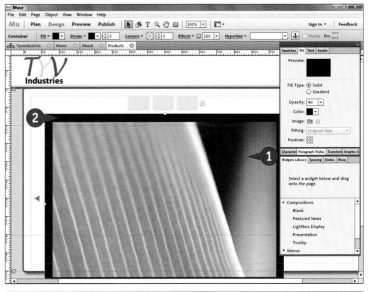

**3** Open the Fill panel.

**4** Select a new fill color.

**5** Set the desired opacity.

The widget updates.

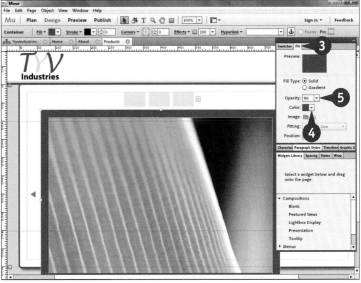

# Update the Content in the Lightbox Display Widget

You can change the content in the widget by replacing the placeholder images with images of your own, and then adjusting the captions accordingly. The easiest way to make this switch is to simply relink the existing images with your own. That way, you can be sure that the new images will fit in the same area as the ones you are replacing. You can relink images by using the Assets panel.

## Update the Content in the Lightbox Display Widget

**1** Click the widget.

**2** Click the image.

**3** Click the image again.

The image is selected.

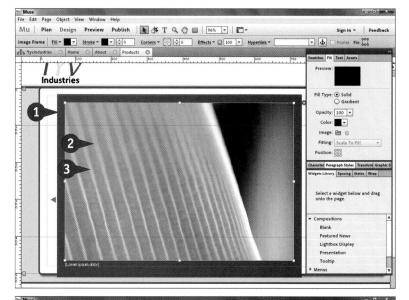

**4** Open the Assets panel.

The panel opens with the currently selected image highlighted.

**5** Right-click the image on the panel, leaves.jpg in this example.

**6** Select **Relink**.

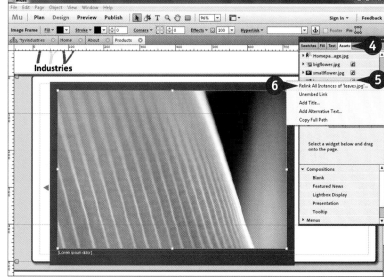

The Relink dialog box opens.

**7** Navigate to the directory that contains your image.

**8** Select the image.

**9** Click **Open**.

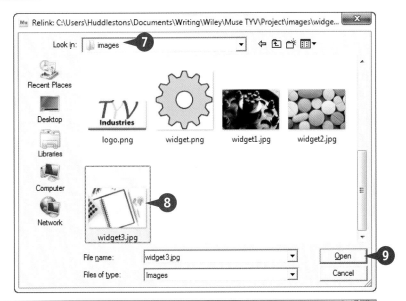

The new image replaces the old one in the widget.

**10** Change the caption text.

**11** Click a trigger button to move to a different element.

**12** Repeat steps **3** to **10** for each additional element in the widget.

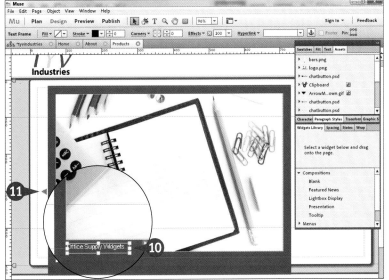

**TIP**

**Can I use the widget for something other than images?**
Yes. Any content can be placed inside the widget; images are just the most popular. You could select the image and caption, delete them, and then insert any other kind of content. You can also mix content, so one page of the widget could be an image and the next could be text. In these cases, you can simply delete the images in the widget and replace them by drawing text boxes and adding content just as you would add it anywhere else in Muse. See Chapter 4 for more information on text boxes.

# Resize the Lightbox Display Widget

You can resize the elements of the Lightbox Display widget, but it contains more elements than appear at first glance, and resizing does not always give you the result you intended. Each page of the widget contains, from the inside out, an image, a caption, a group of the image and the caption, and a background. You can resize the image or the caption by clicking until you select the item itself, but remember that the purpose of the lightbox is to display an item in an overlay. Do not resize to make it fit in your page layout.

## Resize the Lightbox Display Widget

**①** Click the widget.

**②** Click the image in the widget.

The group containing the image and the caption is selected.

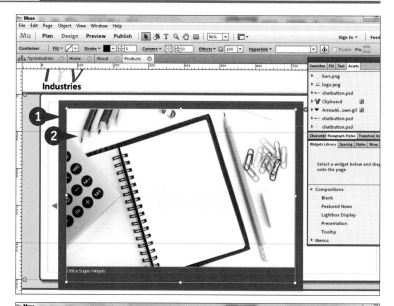

**③** Click the image again.

The image is selected.

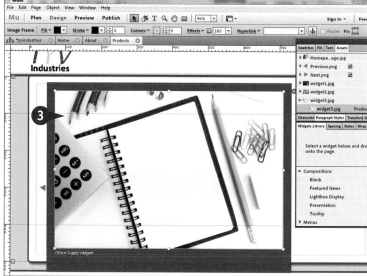

**4** Resize the image by clicking and dragging a corner handle.

**5** Move the caption.

**6** Click a trigger button.

**7** Repeat steps **2** to **5** for each additional image in the widget.

**8** Resize the outer boundary of the widget by clicking and dragging a corner handle.

The widget resizes.

## TIPS

**Is there an easy way to ensure that all the images are the same size?**
You cannot resize all the images in the widget together. However, you can resize the first image and note its width and height on the Control bar. Then, you can simply enter those values for each additional image, instead of trying to drag them to be the same size.

**Can I reorder the content in the widget?**
Not automatically. You can reorder the content only by manually changing the content on each page of the widget to the new content. Because this is obviously a considerable amount of work, carefully planning the content you need for your widget in advance to ensure that it is added in the correct order is highly recommended.

# Update the Trigger Buttons

The trigger buttons for the Lightbox Display widget begin as blank gray rectangles. You definitely must edit those to make them meaningful to your users. If you are using the widget for images, you will likely want to populate the buttons with thumbnails of the images. If you are using text, you must come up with something logical to use on the buttons such as simple labels.

## Update the Trigger Buttons

① Click the widget.

② Click the first of the trigger buttons.

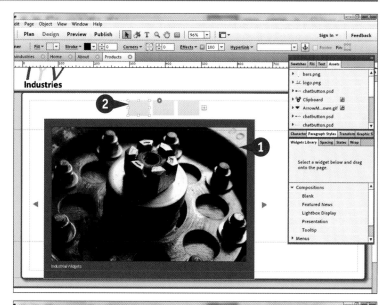

③ Open the Fill panel.

④ Click the **Choose background image** button ( 📁 ).

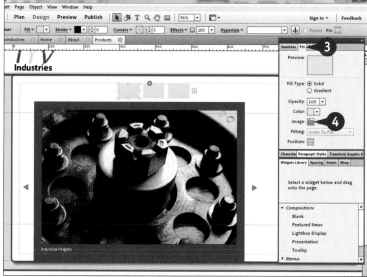

The Import dialog box opens.

**5** Navigate to the folder that contains your images.

**6** Select the image to use as the thumbnail.

**7** Click **Open**.

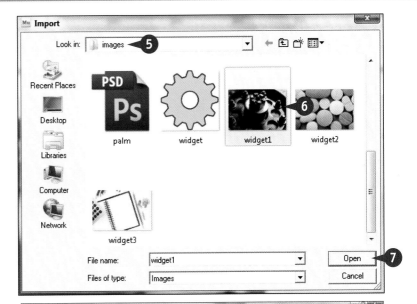

**8** Change the Fitting option to **Scale to Fit**.

**Ⓐ** The thumbnail updates.

**9** Repeat steps **2** to **8** for each additional button.

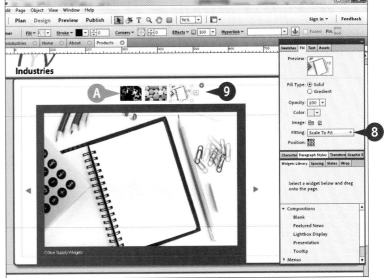

**Instead of making the image fit, can I show a cropped version?**

Yes, but only to a point. You can leave the Fitting option at Original Size, and then change the Position to one that shows more of the image. You could then adjust the size of the button itself to show more or less of the cropped image.

**If I change the main image, will I have to manually change the thumbnail?**

Possibly. No internal association exists between the content in the widget and the background image on the button, so if you change the main content you must manually change the button. The one exception is with images. If the main content and the button are using the same image, then relinking the image in the Assets panel updates both simultaneously.

# Add a Presentation Widget

The Presentation Widget, as its name implies, gives you a widget whose display is similar to PowerPoint or Keynote or other presentation software. The filler content consists of a large image with two overlaid text boxes. However, once you begin working with the widget, you will quickly discover that it functions the same as the Featured News and Lightbox Display widgets, and it contains all the same settings and options.

## Add a Presentation Widget

**1** Open the Widgets Library panel.

**2** Expand the Compositions section.

**3** Drag the Presentation widget to the canvas.

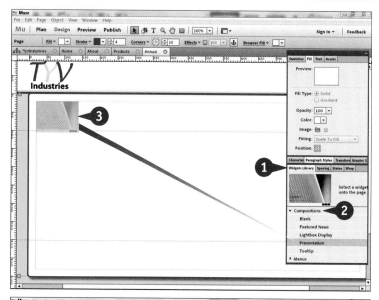

The widget is added to the canvas.

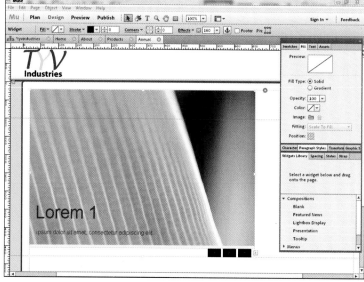

# Add a Blank Composition Widget

The Featured News, Lightbox Display, and Presentation widgets all contain sample filler content to help get you started, but the filler content is in fact nothing more than different default settings for the same widget. The Blank composition widget is another example of this, but it does not contain filler content. Once you are familiar with the configuration options available, you may find using this widget is faster because it saves you from having to delete the sample content.

## Add a Blank Composition Widget

**1** Open the Widgets Library panel.

**2** Expand the Compositions section.

**3** Drag the Blank widget to the canvas.

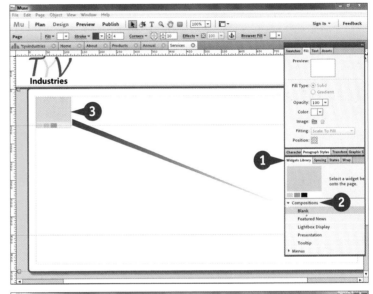

The widget is added to the canvas.

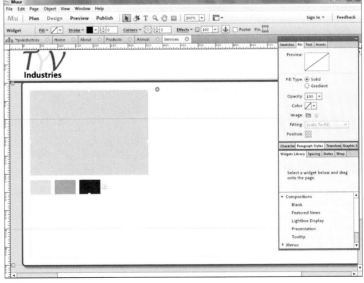

# Using the Tooltip Widget

The Tooltip is another widget with the same basic functionality as the other Composition widgets, but it contains one important additional setting: the ability to control whether the content, in this case pop-up tooltips, remains visible when the user moves the mouse pointer away from the trigger, or if it disappears. Otherwise, the widget works the same as the others.

## Using the Tooltip Widget

### Add the Widget

1. Open the Widgets Library panel.

2. Expand the Compositions section.

3. Drag the Tooltip widget to the canvas.

   The widget is added to the canvas.

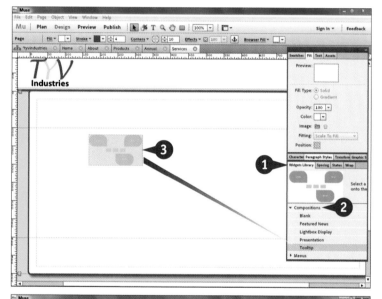

### Configure the Rollout Behavior

1. Click the widget.

2. Click the editing options icon ( ○ ).

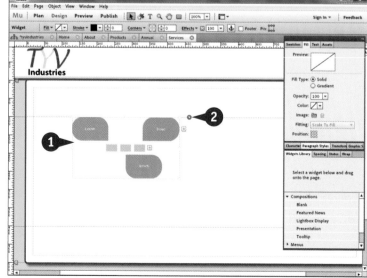

**③** Select either **Hide on Rollout** or **Stay on Rollout**.

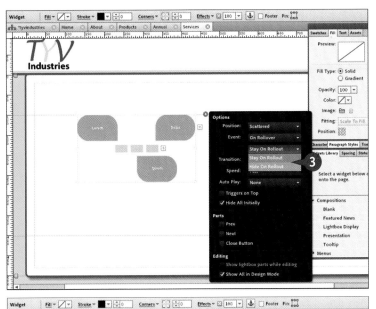

The widget is configured on the page.

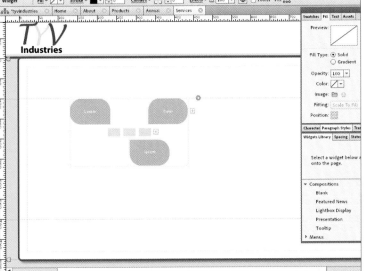

**When might I use a Tooltip widget?**
Anytime you want to have content appear when the user positions his mouse pointer over the trigger button. This can be useful for displaying small help information for content, such as the tooltips that appear when you mouse over tools and other items in Muse and other software. Most of the time, the content you put in the tooltip will be small or short, but you can put large quantities of information or large images in the content if you want.

# Create an Accordion Panel

Muse contains two panel widgets. Both are intended to allow you to add large amounts of data in small spaces. The Accordion panel groups its content into vertical pieces that contain a selection bar and a content area. As the user clicks each selection bar, it expands to fill the accordion, causing the others to collapse. The accordion can contain any information, and each panel within the accordion can contain different data. Each panel can be a different size, but the accordion will be as wide as the widest content.

## Create an Accordion Panel

1. Open the Widgets Library panel.

2. Expand the Panels section.

3. Drag the Accordion widget to the canvas.

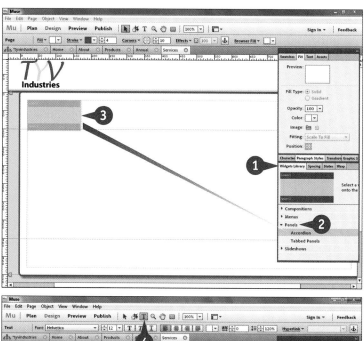

The widget is added to the canvas.

4. Click the **Text** tool ( T ).

5. Click the label.

6. Edit the label.

7. Repeat steps **5** and **6** for the other label.

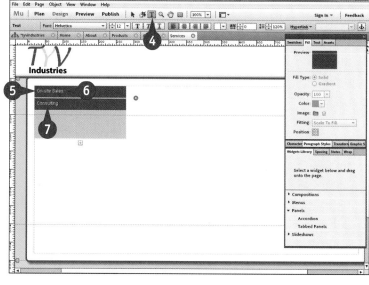

**8** With the Selection tool (↖), click a label.

**9** Insert content into the panel.

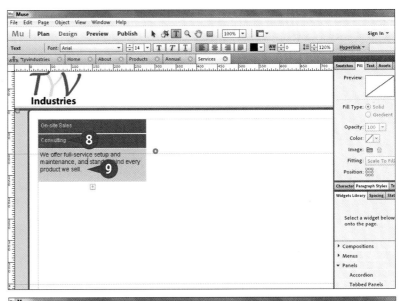

**10** Click the plus sign at the bottom of the widget.

**Ⓐ** A new panel is added.

**11** Edit the new label.

**12** Add content to the new panel.

The panels are set up.

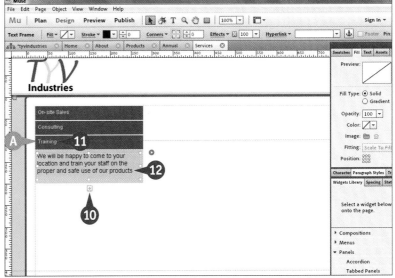

**Are there any configuration options for the accordion?**

Yes. As with other widgets, you can click the editing options icon ( ● ) to view a menu of options. The accordion has only three: You can allow your user to close all panels at once, and if you enable that you can also set up the accordion to have all panels closed initially. You can also enable or disable the ability to edit all the panels at once, so for example if you have this enabled and you change the background color on one panel, they all change.

# Using a Tabbed Panel

The other panel widget is the Tabbed panel, which stacks the content but provides a set of tabs at the top of the widget for navigation. As with the accordion, you can edit the labels and add content to each panel. You can add as many tabs as you need. The Tabbed panel is useful for situations where you have a lot of content you need to fit into a small area, but where you want to make sure that all the navigation remains at the top of the page.

## Using a Tabbed Panel

**1** Open the Widgets Library panel.

**2** Expand the Panels section.

**3** Drag the Tabbed widget to the canvas.

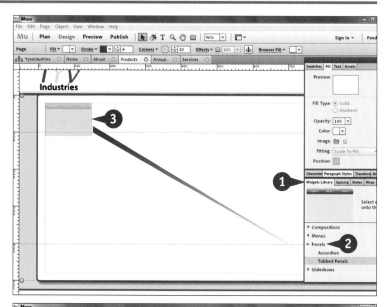

The widget is added to the canvas.

**4** Click the **Text** tool ( **T** ).

**5** Click the label.

**6** Edit the label.

**7** Repeat steps **5** and **6** for each other label.

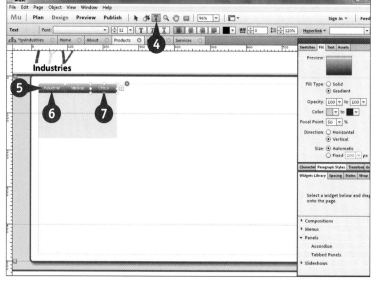

**8** With the Selection tool ( ），
click the first label, and
insert content into the first
panel.

**9** Click the next label.

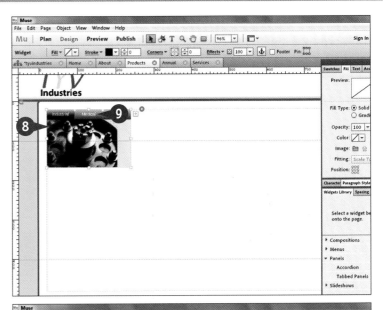

**10** Insert content into the next
panel.

**11** Repeat steps **9** and **10** for
each other panel.

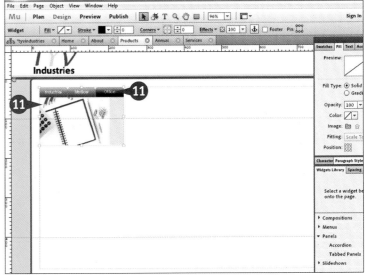

**What configuration options exist for the tabbed panels?**

You can click the editing options icon ( ● ) to access a menu of additional options. They include the ability
to edit all the panels together, change the event that moves between panels to either On Click or On
Rollover, and set whether the total width is uniform or sizes to fit the content. You can add icons to the
left or right of the tabs, which can then be replaced by images, and you can change the position of the
labels within the tabs.

# Add a Slideshow Widget

The final category of widgets in Muse is slideshows. There are four Slideshow widgets, but all have the same basic functionality and the same options. The Basic slideshow displays each full-size picture, called the Hero image, with a caption and navigation controls. The Blank slideshow is the same as the Basic, but lacks sample filler content. The Lightbox slideshow requires thumbnail navigation, and opens the Hero image in a browser overlay. The Thumbnails slideshow is similar to the Basic and Blank, but has thumbnail navigation on by default.

## Add a Slideshow Widget

① Open the Widgets Library panel.

② Expand the Slideshows section.

③ Drag the Basic widget to the canvas.

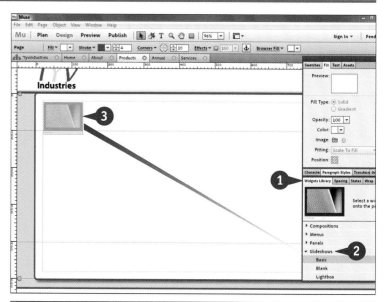

The widget is added to the canvas.

④ Click the editing options icon (○).

⑤ Click the **Choose images to add to this photo gallery** button (▣).

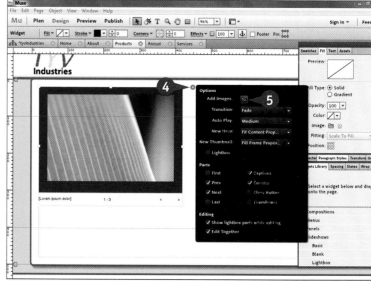

The Import dialog box opens.

**6** Select images to use.

**Note:** You can use Shift to select multiple consecutive images, or Ctrl (⌘) to select nonconsecutive images.

**7** Click **Open**.

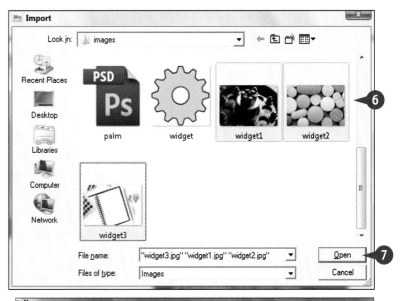

**Ⓐ** The images are imported. The slideshow updates to display the correct number of images.

**TIPS**

**Can I add more images later?**
Yes. Simply click the widget, and then navigate within the widget to the image after which you want to add more pictures. Click the editing options icon ( ⊙ ), and then click the **Choose images to add to this photo gallery** button (▣). Select additional images and click **Open**. Muse adds them to the slideshow after the current image, and the navigation automatically updates.

**Can I delete images?**
Yes. All you need to do to delete an image is navigate to it in the Slideshow widget, select the image, and press Delete on your keyboard. Be careful and make sure that you have the image, and not the widget, selected. If you should happen to delete the widget, click **Edit**, and then **Undo Delete Item**.

# Configure the Slideshow

The Slideshow widgets have a large set of configuration options. You can set the type of transition, turn on auto play, and set the alignment of the Hero image and thumbnail. You can add additional parts such as navigation buttons, captions, a counter, and thumbnails. Finally, you can choose whether to show the lightbox parts, such as the fill color, and choose whether or not to edit all the slides on the widget together. All these options can be accessed by clicking the editing options icon.

## Configure the Slideshow

**1** Click the Slideshow widget.

**2** Click the editing options icon ( ● ).

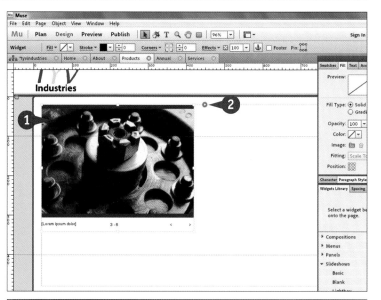

The Options menu appears.

**3** Set a transition.

**4** Set a desired auto play option.

**5** Set a desired alignment for new images.

**6** Set a desired alignment for new thumbnails.

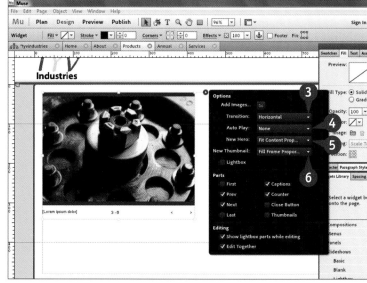

**7** If desired, show additional parts (■ changes to ☑).

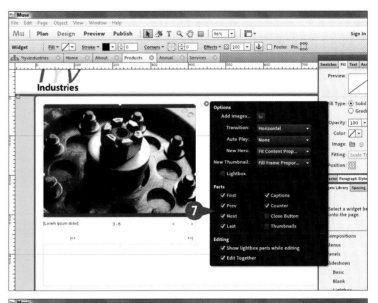

**8** Select whether to show or hide the lightbox parts (■ changes to ☑).

**9** Select whether to edit the slides together (■ changes to ☑).

The widget is configured.

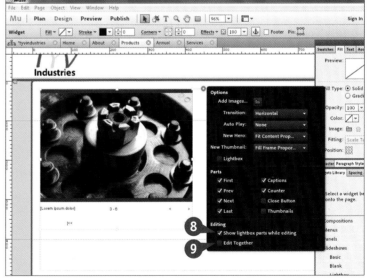

---

**If I choose to add thumbnails, will I have to create them all individually as I did with the Composition widgets?**

No. The Composition widgets are designed to allow you to use many different types of content, and so do not create thumbnails automatically because it would be impossible to know what the thumbnail should display. The Slideshow widgets, on the other hand, are built specifically to work with images, so if you turn on the Thumbnails option, smaller versions of each slide are created for you.

# CHAPTER 11

# Using Content from Other Sources

Adobe Muse's arbitrary HTML feature lets you add a Google map of your location, a Facebook Like button, a Flash animation, and much more.

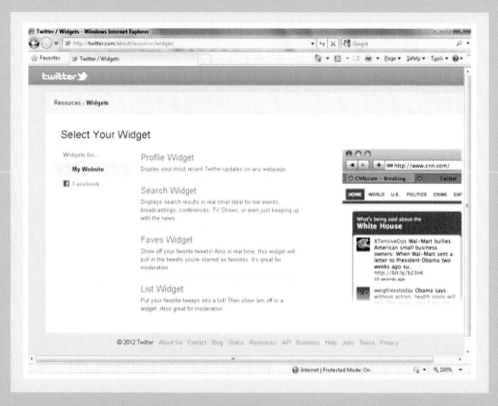

# Add a Google Map

I f your website is for a business with a physical location, providing a map can be much more helpful than simply printing your address on the site. Instead of simply taking a screenshot from a mapping site and placing that on your page, you can add a live Google map to your site which allows your user to interact and get directions. The process is fairly simple once you have the map set up in Google.

## Add a Google Map

### Get the Code for the Map

**1** In your web browser, go to http://maps.google.com.

The Google maps page appears.

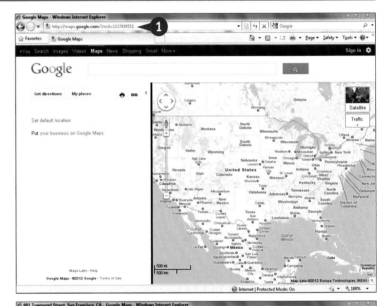

**2** Type the address.

The location appears on the map.

③ Click the **Link** button ( ).

④ Click **Customize and preview embedded map**.

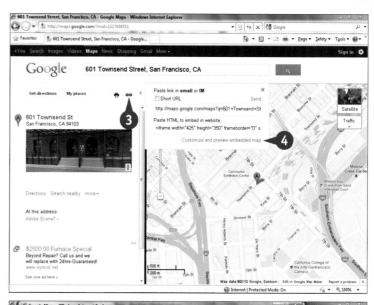

The Customize page opens.

⑤ Click **Custom**.

⑥ Enter a size for the map.

⑦ Select the code.

⑧ Right-click in the code window.

⑨ Choose **Copy**.

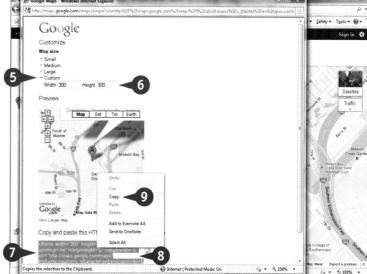

**Can I create a map with several locations?**

Yes. If you sign in with a Google account, which can be created for free if you do not already have one, you can create custom maps that can contain multiple saved locations. Step-by-step directions for this process can be found at http://maps.google.com/help/maps/getmaps/quick.html#multiple-locations.

**Can I use the Satellite view or Street view rather than the Map view?**

Yes. Before you click the **Customize and preview embedded map** link, switch to Satellite view. To use Street view, drag the Street View icon to the desired location. Then, click the **Customize and preview embedded map** link, and the code for whatever view you had set up appears.

Once you have the map code copied from Google's website, you can switch back to Muse. There, open whatever page you want the map to appear on, and then use the Selection tool to click the canvas and paste the map. While in Design view, the map appears as a static image, but when you preview the page you will see that the map is fully interactive.

## Add a Google Map (continued)

### Paste the Map into Muse

1 Switch to Muse.

2 Open the page on which you want the map.

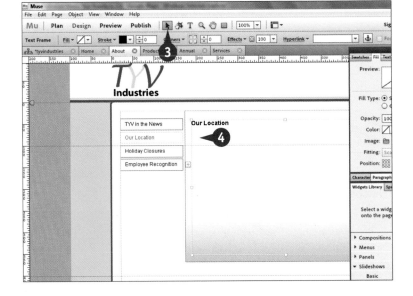

3 Click the **Selection** tool ( ).

4 Click the canvas where you want the map.

**5** Click **Edit**.

**6** Click **Paste**.

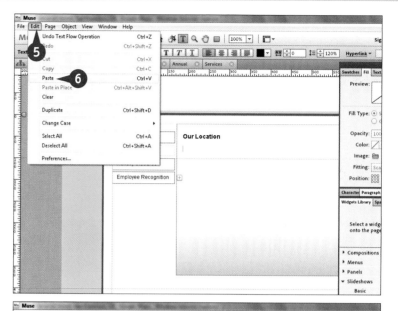

**A** The map is pasted onto the page.

**7** Move the map to the desired location.

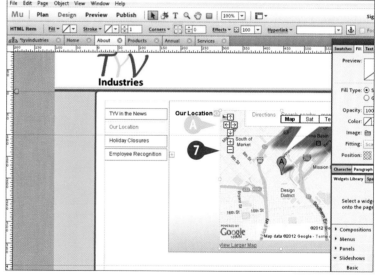

TIPS

**If I discover that the map is not quite right, can I fix it?**

Yes. Return to Google and repeat the steps to get a new map. Copy the code from Google. Then in Muse, right-click the existing map and select **HTML**. Select the code in the HTML Code dialog box and paste the new code from Google.

**Can I resize the map? Dragging the control handles does not seem to work.**

To resize the map, you need to first resize the embedded map through code, and then resize the container. Right-click the map and select **HTML**, and then change the width and height values in the first line of code. Click **OK** and the map resizes. You can then drag the control handles on the container to get it to fit.

# Using YouTube Video

You can very often convey meaning through video much easier than you can through text. This has never been easier thanks to the low cost of high-quality video cameras and microphones. To add video to your site, one of the easiest ways is to record and upload the video to YouTube, and then embed the YouTube video into your page. The embedded video looks like a black rectangle in Design view, but works when you preview.

## Using YouTube Video

**1** In your browser, go to www.youtube.com.

**2** Search for the video you want to embed.

**3** Click **Share**.

**4** Click **Embed**.

**5** Select the code.

**6** Right-click the code.

**7** Click **Copy**.

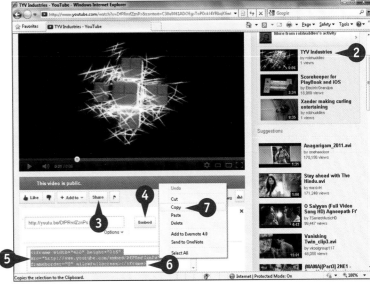

**8** Switch to Muse.

**9** Open the page onto which you want to embed the video.

**10** Click the canvas.

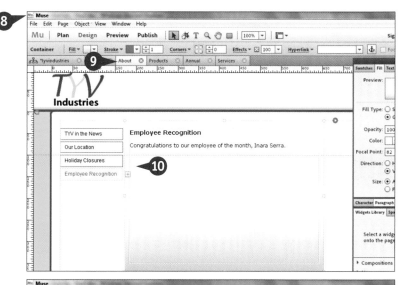

**11** Click **Edit**.

**12** Click **Paste**.

Ⓐ The video is embedded onto the page.

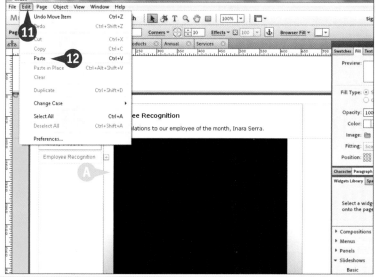

**Can I embed any video from YouTube?**
Technically, yes, but you need to assume that any video you see on YouTube is protected by copyright, so it may not be legal to do so. To be safe, you should embed only video that you personally created, although if you look on the page for other videos you may see permission to embed. You can also contact the owner of the video and ask for permission.

**Can I upload video to YouTube but keep everyone from seeing it?**
Yes. When you upload video to YouTube, you have the option of making it public or private. If you select private, only you and others you designate can see the video. However, you cannot embed this video in a public website. For more information on creating video and uploading it to YouTube, see *YouTube and Video Marketing: An Hour a Day,* 2nd Edition (John Wiley & Sons, 2011).

# Add a Facebook Like Button

Facebook has become so popular over the last few years that some companies and organizations have abandoned having their own sites in favor of creating pages on Facebook. Many companies find a combination of both is a better approach. You can effectively leverage both by adding a Facebook Like button to your website, so that users visiting your website can instantly subscribe to your Facebook page.

## Add a Facebook Like Button

① In your browser, go to http://developers.facebook.com/docs/reference/plugins/like.

② Fill out the form on that page under the heading Step 1 – Get Like Button Code.

**Note:** Be sure to deselect the **Send Button** option ( ☑ changes to ☐).

③ Click **Get Code**.

The Your Like Button Plugin Code screen opens.

④ Click **IFRAME**.

⑤ Click in the code.

The code is selected.

⑥ Right-click the code.

⑦ Select **Copy**.

**8** Return to Muse.

**9** Open the page onto which you want to add the Like button.

**10** Click the canvas.

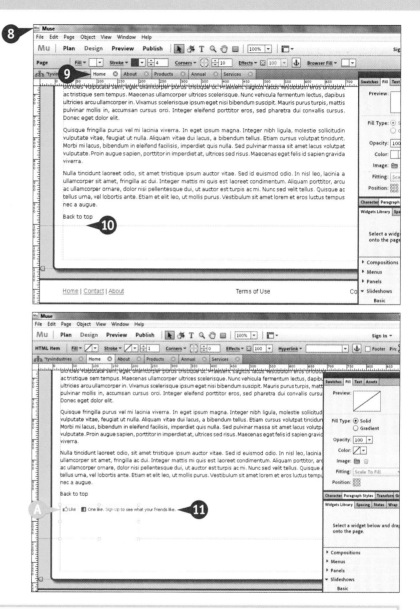

**11** Paste the code.

Ⓐ The Like button is added to the page.

**I see that Facebook's Open Graph service gives me many more options on how my users interact with my page. Can I use Open Graph?**

Unfortunately, not at this time. Open Graph requires that you place a set of HTML tags in the head section of your document, which you cannot yet do in Muse. The Muse team has stated they are looking into this feature, so hopefully you will be able to in a future version.

**How can I create a Facebook page for my company or organization?**

Go to www.facebook.com/pages/create.php and follow the simple on-screen directions to create a page. You can learn much more about using Facebook to enhance your business' online presence in *Facebook Marketing For Dummies*, 3rd Edition (John Wiley & Sons, 2012).

# Using Twitter Buttons

lthough not as big as Facebook, Twitter has become almost as important in social networking. Twitter provides an easy way to users to follow you and get immediate, up-to-the-minute updates. Twitter can be a very effective way to communicate sales, special offers, or breaking news. Best of all, it is entirely free. You can add buttons to your site that allow users with their own Twitter accounts to share the link to your page with their followers, follow you, or mention you in their Twitter stream.

## Using Twitter Buttons

**1** Use your browser to go to https://twitter.com/about/resources/buttons.

**2** Select what kind of button you want to use ( ○ changes to ◉ ).

**3** Fill out the form.

**4** Right-click in the code box.

**5** Select **Copy**.

The code is placed on the clipboard.

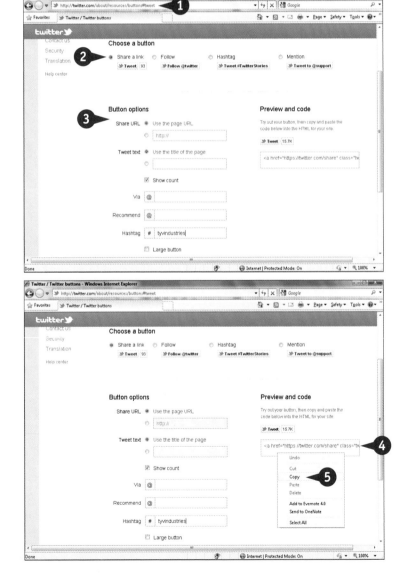

**6** Return to Muse.

**7** Open the page onto which you want to add the button.

**8** Click the canvas.

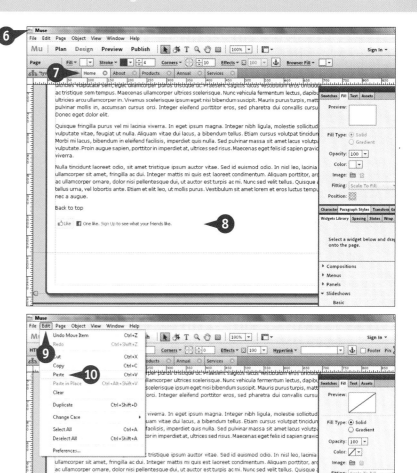

**9** Click **Edit**.

**10** Click **Paste**.

Ⓐ The button is added to the page.

**Why are tweets limited to 140 characters?**

Twitter was originally conceived as a service that would allow users to send SMS or text messages to groups of people, rather than to individuals. Text messages have long been limited to 140 characters due to early technical reasons. Because of this background, Twitter began with a 140 character limit. Today, they probably maintain it because it makes the platform unique.

**What is a hashtag?**

Hashtags are a method by which Twitter users can mark a post by putting a pound sign (#) before a word. Often, hashtags are used as a way of identifying a set of related posts — so for example on many Twitter streams in January and February, you see posts related to the Academy Awards tagged with #oscars. Hashtags are sometimes used to make ironic statements in the posts.

# Display a Twitter Feed

I n addition to having your users follow you on Twitter, you can embed a live Twitter feed, so your
 website visitors can see in real time what other Twitter users are saying about your company or
product. Twitter provides an easy-to-use widget generator to make setting up the feed easy, and just
like with the other topics in this chapter, you can simply copy and paste the code from Twitter into
your Muse page.

## Display a Twitter Feed

1 Use your browser to go to
https://twitter.com/about/
resources/widgets.

2 Click **My Website**.

3 Click **Search Widget**.

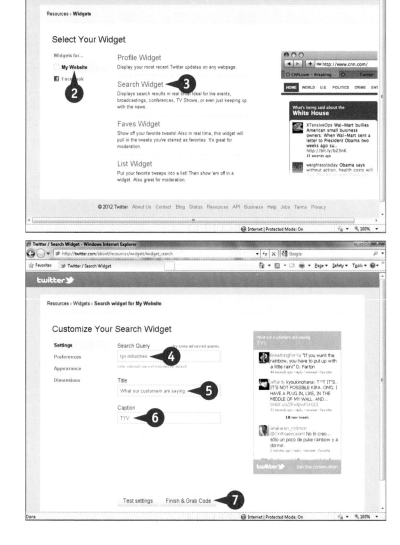

4 Type a term or terms for
which you want to search
Twitter.

5 Type a title for the widget.

6 Type a caption.

7 Click **Finish & Grab Code**.

**8** Click in the code window.

**9** Right-click the code.

**10** Select **Copy**.

The code is placed on the clipboard.

**11** Return to Muse.

**12** Right-click the canvas.

**13** Select **Paste**.

Ⓐ The widget is added to the page.

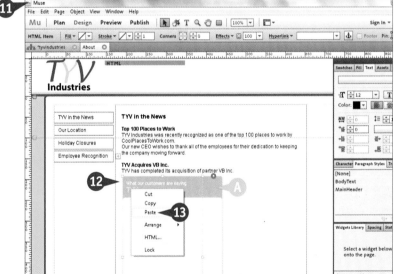

TIP

**Can I customize the widget to match my website's look and feel?**
Yes, the Twitter widget is highly customizable. On the Twitter page, click **Appearance**. You can use the page to change the background of the shell, the tweets, and the links, and well as the text color. You can also click **Preferences** to set how often the widget gets results from Twitter and display settings such as whether or not to display a scrollbar. Finally, use the Dimensions page to change the size of the widget before you paste it into Muse.

# Add a Flash Movie

A dobe Flash has long been the standard for creating interactive animations on the web. Although creating Flash content can be quite difficult and often requires writing code, adding content already created to a Muse project is fairly simple. To add Flash content to your site, you must have a Flash developer create the content and give you the HTML document and an SWF file that she published from Flash. Then, you can copy and paste the relevant code into your Muse project.

## Add a Flash Movie

1 Open the HTML file you got from your Flash developer in a text editor.

2 Find the code beginning with `<object`.

3 Select the code through the line that reads `</object>`.

4 Copy the code to the clipboard.

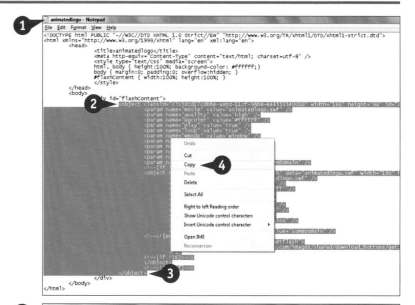

5 Return to Muse.

6 Click **Object**.

7 Click **Insert HTML**.

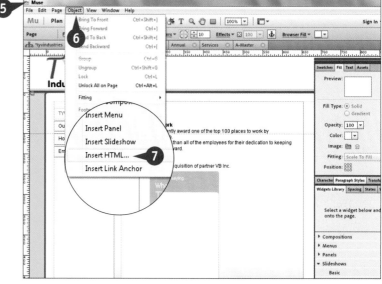

The Insert HTML dialog box opens.

**8** Right-click in the dialog box.

**9** Select **Paste**.

The code is pasted into the dialog box.

**10** Click **OK**.

The Flash content is added to the page. It will appear correctly after the project is published.

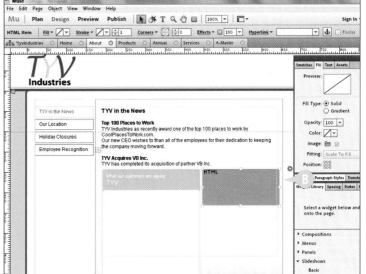

**My Flash content does not show up correctly when I preview the page. Why?**

The HTML `<object>` tag includes a reference to the SWF file, which is the actual Flash content. When you first copy and paste the code into Muse, this reference to the SWF file is not correct. When you publish the project, you must manually upload the SWF to the web server, at which point it will appear correctly. See Chapter 13 for details on publishing and manually uploading the project.

**Where can I learn more about creating sites in Flash?**

One of the best resources for learning to use Adobe Flash is *Flash Professional CS6 Digital Classroom* (John Wiley & Sons, 2012). This book provides a comprehensive look at Flash and takes you through the entire process of creating animation in it, from the very beginning steps of learning the interface through advanced coding techniques.

# Add HTML5 Animation

Within the last few years, significant advances in HTML, CSS, and JavaScript — the languages that most web pages are written in — have allowed a lot of improvements in the techniques used for building sites, including the growing ability to create animation and interactivity without the need to use external tools like Flash. Adobe Edge is a new tool that makes it easy to create animation and interactivity using these new technologies. As with Flash, you will likely need a developer familiar with Edge to create the content and then simply publish an HTML file that you add to your Muse project.

## Add HTML5 Animation

① Open the page onto which you want to place the content from Edge.

② Click **Object**.

③ Click **Insert HTML**.

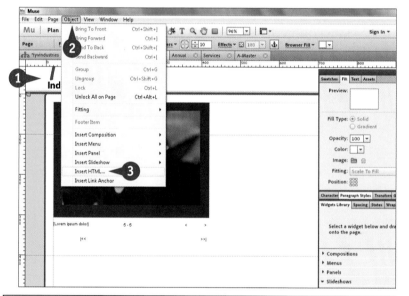

The Insert HTML dialog box opens.

④ In the dialog box, type `<iframe src=".`

⑤ Type the filename of the HTML file you received from your Edge developer, such as `animatedhtmllogo.html`.

⑥ Type `"`.

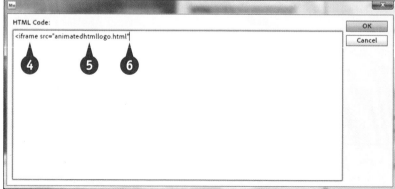

**7** Type width="100%"
height="100%"
frameborder="0"
scrolling="no">
</iframe>.

**8** Click **OK**.

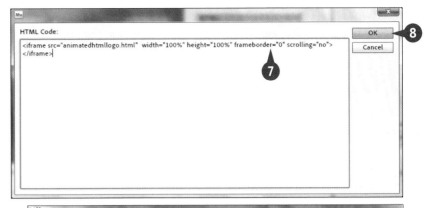

**A** The Edge content is added to the page. It will appear correctly after the project is published.

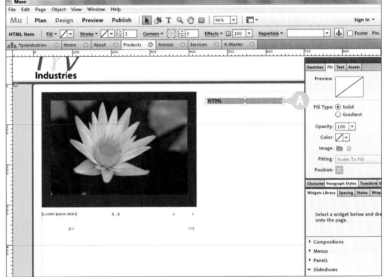

**Why is my Edge content not appearing in Design view or when I preview the page?**
Previewing Edge content represents the exact same issue faced when importing Flash content: The path to the HTML page you inserted into the code is not correct. When you publish the project, you manually upload that file and a few supporting files to the server, which causes the page to function properly.

**Where can I learn more about using Edge?**
Because Edge is a brand new tool like Muse, not a lot of resources are available for it yet. You can find a set of excellent video tutorials on Edge at http://webdesign.tutsplus.com/tutorials/applications/introducing-adobe-edge-user-interface that should get you started with the tool.

# Display Excel Data

Although Muse does not currently support directly importing tables and charts from Excel, its ability to add HTML code provides a workaround, albeit a workaround that, like many of the other topics in this chapter, does not work until you publish the site. To get Excel data into your page, you must save the Excel spreadsheet as an HTML page, and then add an `<iframe>` to your Muse document to display that page.

## Display Excel Data

**1** Open the spreadsheet you want to use in Excel.

**2** Click **File**.

**3** Click **Save As**.

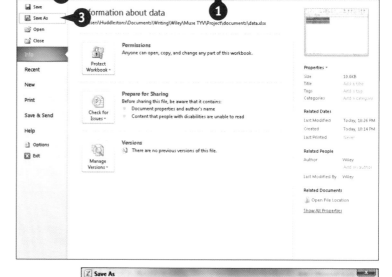

**4** Set the file type to **Web Page**.

**5** Navigate to the directory into which you want to save the file.

**6** Type a filename.

**Note:** The filename cannot contain spaces.

**7** Click **Save**.

8 Return to Muse.

9 Click **Object**.

10 Click **Insert HTML**.

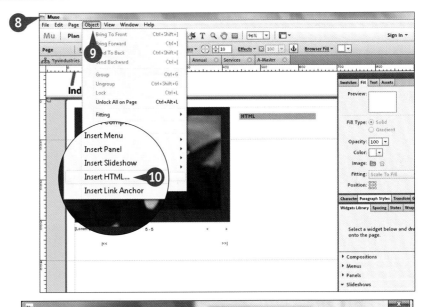

11 In the dialog box, type
`<iframe src="`.

12 Type the filename of the
HTML file you created in
steps **4** to **7**.

13 Type `"`.

14 Type `width="100%"`
`height="100%"`
`frameborder="0"`
`scrolling="no">`
`</iframe>`.

15 Click **OK**.

The Excel content is added
to the page. It will appear
correctly after the project
is published.

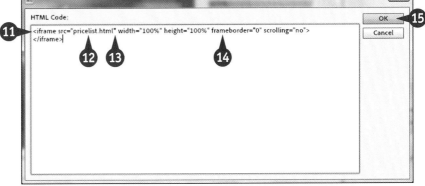

---

## TIPS

**What does an <iframe> do exactly?**
An `<iframe>` is an HTML element that allows web
pages to create a window within the page to display
another page altogether. Although they are not used
that widely on the web as a whole, they provide a
nice way for Muse users to add content that the
program does not otherwise support.

**Could I just open the page Excel creates and copy
and paste the code instead of using an iFrame?**
Yes, but you will lose all of your formatting, and
because Muse does not currently support tables, you
will not have a way to restore the formatting.
Therefore, you are better off using an iFrame.

# Insert Arbitrary HTML

Ideally, you could build a website in Muse without ever seeing or even thinking about the underlying code. Unfortunately, however, Muse does not yet support everything that HTML makes possible, so you may find times when you need to add bits of code. Two common requests are for the ability to add tables and bulleted lists, both of which are very common on web pages and as yet have no support in Muse. Adding these elements requires that you either write basic HTML yourself or partner with a designer who knows the code.

## Insert Arbitrary HTML

1 Open an HTML document that contains the code you want to copy.

This example adds a table.

2 Select the code.

3 Using the editor you are in, copy the code to the clipboard.

4 Return to Muse.

5 Click **Object**.

6 Click **Insert HTML**.

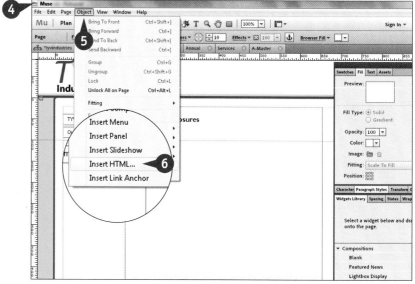

The Insert HTML dialog box opens.

**7** Paste the code.

The code is inserted into the dialog box.

**8** Click **OK**.

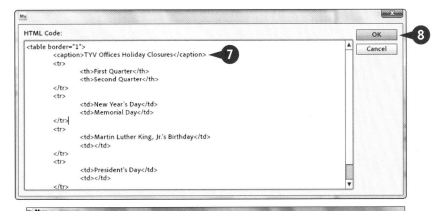

The result of the code is displayed on the page.

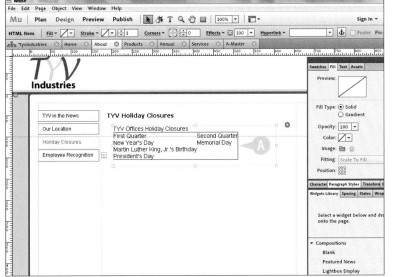

**When I insert arbitrary HTML, can I format the result?**

Not easily. Most web designers would use Cascading Style Sheets (CSS) to apply formatting. Muse creates CSS when you format objects, but because it does not allow you to directly edit the styles, you cannot add your own code to it. You can, however, use something called *inline styles*, where the formatting instructions are embedded directly within the HTML, to apply formats, but this requires that you know CSS and are comfortable editing the HTML directly yourself.

# Add Google Analytics Code

Google Analytics is a free service that provides a wealth of information about how many people visit your site, where they come from, what browsers they use, and much more. It is an invaluable resource for professional web developers. Although Muse does not have a way to directly add Google Analytics code, you can add it yourself to begin tracking your website's traffic.

## Add Google Analytics Code

**1** Using your browser, go to www.google.com/analytics.

**2** Click **Access Analytics**.

**Note:** If the Google Sign In page appears, enter your Google account information or create a free Google account to continue.

The Start Using Google Analytics page opens.

**3** Click **Sign up**.

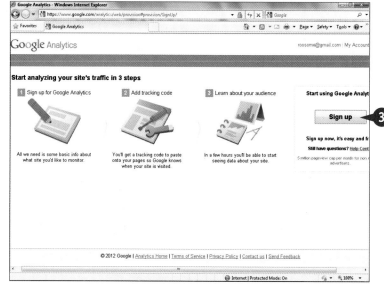

The Create New Account page opens.

**④** Fill out the requested information.

**⑤** Be sure to click **Yes, I agree to the above terms and conditions** (☐ changes to ☑).

**⑥** Click **Create Account**.

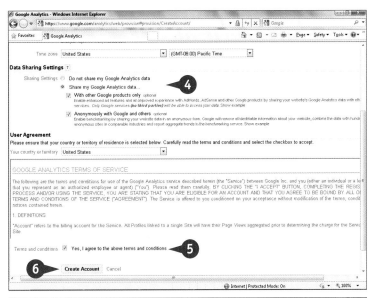

Your account is created and the Google Analytics dashboard appears.

**⑦** Scroll down the page.

**⑧** Click in the code box.

**⑨** Right-click.

**⑩** Choose **Copy**.

The code is copied to the clipboard.

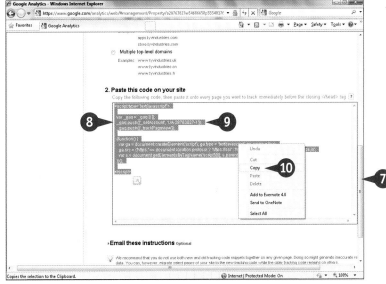

continued ▶

---

**TIPS**

**Can I use the same Analytics account to track more than one site?**
Yes. You can only enter a single domain name on the sign-up form, but once you are in the dashboard you can add additional domains. To add more domains, you need to click **All Accounts** and then click your account name. From that page, you can click **New Property** to add a new domain to the account.

**What kinds of information does Analytics provide?**
The standard reporting section shows you the number of visitors on your site, how many pages they view, and how long they stay on the page. It also provides demographic information including the country your visitors are from and their operating system and browser, broken down by desktop and mobile.

# Add Google Analytics Code (continued)

Once you have registered for Analytics, Google provides you with code that you need to add to your page. The code is a bit of JavaScript that communicates information about your user back to Google's servers. This information then gets aggregated and presented to you on the Analytics dashboard. In Muse, you must manually add the Analytics code to each page that you want to track. If you do not include a page, it will not be tracked. Unfortunately, you cannot add this code to the Master, so you have to open each page individually.

## Add Google Analytics Code (continued)

⑪ Return to Muse.

⑫ Open the first page onto which you want to add the tracking code.

⑬ Click in the header section of the page.

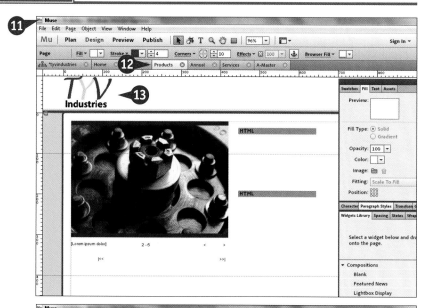

⑭ Click **Object**.

⑮ Click **Insert HTML**.

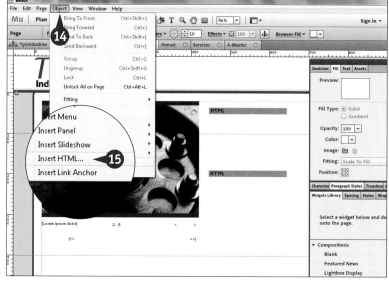

The Insert HTML dialog box opens.

**16** Right-click in the dialog box.

**17** Choose **Paste**.

Ⓐ The code is inserted into the dialog box.

**18** Click **OK**.

Ⓑ The Analytics code is added to your page. It will appear correctly after the project is published.

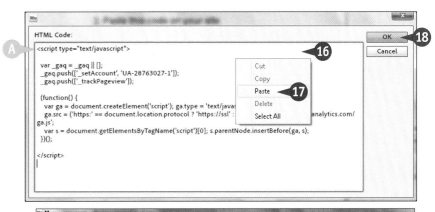

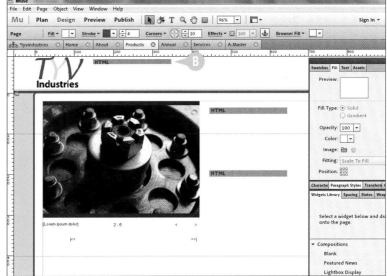

TIP

**The Google Analytics page said to add their code to the <head> of the document. Is that why I need to click in the header?**
No. The header in Muse and the <head> in HTML are different. HTML documents are divided into two sections: the head and the body. The body contains all the visual display of the page, and is the only thing that you can access in Muse, so in the steps in this section you are inserting it into the body, not the head. Thankfully, the Analytics code works if inserted here, but you do want it as close to the top of the page as you can get, which is why the steps have you click in the header section.

# Using Web Fonts

Typography on the web has been a struggle since its earliest days, but it is quickly improving. Today, a variety of services exist that allow you to use any one of hundreds, and sometimes thousands of fonts. Unfortunately Muse does not yet fully support using these fonts, and as was noted in Chapter 5, Muse makes an image out of any text that uses fonts it deems unsafe for the web. Thankfully, the Insert HTML feature provides a workaround. Although not the most graceful solution, it allows you to use the wider variety of fonts available until Muse directly supports web fonts.

## Using Web Fonts

1 Use your browser to go to www.google.com/webfonts.

2 Click **Add to Collection** for a font you want to use.

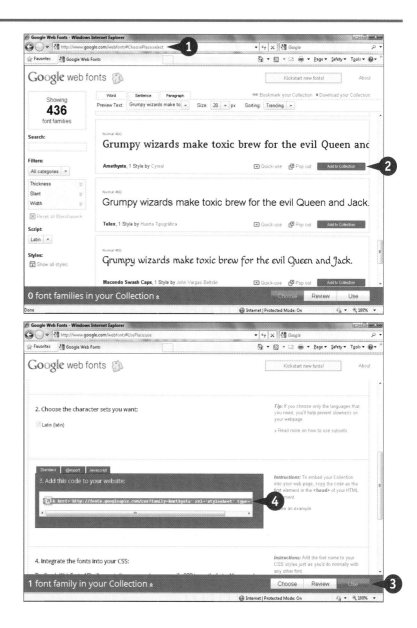

3 Click **Use**.

4 Select the line of code.

**5** Right-click the code.

**6** Select **Copy**.

**7** Return to Muse.

**8** Ensure that all your text is set to a web-safe font in Muse.

**Note:** See Chapter 5 for details on using web-safe fonts.

TIP

**I did not find a font I want on the Google Web Fonts page. Are there other resources available?**

Yes. Typekit is a popular source for web fonts, and was recently purchased by Adobe, but they limit usage of their fonts unless you are willing to pay a yearly fee. You can read about their policies and view their fonts at http://typekit.com. Fonts.com also offers web fonts for a fee. A big advantage of Google's fonts over either of those, beyond the fees, is that Google uses only CSS to implement fonts, whereas both of the other two use a combination of JavaScript and CSS, so you have to deal with more code.

continued ▶

Once you have selected the fonts you want to use, you need to copy the code you got from Google into your page. If you want a font to apply to all of your pages, you can place it in the Master. You must also write a small amount of Cascading Style Sheets (CSS) code to apply the font to your text. If you have never worked with CSS before, the code may seem a little strange, but it is fairly straightforward. You must apply the text to the regular text on your page and to any styles you have created.

## Using Web Fonts (continued)

**9** Open the Master.

**10** Click **Object**.

**11** Click **Insert HTML**.

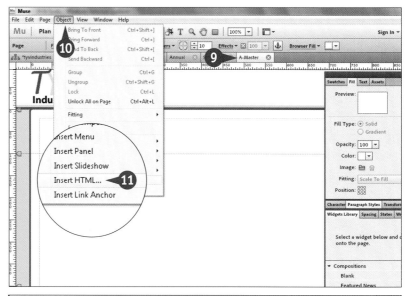

The Insert HTML dialog box opens.

**12** Right-click in the dialog box.

**13** Choose **Paste**.

Ⓐ The code from Google is inserted into the dialog box.

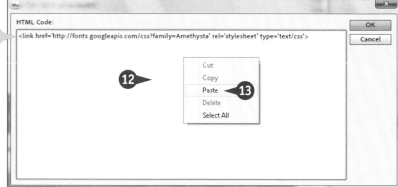

**14** Below the code, type
`<style>`.

**15** Type `body, h1, h2, h3, p`.

**16** Type a period followed by a style name, followed by a comma.

**17** Repeat step **16** to add any additional style names.

**18** Type `{`.

**19** Type `font-family:`.

**20** Type the name of the font in quotation marks.

**21** Type `;`.

**22** Type `}`.

**23** Type `</style>`.

**24** Click **OK**.

The font is applied to your text. It will be visible when you preview the page in a browser.

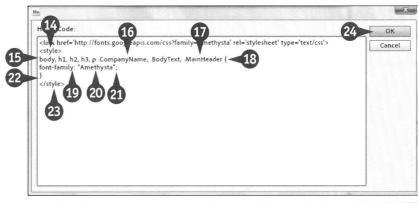

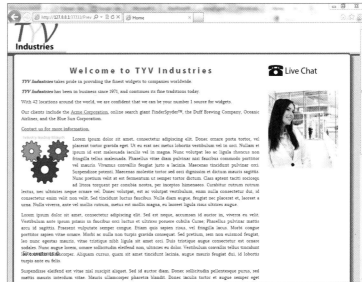

**TIP**

**Can I just use fonts I have on my system?**
No. Fonts are protected by copyright, and you cannot use a font on a website unless you have a specific license for that use. Most fonts you have on your computer likely came with a program, such as Microsoft Office or Muse itself, and are almost certainly licensed only for desktop and print use. Another advantage of using a service like Google Web Fonts or Typekit is that you can be assured that you are getting fonts that you can use legally.

# CHAPTER 12

# Designing for Mobile

Few innovations have changed the way we get online more than mobile. Even fewer have changed it as fast. Smartphones and tablets, for all practical purposes, did not exist five years ago; today, more and more of your users will likely use them to visit your site.

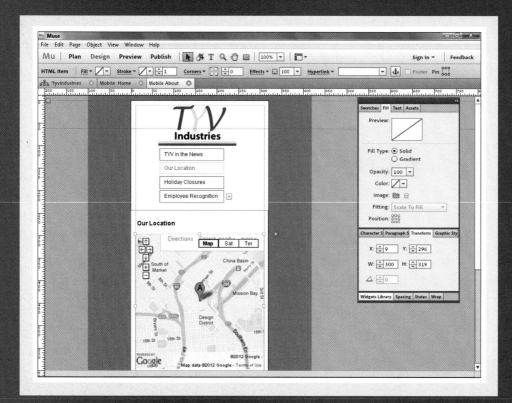

# Understanding the Mobile Web

When he introduced the original iPhone in 2007, Steve Jobs made a point of talking about how users could use the phone to access what he called the "whole web." Although some sites had been presenting stripped-down versions of their content to phones before that, the devices generally could not handle the demands of normal websites. Today, many users fully expect to be able to view your full site on their device. The successful sites of the future will be those that appear as well on a small phone screen as they do on large desktop monitors.

## Mobile Operating Systems

The mobile market is dominated by two operating systems: Apple's iOS, used by iPhones, iPods, and iPads, and Google's Android, which runs the popular Verizon Droid devices and hundreds more. You also need to think about the many users who continue to use their Blackberry devices, along with those running Microsoft's Windows Mobile.

## Phones and Tablets

More and more users are turning to tablets for their larger screens and generally more powerful abilities. Apple's iPad continues to dominate the tablet world, but as the number of tablets running Android increases, you can expect its share to grow. Blackberry's experiment with tablets, the Playbook, generally regarded as a failure, is still out there and being used by a few people.

## Mobile Market Share

According to most analysts, less than one third of all web users in 2007 used mobile devices. Those same analysts predict that by 2014, and possibly as early as 2013, the majority of web traffic will come from phones and tablet. The simple reality is that the successful sites of the future will be those that appear as well on a mobile device as they do on a desktop screen.

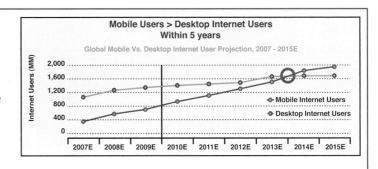

Mobile Users > Desktop Internet Users Within 5 years

Global Mobile Vs. Desktop Internet User Projection, 2007 - 2015E

Internet Users (MM)

- Mobile Internet Users
- Desktop Internet Users

2007E 2008E 2009E 2010E 2011E 2012E 2013E 2014E 2015E

## Mobile Design Considerations

The most obvious difference between mobile and desktop is screen size. You need to consider what your site will look like on a 3-inch screen as well as a 19-inch monitor. Beyond that, also consider that your mobile users will interact with the site with their fingers, not a mouse. Rollover actions simply will not work, and a user's hand may obscure large portions of the screen at any given time.

## Mobile-Only Sites

Many organizations have decided that they can best serve their mobile customers by creating separate versions of their site for mobile and desktop users. Although this obviously means that they must maintain and update two individual sites, it can be easier to create initially. Muse currently only supports the creation of separate mobile sites.

## Responsive Design

Rather than maintain two sites, some designers have opted for a technique known as responsive design, whereby they create a single site but use a combination of JavaScript and Cascading Style Sheets to change the layout and size of the site for different screens. Because this can be done only with extensive coding, creating a responsive site is not currently possible in Muse.

# Create a Master for Phones

Although support for mobile development is not officially supported at all in the current version of Muse, it is possible to work with its tools as they exist to create a mobile version of your site. The first step in this process is creating a Master page to define the size and overall layout of your mobile site. The mobile world today contains many dozens of possible screen sizes, so you should generally create a design that works well with lower-end phones and let newer models scale the site up for you.

## Create a Master for Phones

**1** Open the site for which you want to create a mobile version.

**2** Click the plus sign next to the Master to create a new Master.

**3** Rename the new Master.

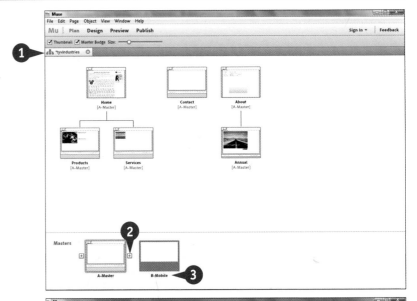

**4** Right-click the new Master.

**5** Choose **Page Properties**.

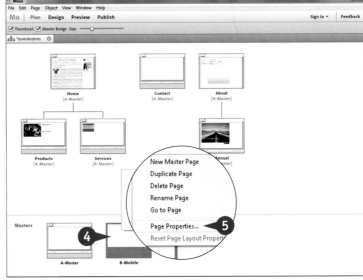

The Page Properties dialog box opens.

6 Set a small width and height. 320 × 480 pixels is recommended.

7 Set columns to **1**.

8 Reduce the margins and padding.

9 Click **OK**.

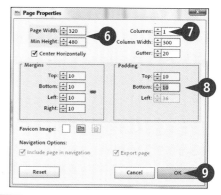

The Master for phones is created.

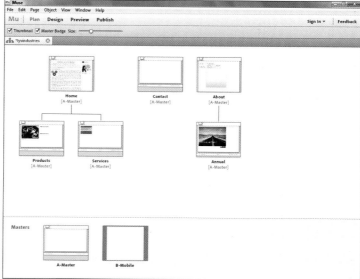

**Why a screen resolution of 320 × 480?**
The three original versions of the iPhone have that resolution. Many lower-end and older Android phones also use it. Even though most newer devices have a higher resolution — the iPhone 4's resolution is 640 × 960, and some of the newer Android phones have similarly high resolutions — the smaller size makes for a nice lowest common denominator, because a newer phone displays a smaller version of a site better than a older phone shows a big site.

**Will my site be able to adjust if my user turns the phone on its side to view the web in landscape mode?**
No. That is possible only with a responsive design, which Muse does not support. To create a site like this today, you must learn Cascading Style Sheets and JavaScript. Hopefully, a future version of Muse will incorporate this capability and remove the requirement to learn and write code to create responsive sites.

# Duplicate Existing Pages to Your Mobile Site

Rather than re-create your pages from scratch, you can duplicate existing pages, apply your mobile Master to the duplicates, and then simply rearrange your content to fit on the smaller screens. You can duplicate any or all of your site's pages for your mobile version; however, if you duplicate child pages, they become children of the original parent, so you may also need to move them into your mobile site plan.

## Duplicate Existing Pages to Your Mobile Site

**1** Right-click on Home page.

**2** Choose **Duplicate Page**.

**A** A duplicate page is created.

**3** Rename the duplicate.

**4** Drag the mobile Master onto the new page.

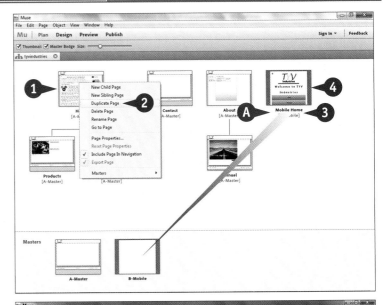

**5** Repeat steps **1** to **4** for any additional pages.

The pages are duplicated for mobile.

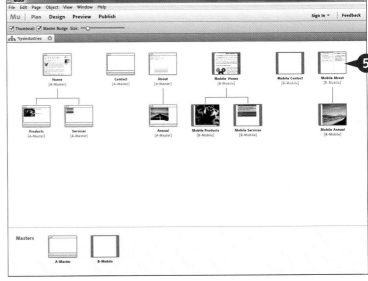

# Prevent Your Mobile Pages from Showing in Your Main Navigation

The Menu Bar widgets generate a set of buttons with links to each page in your site. (See Chapter 8 for details on using the menu bars.) In a normal website, this behavior is beneficial, but when you add mobile versions of pages, you do not want them showing on the buttons in the rest of your site. Therefore, you must tell Muse to exclude them from the navigation.

## Prevent Your Mobile Pages from Showing in Your Main Navigation

**1** Right-click on your Mobile Home page.

**2** Click **Include Page In Navigation**.

The option is deselected.

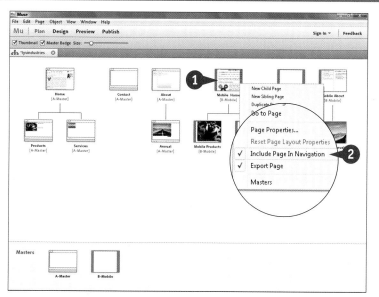

**3** Repeat steps **1** and **2** for each additional mobile page.

The pages are excluded from the navigation and menu bars in the main site.

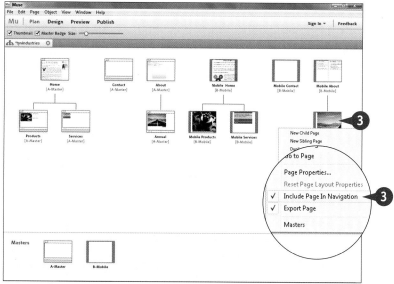

# Optimize Your Content for Your Mobile Pages

Once you have duplicated the pages you need, you must open each one and rearrange the content to fit the smaller space. This mostly involves sizing elements down and moving them to new locations. You should almost always maintain a single-column layout in a mobile site. You may also want to provide smaller versions of images, which you can create in Fireworks or a similar tool, so that your graphics fit nicely on a mobile screen.

## Optimize Your Content for Your Mobile Pages

**1** Double-click your **Mobile Home** page.

The page opens in Design view.

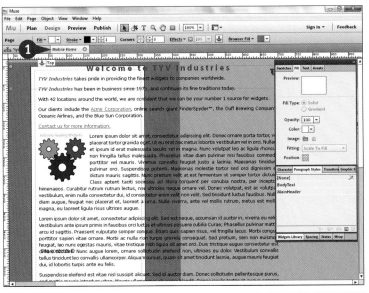

**2** Resize and reposition your main text frame to fit in the mobile screen.

**3** Resize and reposition any other text frames.

**Note:** See Chapter 4 for details on repositioning and resizing text frames.

**4** Delete the large versions of graphics.

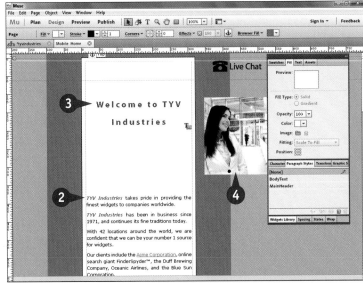

**5** Place mobile versions of your graphics.

**Note:** See Chapter 7 for details on placing graphics.

**6** Finalize the arrangement of the content on the page.

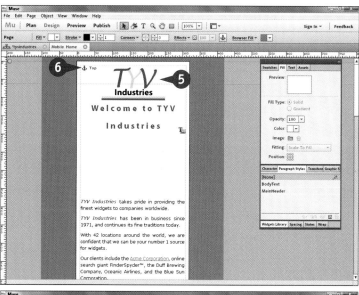

**7** Repeat steps **2** to **6** for any additional pages in your mobile site.

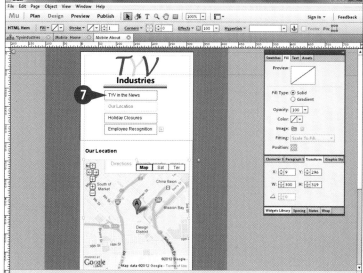

## TIPS

**Is there a limit as to how much content I should put on a mobile page?**

Not really, but in general users will likely appreciate smaller pages. Mobile browsers are often on slower connections than desktop users, so larger pages may take too long to load. You might want to consider taking long pages and breaking them up into multiple, smaller pages to help this.

**What size should I make my graphics?**

Desktop users have long had an aversion to horizontal scrolling on web pages, but mobile users will almost certainly like it even less. You should take your page width, subtract the margins, and make sure that none of your images are wider than that. In the example above, the Master page is set to 320 pixels, with left and right margins at 10 pixels each, so all images should be kept at 300 pixels or less.

# Design Mobile Navigation

**B**ecause you removed all of your mobile pages from Muse's navigation structure, you must manually create all the navigation in your mobile site. You can either use the Menu Bar widgets, set to Manual mode, or you can use simple hyperlinks. If you do use the Menu Bar widgets, you need to avoid adding submenus, because the only available trigger is Rollover, which is impossible to activate on a mobile device.

## Design Mobile Navigation

1. Open your Mobile Home page.

2. Open the Widgets Library panel.

3. Expand the Menus section.

4. Drag Vertical to the canvas.

5. Click the editing options icon ( ).

6. Click the Menu Type dropdown and select **Manual**.

7. Double-click **[Name]**.

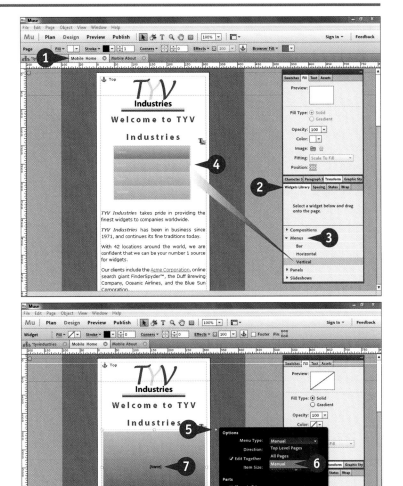

**8** Type **Home**.

**9** Click the **Selection** tool ( ▶ ).

**10** Select the button.

**11** From the Hyperlink dropdown, select your Mobile Home page.

**12** Click the plus sign to add a new button.

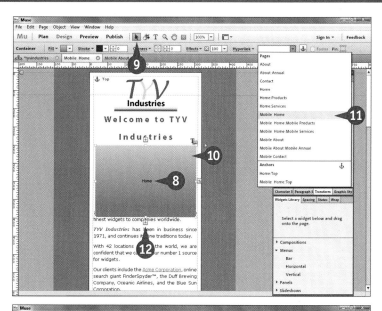

**13** Repeat steps **7** to **12** to create links for the remaining pages.

The mobile version of the navigation is created.

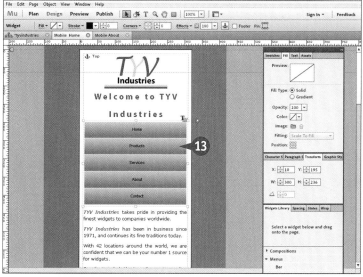

---

## TIP

**Can I use other widgets on my mobile pages?**

Yes. Any of the widgets can be used. The Tabbed Panels and Accordion can be used to present your content in a format that more closely resembles mobile apps. The Composition widgets might be useful to fit more content on the smaller screen. With all widgets, be careful to ensure that any events are set to On Click, and make sure that all content in the widgets are sized correctly. Keep in mind that on many of the widgets, you need to manually resize any content within the widget before you can resize the widget itself.

# Add a Mobile Redirection Script

Once you have your mobile pages created, you must add a method by which all the pages in your site can detect whether a desktop or a mobile browser is requesting them. If a user visits your site using a mobile browser, your pages can redirect the request to the mobile version of the page. You should add the script individually to each page in your site so that it can redirect to the correct mobile page and not just your home page.

## Add a Mobile Redirection Script

**1** In your browser, go to http://detectmobilebrowsers.com.

**2** Click **JavaScript**.

**3** Click **Save** in the dialog box that appears.

The file downloads to your computer.

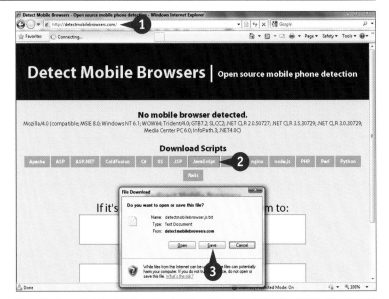

**4** Open the file you downloaded from the website in a text editor.

**5** Copy all of its contents to the clipboard.

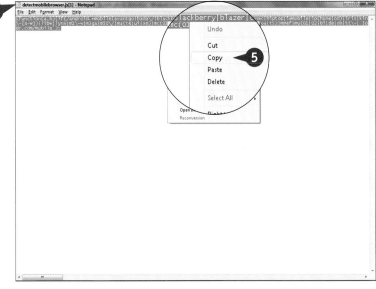

**6** In Muse, open one of the
pages.

**7** Click **Object**.

**8** Click **Insert HTML**.

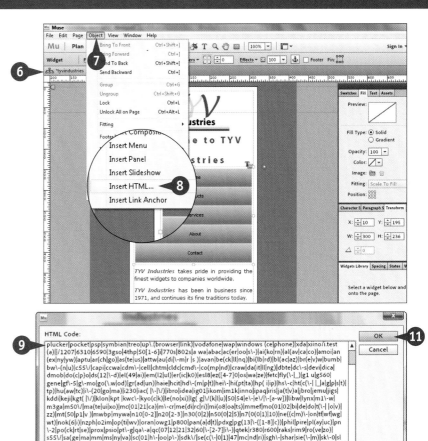

**9** Paste the code into the
dialog box that appears.

**10** At the very end of the script,
change `'http://detect
mobilebrowser.com/
mobile'` to the filename of
your page. For example, type
`'mobile-home.html'`
for the home page.

**Note:** Be sure to keep the single
quotes.

**11** Click **OK**.

**12** Repeat steps **7** to **11** for
all remaining pages.

The script is added to
the site.

## TIPS

**Is adding JavaScript to each page the only way to do
mobile redirection?**
Most sites use a redirection script that works on their web
server. This method is considerably more accurate and saves
you from having to add it to every page, but requires that you
know and understand a server-side language such as PHP.
Inserting a JavaScript function like the one from http://
detectmobilebrowser.com is the only way to avoid learning
how to program.

**How can I test to make sure this
worked?**
You can test this process only by
publishing your site to a live web server
and then visiting the site from a mobile
device. If you do not have a smartphone
or tablet, you must borrow one from
someone else to test your pages.

# CHAPTER 13

# Publishing Your Site

Your site is designed. Your content added, and your navigation complete. The one final step is to get it all online, either by publishing it directly from Adobe Muse to the Adobe Business Catalyst platform, or uploading it yourself to your own site.

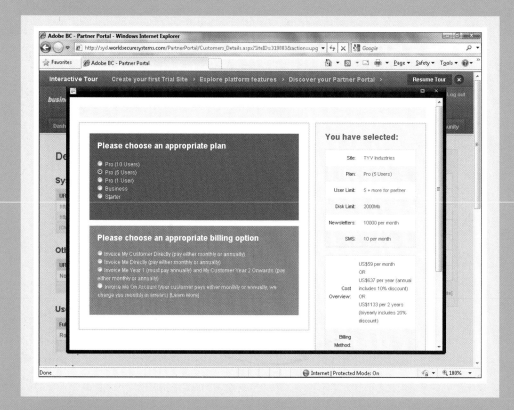

# Add Metadata

Metadata allows you to add information about your page to help some search engines find and index it. Muse provides two kinds of metadata: keywords and description. Keywords should be a comma-separated list of the words by which you think users are likely to search for your site. Common misspellings or alternate forms of the company's name or primary purpose should be included. The description should be a brief, human-readable paragraph describing the site. Some search engines display this description under the link to the site on the results page, so a well-written description can create a higher click-through rate.

## Add Metadata

**1** Open the page into which you want to add metadata.

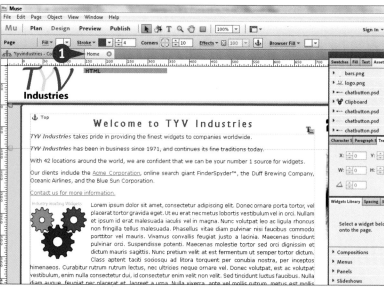

**2** Click **Page**.

**3** Click **Page Properties**.

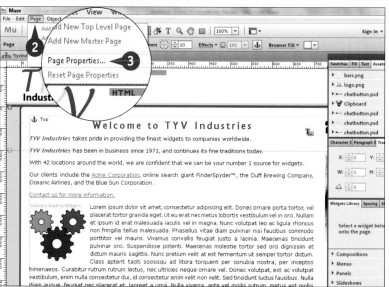

The Page Properties dialog box opens.

**4** Click **Metadata**.

**5** Enter a description.

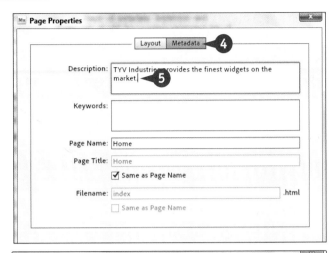

**6** Enter a set of keywords for the page.

**7** Click **OK**.

The metadata is added to the page.

## TIPS

**I read that modern search engines ignore metadata. Is that true?**

Search engines are constantly fighting against unscrupulous designers who want to manipulate the rankings to ensure that their page appears first even if it does not relate to the search. Therefore, search engines are very secretive about what they do and do not support. Google has publicly stated that they do not use the keywords metadata, and only sometimes use the description. Other search engines, however, still rely on both.

**Do I need to add metadata to each page individually, or can I add it to the Master?**

You need to do it for each page because the data is supposed to describe that page, not your site. Muse does not allow you to add metadata to the Master. It may be tedious to add it to each page, especially considering that search engines may not even use it, so you must decide whether or not adding the metadata is worth your effort.

# Understanding Adobe Business Catalyst

Asimple website is fairly easy to create and maintain, but many business owners want far more from their site than a set of static web pages. They want to sell products online, or track their site's users and be able to contact those users with special offers. They will almost certainly want to know who is visiting, when, and from where. All of these are relatively difficult tasks to create by hand, but very easy to implement in Business Catalyst.

## Adobe's CRM

Most successful companies understand that making sure existing customers keep coming back is far more profitable than constantly getting new customers. Keeping track of these existing customers, however, can be difficult. Customer relationship management (CRM) software is designed to make it easier for companies to know who their customers are and to try to meet the needs of those customers. Business Catalyst is a CRM acquired by Adobe in 2009, and provides an integrated hosting and management system for Muse sites.

| First Name | Last Name | City | State | Zip |
|---|---|---|---|---|
| Ronda | Davies | Anderson | IN | 46016 |
| Colin | Clarke | Downing | IL | 60452 |
| Phil | Moyles | Haverstock | OH | 43017 |
| Jon | Hilton | Alexandria | IN | 46001 |
| Ruthann | Blackburn | South Bend | IN | 46613 |
| Cheryl | Curran | Muncie | IN | 47302 |
| Ron | Barbrook | Davendale | OH | 43522 |
| Rhys | Ackart | Swindonbank | IL | 60038 |
| David | Asbury | Conway | IL | 43524 |
| Fiona | McKenna | Newcombe | OH | 43524 |

## Key Business Catalyst Features

Business Catalyst offers e-commerce solutions, customer databases, e-mail marketing, and powerful analytic and reporting tools. The service is entirely based on the web, so as a user you never need to download or install software, and you can access your Business Catalyst data from anywhere.

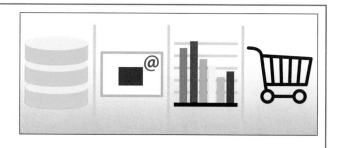

## Easy Site Maintenance

Most of the maintenance of your site can be done online, through a series of easy-to-use web forms. The Business Catalyst website lets you set up shopping carts and manage e-mail campaigns without you needing to write any code. Muse maintains the visual aspects of your site, and the platform makes sending updates from Muse very easy.

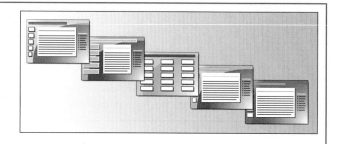

# Designate Pages to Not Export

Although most of the time you will want your entire site online, you may have some pages that you want to keep offline. These could be pages that you have not yet finished designing, or they may be pages that you are not sure fit into the overall scheme of the website. Before you publish your site to Business Catalyst, you should designate what pages you do not want to export.

## Designate Pages to Not Export

**1** Open the site you plan to publish.

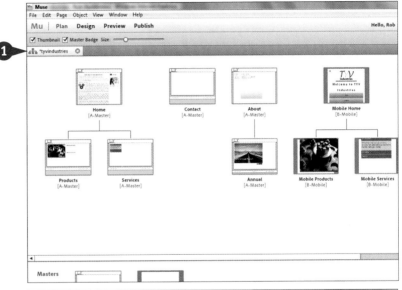

**2** Right-click a page you do not want to export.

**3** Click **Export Page**.

The option is deselected, and the page does not export with the site.

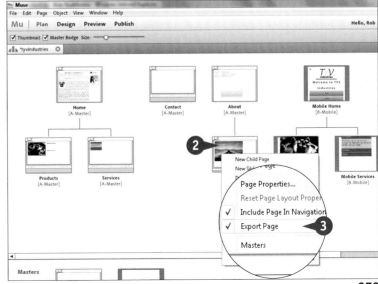

# Create a Free Trial Business Catalyst Site

Taking your site public on Business Catalyst requires a monthly fee, but before you commit you can upload your site and test it and the Catalyst features free for 30 days. You can have as many sites running on your free trial as you want, and at the end of the 30 days you can choose to upgrade to a paid subscription or allow your trial to expire. Setting up a trial subscription is a very easy process.

## Create a Free Trial Business Catalyst Site

1 In your browser, go to www.businesscatalyst.com.

2 Click **Try for Free**.

The Create Your Free Trial Site screen opens.

3 Click **Continue**.

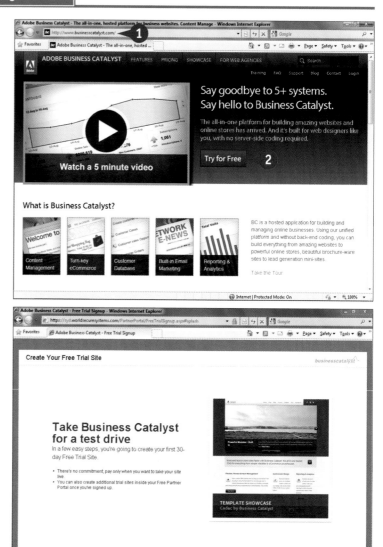

The Choose a Site Template screen opens.

④ Click **Blank Template**.

⑤ Click **Continue**.

The Site Details screen opens.

⑥ Fill out the form.

⑦ Click **Create Free Trial Site**.

Your trial account is created.

**TIPS**

**Will I be charged if I create the free trial but do not cancel within 30 days?**

No. Adobe does not collect any payment information from you until you decide to upgrade to a paid account, so if you create the trial site and then abandon it, your Business Catalyst site never becomes fully functional and you are not charged anything.

**Can I change my site name or other account information later?**

Yes. All the information in your account can be changed at any time via the Business Catalyst web administration site. All you need to do is log in, click **My Details** or **My Account**, and change whatever information you need to change. You can do this at any time, and as often as necessary.

# Publish Your Site to Business Catalyst

Once you have created your Business Catalyst account, you can upload your site from Muse. You can publish your site directly from Muse to Business Catalyst without any additional software; you only need to provide the e-mail address and password you used when you created your Business Catalyst account. Once you log into Business Catalyst from Muse, all the pages from your site upload, minus those you designated to not export.

## Publish Your Site to Business Catalyst

**1** Click **Publish**.

The Sign In window opens.

**2** Enter the e-mail address you used to sign up for your Business Catalyst account in the User Name field.

**3** Enter your password.

**4** If you are not on a shared computer, click **Remember user name and password** (☐ changes to ☑).

**5** Click **Next**.

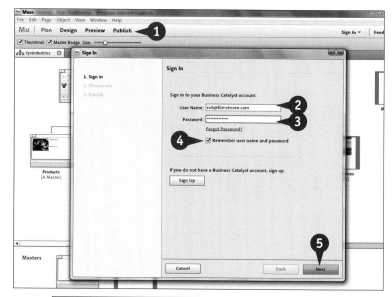

The Choose Site window opens.

**6** Click **Existing Site** (○ changes to ◉).

**7** Click the site you created when you signed up with Business Catalyst.

**8** Click **Next**.

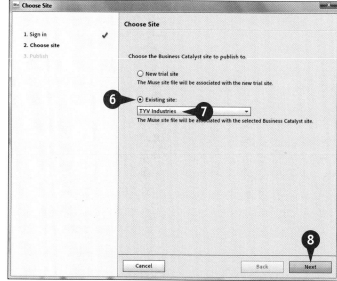

The Publish window opens.

**9** Click **Next**.

The site publishes to Business Catalyst.

**10** In the Publish Confirmation window, click **View site**.

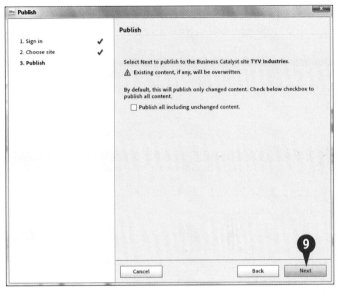

The site opens in your browser.

**How soon after I publish is my site available online?**

Your site is available online immediately after publishing. You can view the site by clicking the **View site** button on the last page of the Publish dialog box, or by simply using your browser. In your browser, go to http://*the-name-of-your-site*.businesscatalyst.com/index.html, replacing *the-name-of-your-site* with your site name. As you work on your site, any changes you make are also visible instantly after you upload the saved changes.

# Upgrade Your Business Catalyst Account

Once you are sure that you want to host your site on the Business Catalyst platform, you can upgrade your account from the free trial to a paid subscription. This allows you to enjoy some or all of the features of Business Catalyst. Currently, three levels of account are available: Starter, Business, and Pro. The Pro level has additional options to allow access from multiple users. The price and features of each are outlined on the Business Catalyst website.

## Upgrade Your Business Catalyst Account

**1** Log into the Business Catalyst administration portal by using your browser to go to http://*your-site-name*.businesscatalyst.com/admin, where *your-site-name* is the name of your site.

**2** Enter your e-mail address and password.

**3** Click **Login**.

The Business Catalyst dashboard page opens.

**4** Click **Upgrade**.

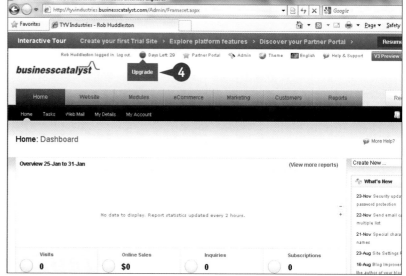

The Choose a Plan page opens.

**5** Select a plan.

**6** Select a billing option.

**7** Scroll down the page and select a billing frequency.

**8** Enter your payment information.

**9** Click **Upgrade**.

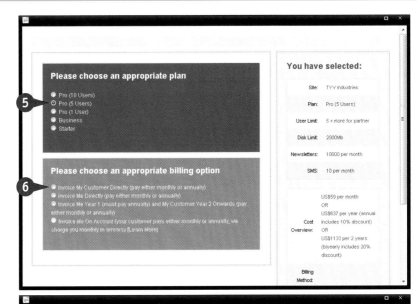

The upgrade confirmation screen appears.

**Can I cancel my account once I upgrade?**
Yes, you can cancel at any time. However, Business Catalyst does not offer refunds for prepaid services, so if you select the annual billing and then cancel after only a few months, you do not get a refund for the unused months.

**Can I change plans?**
Yes, you can change plans whenever you want, although if you change from a higher-priced plan to a lower-priced plan in the middle of a billing period, you do not get a refund on the difference between the plans. To change your plan, go to www.businesscatalyst.com/Default. aspx?PageID=988650 and fill out the form.

# Manually Upload Additional Files to Business Catalyst

If you have added links to other files such as PDF or Word documents, you must manually upload those files to the Business Catalyst site to make them available on the web for your users to download. See Chapter 8 for details on creating links to these file types. The Business Catalyst dashboard page provides a file manager interface that makes it very easy to upload your files and requires no special software or technical knowledge.

## Manually Upload Additional Files to Business Catalyst

**1** Log into the Business Catalyst dashboard interface.

The Business Catalyst dashboard page opens.

**2** Click **Website**.

The Web Pages page opens.

**3** Click **Use File Manager**.

The File Manager page opens.

**4** Click **Upload File(s)**.

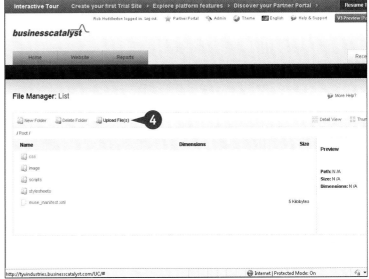

TIP

**Can I upload any file type?**
No. Business Catalyst does not support all file types, and unfortunately they also do not publish a complete list of the file types they do support. Web pages, plain text, Flash movies, PDF, common media files such as MP3, and Word files are all supported. If you attempt to upload another file and get an error, you can contact Business Catalyst support at www.businesscatalyst.com/support/home for more assistance.

continued ▶

Within the Business Catalyst dashboard, you can upload as many files as you need, as long as they are supported file types. Each file can be up to 100 megabytes each, and they can be of any type. You must make sure that you upload the file into the correct directory for the links you created in Muse to work; most of the time, uploading into your site's top-level or root folder works best.

## Manually Upload Additional Files to Business Catalyst (continued)

The page updates to show the Upload Pages page.

**5** Click **Select**.

The Choose File to Upload dialog box opens.

**6** Navigate to the document you want to upload.

**7** Click **Open**.

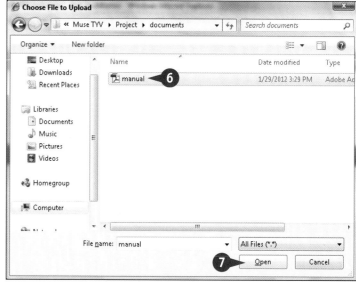

A The file is added to the upload list.

**8** If necessary, repeat steps **5** to **7** for each additional document you need to upload.

**Note:** You can click the Add button to insert additional file upload fields.

**9** Click **Upload**.

B The file or files are uploaded to the Business Catalyst server and are now able to be downloaded from your site.

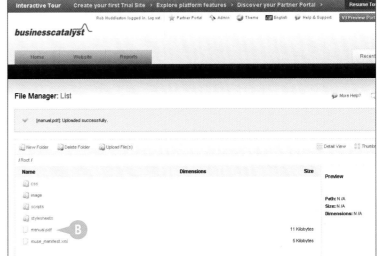

## TIPS

**What can I do if I have a very large file I need to upload?**
You may be able to compress the file with a Zip utility to get it below the 100MB file limit. If that still does not work, you cannot upload it to your Business Catalyst site. Instead, you might try a service such as Dropbox, which allows you to upload files of almost any size. You could make the file public on Dropbox and provide a link to it from your site. More information can be obtained at www.dropbox.com.

**After uploading a file, I get a Page Not Found error when I click the link from my website. Why is that happening?**
Almost always, problems like this are caused by incorrect file paths in links. On the website, check the location from which the browser is trying to access the file. If there are any folders in the path, you must return to the File Manager in Business Catalyst and move the file into that folder.

# Update Changed Pages

Once you have published your site, you can update the content on your site in Muse and then upload the changed files to your server. By default, the publish utility in Muse detects what pages you have changed and uploads only those files, saving you from having to wait while files you have not changed are needlessly uploaded. You can also add additional pages to your site and then upload them to make them live. If you are using a Menu Bar widget, your site's navigation automatically updates on all pages.

## Update Changed Pages

**1** Make any needed changes to your pages.

**2** Click **Publish**.

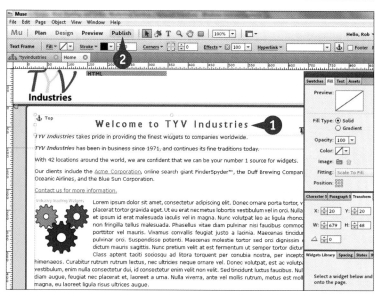

The Choose Site window opens.

**3** Click **Currently associated site** ( ○ changes to ⊙ ).

**4** Click **Next**.

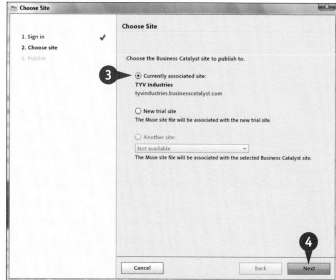

The Publish window opens.

**5** Click **Next**.

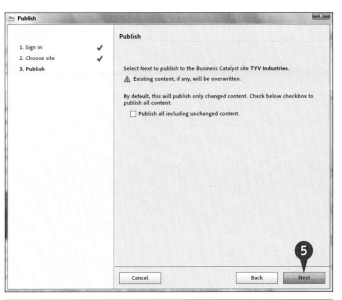

The Publish Confirmation window opens.

Ⓐ The changed files are uploaded to the server.

**TIP**

**I have a friend who knows how to code web pages. I had him log into the Business Catalyst site and make some manual changes to my site. When I later uploaded files from Muse, I lost those changes. Why?**

Although the Business Catalyst site does allow those who know how to code to make manual changes to pages, the local copies of the page in Muse remain unchanged. If you make changes to those pages in Muse and publish the site, that file, which does not contain the changes made through Business Catalyst, overwrites the file on the server. Therefore, you need to make sure that you edit your pages only in Muse, and never manually make edits on Business Catalyst.

# Find a Web Host

If you do not want to host your site through Business Catalyst, you can find a different host. Business Catalyst offers many advantages to users who need all of its extra features, but if you do not want or need the services it offers, you may be able to find a cheaper alternative. Rather than deal with the technical and cost issues of trying to run your own web server, you can contract with a commercial web host. Once you find a host, you can transfer your files to their servers to get your site online.

## Shopping for a Host

Literally millions of web hosts are available — a Google search for "web hosting" in February 2012 returned 462 million results. Therefore, you should spend some time comparison shopping. Hosts have widely varying fees for their services, from free to thousands of dollars per month. They also offer a wide range of services for these fees, so you will need to investigate which ones offer the services you want for the price you can afford.

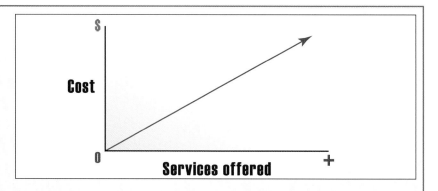

## Shared versus Dedicated Hosting

Many web hosts offer two basic services: shared hosting and dedicated hosting. With shared hosts, your site is on a server with many other sites. If one or more of those sites begins to use too much bandwidth or server resources, the performance of your site might suffer. Dedicated hosting allows you to rent an entire server for your site, so yours will be the only one running on the machine. This is, for obvious reasons, a much more expensive alternative, but generally offers better performance.

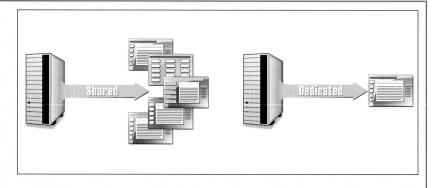

## Hard Drive Space and Bandwidth

All hosts should offer a certain amount of disk space, a maximum allowed amount of monthly bandwidth, and some sort of control panel interface to allow you to administer your site. Usually, the hard drive space and bandwidth is more than sufficient for most sites, although hosts generally offer à la carte options for additional space and bandwidth should you need them.

## Extra Services

Hosts generally offer e-mail services as well, allowing you to use e-mail accounts attached to your domain name. They may also offer server-side scripting features, such as support for PHP, ASP, ASP.NET, and ColdFusion, as well as space on database servers. All hosts should offer some sort of backup system to protect against data loss on their side, and many make the web server logs for your site available, either as a raw data file that you need to analyze yourself or through a graphical interface on the control panel.

## Signing Up with a Host

Once you have found the host you want to use, you can sign up through their website. Most ask for basic contact and billing information. Many offer monthly or yearly billing, with a discount for longer terms. Once they receive your information, you should receive an e-mail from them with the login information and details on how to log into the control panel and set up other details of your site so that you can upload your files to them.

Login details as follows:

ELECTRONIC MAIL

# Buy a Domain Name

A domain name is the recognizable identifier for your site, and becomes an important part of your overall brand. You can purchase a domain name by searching for one that is still available and then purchasing it for a small yearly fee from a company called a domain registrar. Thousands of domain registrars exist, so you need to do some comparison shopping to find the best price. Unfortunately, you may have difficulty finding a domain name ending in .com still available.

## Buy a Domain Name

**1** Use your web browser to go to www.networksolutions.com.

**Note:** Network Solutions is merely one of the more popular registrars. You may want to shop around before you purchase.

**2** Type a domain name you would like to purchase.

**3** Click **Search**.

The next page opens, either informing you that the name is available or prompting you to search again.

**4** When you have found an available name, click **Add Selected to Cart**.

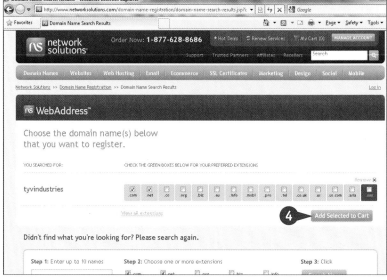

The next page opens, offering domains.

**5** Click **No, Thanks**.

**6** Complete the remainder of the steps for the checkout process.

Your domain name is now purchased.

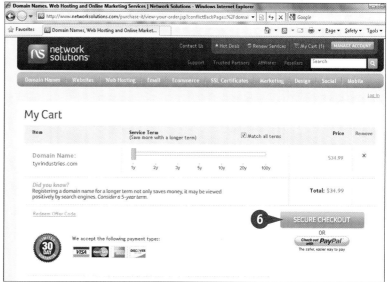

**I see a lot of other domains that end in .edu, .gov, and .mil. I also see a lot with two-letter endings such as .us or .uk. What are these?**

When the domain name system was developed, six of these so-called top-level domains were created. Three were designed to be open to anyone: .com, .net, and .org. The other three were reserved, and so only educational institutions can use .edu, only governmental entities within the United States can use .gov, and only branches of the United States military can use .mil. The two-letter top-level domains designate countries; .us is for the United States and .uk is Britain. The popular .tv domain actually belongs to the Pacific island nation of Tuvalu. Today, many other top-level domains exist, such as .aero and .name, but .com remains the most popular.

# Export Your Files to HTML

If you have chosen to use your own hosting and domain name and not use Business Catalyst, you must export your site to individual HTML files so that you can manually upload the site to a server. Once exported, all the files in your site, which will include HTML pages of the content, CSS documents for formatting, JavaScript documents for behaviors, and all of your site's images, are extracted to a folder on your computer.

## Export Your Files to HTML

**1** Click **File**.

**2** Click **Export as HTML**.

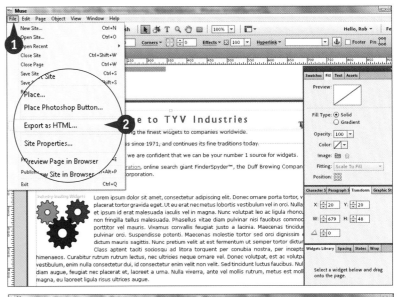

The Export to HTML dialog box opens.

**3** Click the file folder icon ( ).

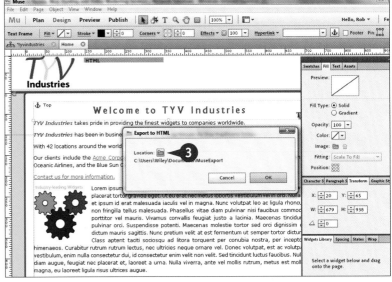

The Browse For Folder dialog box opens.

**4** Select the folder into which you want to export the files.

**5** Click **OK**.

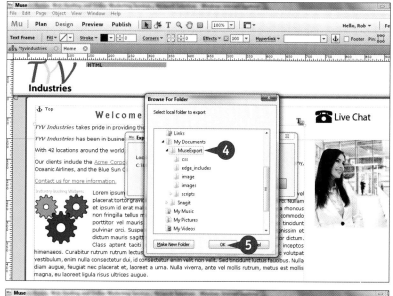

**6** Click **OK** in the Export to HTML dialog box.

The site exports to HTML.

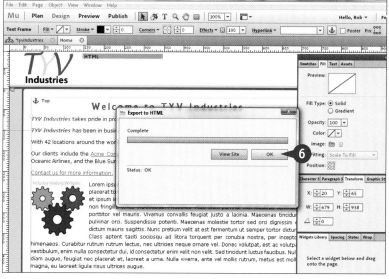

**When I look in the folder of the exported files, I am surprised by how many files there are. Do I really need all of them?**

Yes. Although Muse hides this complexity from you by allowing you to work with a single MUSE file, even simple websites are made up of many dozens of files. Complex, larger sites may need tens of thousands of files. Thankfully, even when you export to HTML, you do not really need to worry about this. If you make any changes in Muse, simply export the site again and replace all the files with the new ones.

# Upload Your Site

In order for your website to be visible to other people, you must transfer the files from your local machine to your web host's servers. Although several different technologies are available to transfer files, by far the most common is FTP (file transfer protocol). FTP has been used for many years to allow for the transfer of files between computers and, in fact, predates the web. You also need an FTP client — software on your computer that you can use to create and maintain the FTP connection. Both Windows and Macintosh include a built-in command line FTP.

## Upload Your Site

**1** From the Start menu, type **ftp**.

On a Mac, open the terminal by clicking **Applications**, **Utilities**, and then **Terminal**.

**2** Click **ftp**.

On a Mac, type **ftp** followed by the address of the server, and skip to step **5**.

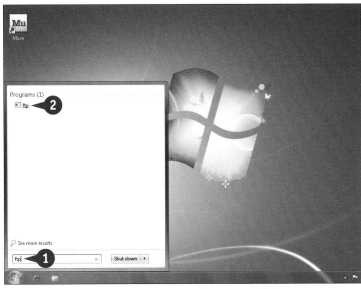

The Windows FTP window opens.

**3** Type **open ?**, replacing **?** with the address of your host's FTP server.

**4** Press Enter.

**5** Type your username.

**6** Press Enter.

**7** Type your password.

**8** Press Enter.

The FTP server logs you in.

**9** Type **hash**.

**10** Press Enter.

**11** Type **lcd** and then the path to the folder on your hard drive that contains your web page files.

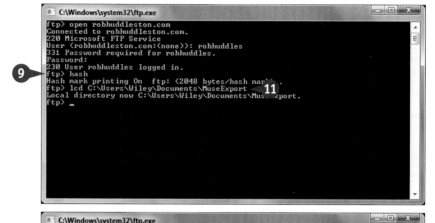

**12** Type **mput \*.\***.

**Note:** This transfers all files in the folder to your server.

**13** Press Enter.

All files in the current directory are uploaded.

**14** Type **Quit**.

**15** Press Enter.

The command window closes.

## TIP

**Many of the commands in FTP seem odd. Where can I find a reference for them?**

Perhaps the biggest disadvantage for using a program such as FTP is that it relies on rather arcane commands. Some common commands are included in the table below.

| Command | Function |
|---|---|
| dir | Displays a list of the files in the current directory on the server |
| cd <path> | Changes to a specified directory on the server |
| lcd <path> | Changes to a specified directory on the client |
| mkdir <directoryname> | Creates a directory on the server |
| hash | Displays hash symbols, or pound signs, to show the progress of a file upload or download |
| get <filename> | Downloads a file from the server |
| put <filename> | Uploads a file to the server |
| mget <*.extension> | Downloads all files with the specified extension |
| mput <*.extension> | Uploads all files with the specified extension |
| ? | Displays a list of accepted commands |

# Index

## A

abbr tag, 78
accordion panels, 216–217
Active setting, 169
adding
    alternate text and titles, 130–131
    background fills, 36–39
    blank Composition widgets, 213
    borders, 30–31
    content to widgets, 202–203
    custom color to swatches, 29
    effects, 34–35
    Facebook Like buttons, 232–233
    Featured News widget, 194
    Flash movies, 238–239
    Google Analytics code, 246–249
    Google maps, 226–229
    graphic styles, 126–127
    horizontal menu bars, 144–145
    HTML5 animation, 240–241
    icons to menus, 150–151
    images to Slideshow widget, 221
    Lightbox Display widget, 204
    links to PDF or Word files, 166–167
    manual menus, 156–159
    metadata, 270–271
    mobile redirection scripts, 266–267
    non-scrolling content, 60–61
    Presentation widget, 212
    Slideshow widget, 220–221
    special characters, 54–55
    text to pages, 46–47
    Tooltip widget, 214
    top-level pages, 21, 22
    YouTube videos, 230–231
adjusting
    browser fill color for Lightbox Display widget, 205
    Business Catalyst account plans, 279
    button appearance, 203
    character styles, 77
    content in widgets, 200–201
    fill colors, 101
    images in Fireworks, 99
    menu
        appearance, 152–153
        orientation/size, 148–149

    opacity of canvas, 29
    paragraph styles, 84
    stroke colors, 101
    text
        alignment, 68–69
        in menus, 145
        properties, 103, 169
        properties in Fireworks, 103
        spacing, 68–69
Adobe Business Catalyst
    about, 272
    creating free trial sites, 274–275
    manually uploading files to, 280–283
    publishing sites to, 276–277
    upgrading accounts, 278–279
Adobe Integrated Runtime (AIR), 7
Adobe Muse. See Muse (Adobe)
Adobe Proto, 40–43
.aero, 289
AIR (Adobe Integrated Runtime), 7
alignment (text), 68–69
anchor links, 172–173
Android Tablet, installing Adobe Proto on, 40–41
animated icons, 137
animation (HTML5), 240–241
appearance
    button, 203
    of content area of Master pages, 180–181
    menu, 152–153
applying
    character styles, 76
    effects to frames, 124–125
    fonts, 66, 67, 250–253
    formats with Text panel, 72–73
    tags, 79, 85
    web-safe fonts, 66, 250–253
arbitrary HTML, 244–245
asset links, 134–135
associating Master pages with pages, 191
audience, understanding your, 13

## B

background fills, 36–39
backgrounds, designing for Master pages, 178–179
backing up sites, 16–17
bandwidth, for web hosting, 287

# Index

# Index

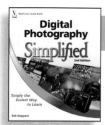

# ...all designed for visual learners—just like you!

## Master VISUALLY®

**Your complete visual reference. Two-color interior.**

- 3ds Max
- Creating Web Pages
- Dreamweaver and Flash
- Excel
- iPod and iTunes
- Mac OS
- Office
- Optimizing PC Performance
- Windows
- Windows Server

## Visual Blueprint™

**Where to go for professional-level programming instruction. Two-color interior.**

- ActionScript
- Ajax
- ASP.NET 2.0
- Excel Data Analysis
- Excel Pivot Tables
- Excel Programming
- HTML
- JavaScript
- Mambo
- Mobile App Development
- Perl and Apache
- PHP & MySQL
- SEO
- Ubuntu Linux
- Vista Sidebar
- Visual Basic
- XML

## Visual™ Quick Tips

**Shortcuts, tricks, and techniques for getting more done in less time. Full color.**

- Beading
- Crochet
- Digital Photography
- Excel
- Golf
- Internet
- iPhone
- iPod & iTunes
- Knitting
- Mac OS
- Office
- Paper Crafts
- PowerPoint
- Quilting
- Sewing
- Windows
- Wire Jewelry

**Visual®**
An Imprint of ⓦ**WILEY**
Now you know.

**For a complete listing of Visual books, go to wiley.com/go/visual**

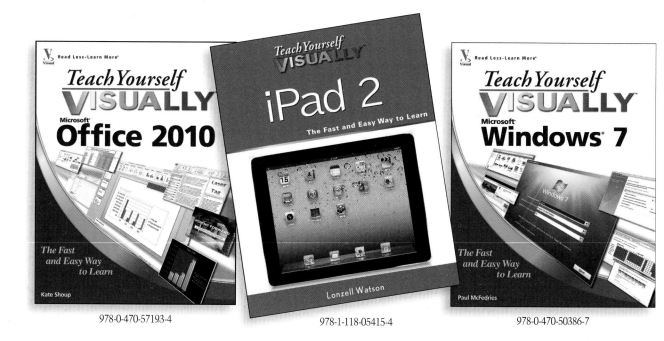